To Gilpin County Library

BLACKS

Through the 'Ayes' of Our American Presidents

— A Political Timeline —

Gwen Scott

By

Gwendolyn Scott, Wallace Tollette,

Jane Taylor

Jane Taylor

The Write Group, LLC

Blacks Through the 'Ayes' of Our American Presidents: A Political Timeline
by Gwendolyn Scott, Wallace Tollette, Jane Taylor

Historical images, paintings, photos,
courtesy of the Library of Congress (unless otherwise noted)

Published by
The Write Group, LLC
Denver, Colorado

Cover and Interior Design: Nick Zelinger, www.nzgraphics.com

ISBN: 978-0-9828661-0-8

Library of Congress Catalog Control Number: 2010933809

First Edition
Second Printing

Printed in the United States of America

Books may be purchased directly from the publisher:
Visit www.TheWriteGroupLLC.com
Jane Taylor: 303 460-7416, jtaylorbiz@msn.com
Wallace Yvonne Tollette: 303 830-1691, westernimages@juno.com

A Special Dedication

Mildred Rainey Jones, life-long friend, who provided inspiration
and who helped keep us on track to finish this book.
Unfortunately, she did not live to see 'Ayes' completed,
having departed this life on October 22, 2009.

CONTENTS

Preface

This book, *Blacks Through the Ayes of Our American Presidents: A Political Timeline,* was serendipitous, a happy accident of three women—two of whom are independent historians and the third, a retired public school history teacher, all with a keen interest in black history—came together. Co-incidentally, the three—Jane Taylor, Wallace Yvonne Tollette and Gwendolyn Scott—are also historical re-enactors who not only portray pioneer black women, but who also have a shared interest in preserving black history collectively and individually.

In our work, frequently our audiences are students. One day, it occurred to Taylor that these students had nothing tangible to take with them at the end of our programs. She felt that this needed to be remedied. So, the three of us brain-stormed, exploring numerous possibilities: paper dolls, bookmarks, timeline charts, and other history-related types of mementos. In our discussions, the timeline chart idea seemed the most plausible; however, as we continued to explore ideas for something appropriate, Taylor posed the questions of why some rights of black people in America are still abridged and, what are, or were, the circumstances leading to this attitude?

For years, Scott had taught Afro-American history to high school students. She distinctly remembered from her experiences that large numbers of the students entered the class with great gaps about American history in general, lacking important prior knowledge. And, as for information about Blacks as to where, and how, they fit into the historical scheme of America, the students' gaps were even greater. However, some students had tangential acquaintances with issues and events such as: slavery, civil rights, the Fourth of July, the Civil War, and the Emancipation Proclamation. Yet, a deep understanding and fundamental knowledge of determining forces stemming from the Founding Fathers' drafting of the Declaration of Independence, the United States Constitution & the Bill of Rights, were woefully absent. Scott realized then that her students needed a way to find a bridge to these documents so that this part of history could come alive, and not only be meaningful, but also memorable. So she decided that using the actions and policies of the presidents supplied the connective link that would foster student learning and understanding. This approach proved to be quite successful—seeing the history of Blacks in America through the ayes—which means an affirmative answer or vote—of our presidents and also answering Taylor's questions about the status of Blacks in America.

To our excitement, carrying this thought forward and developing a timeline, Scott was able to organize the issues and actions of all the presidents into fourteen eras emphasizing each one which either helped Blacks move ahead in American society or kept them from being an integral part of it. Although not being formally educated historians like Scott, Taylor and Tollette decided that this historical perspective was the key, and it needed to be heard by a broader audience. After thoroughly researching and developing support materials, we were able to present the program in five two-hour sessions: twice in abbreviated form of an all-day session and also in a four-hour session. We also had the opportunity to present an overview of the timeline to young students in an hour-and-a-half session which was well-received. We planned time to present information and hold group discussions. From these programs grew an outline for this book which was originally designed to be used with the presentation. As we continued to refine our work, we decided to compile the information into a stand-alone book presenting the material in a concise, yet thorough, and easily understandable manner.

The timeline idea was the key for a perfect historical memento because these questions, we determined, could not accurately and historically be answered without closely examining each of the United States presidential administrations from George Washington to George Bush. From this grew the outline for *Ayes*, the public program, and this book. Then we organized ourselves into a legal entity, The Write Group. And as the saying goes, "The rest is history."

By applying the same approach to *Blacks Through the Ayes of Our American Presidents: A Political Timeline*, which centers the historical narrative through the presidents, it is hoped that you, the reader, will experience a similar kind of success as many of Scott's students did. This fostered their understanding and knowledge of how Blacks fit in American history more poignantly.

And, further, you will also find answers to the questions as to why black people continue to be viewed less favorably by America's leadership and majority population and what the forces were then and continue to be, behind such attitudes and actions.

We hope that you will find this book, which explores the cultural, political, social and economic journey of Blacks in America, to be a helpful, enlightening, and useful tool to facilitate understanding of the underpinnings of all that has happened to black people in America—from 1619 to 2008.

———

To book a presentation or to obtain a copy of the book, please call:
The Write Group, LLC: 303-756-0198, www.thewritegroupllc.com
or
Jane Taylor: 303-460-7416, jtaylorbiz@msn.com
or
Wallace Yvonne Tollette: 303-830-1691, westernimages@juno.com

Introduction

It has been said that one of the most effective ways in which dominant groups maintain their power is by depriving the people they dominate of the knowledge of their own history and culture. In addition, the oppressors discredit, distort and disfigure those oppressed. America evolved in this manner. It is evident: during the formation of our national government, and the drafting of the Declaration of Independence, the U.S. Constitution and the Bill of Rights, this strategy, based on a racist premise, heavily influenced the Founding Fathers. They used it to rationalize the American system of slavery, and to justify the inhumane treatment of Black people. This perverse logic damaged both America and Americans for generations to come. *Blacks Through The 'Ayes' Of Our American Presidents: A Political Timeline*, looks at and examines some of the history and the political actions taken by presidents that profoundly affected Blacks and America.

Organized around fourteen eras in American history, "Ayes" sorts and traces issues and actions that dominated and earmarked the various presidential administrations. Black people are the focus of the discussion on the presidents' actions. Each era is formatted as a panel (from the original political time chart Scott created), which represents a chapter.

Panel 1, for example, "Background," deals with the Colonial Period. It opens with a picture and profile chart of some of the Founding Father-delegates who attended the Constitutional Convention at Philadelphia in 1785. A brief sketch of their background roles in conceiving, creating and crafting of the United States Constitution & the Bill of Rights follows. A narrative detailing Issues & Actions that impacted black people during these times is centralized in this section. Wrapping up the "Background" Panel is the analytical summary feature: "Effects on Blacks."

Beginning with Panel 2, "Nation Building," and included in the subsequent other twelve panels, the features are similar to the Panel 1 format, except, instead of the Founding Fathers, the presidents of each era are showcased in each panel. Their pictures precede the President Profile chart and brief biographies. The bios cite some possible factors – cultural/social history of the times, family background, personal makeup and experiences, plus their political ideology – that bore considerably, as definitive determinates, explaining or influencing the whys and wherefores of their decisions and actions. Followed are the bulleted introductory areas to the "Issues & Actions" section. In this portion of each panel, the narrative details the issues and frames how Blacks were impacted by them. After which the actions taken – or not taken – by the incumbent president are traced. The wrap-up to each panel comes with the "Effects on Blacks" feature. It is an analytical summary of each of the eras.

Presidents take the oath of office to uphold the U.S. Constitution. From its conception, and inception, until the ratification of the Civil War Amendments, presidents swore to uphold and maintain a racist form of government; one that denied the humanity of black people. It is in this light that *Blacks Through The 'Ayes' Of Our American Presidents: A Political Timeline* was written. Its purpose is to provide knowledge and insight which will foster an enhanced and a broader understanding of not only America's history, but also knowledge of, or about America and Americans in general.

It has often been said, "To know one's history is to know one's self..."

And So It Begins...

As we journey through history, be watching the social, economic, and political times, as well as the political parties' actions which influenced how each president proceeded.

AN OVERVIEW OF OUR AMERICAN PRESIDENTS

1. George Washington

2. John Adams

3. Thomas Jefferson

4. James Madison

5. James Monroe

6. John Quincy Adams

7. Andrew Jackson

8. Martin Van Buren

9. William Henry Harrison

10. John Tyler

11. James K. Polk

12. Zachary Taylor

13. Millard Fillmore

14. Franklin Pierce

15. James Buchanan

16. Abraham Lincoln

17. Andrew Johnson

18. Ulysses S. Grant

19. Rutherford B. Hayes

20. James Garfield

21. Chester A. Arthur   22. Grover Cleveland   23. Benjamin Harrison   24. Grover Cleveland   25. William McKinley

26. Theodore Roosevelt   27. William Howard Taft   28. Woodrow Wilson   29. Warren G. Harding   30. Calvin Coolidge

31. Herbert Hoover   32. Franklin D. Roosevelt   33. Harry S. Truman   34. Dwight D. Eisenhower   35. John F. Kennedy

36. Lyndon B. Johnson   37. Richard M. Nixon   38. Gerald R. Ford   39. James Carter   40. Ronald Reagan

41. George H. W. Bush   42. William J. Clinton   43. George W. Bush

Background
1619~1789

"Those who cannot remember the past are condemned to repeat it."
~ George Santayana 1905

"Perhaps oppression dehumanizes the oppressor as much as,
if not more than, the oppressed. They need each other to become
truly free, to become human. We can be human only
in fellowship, in community, in koinonia, in peace."
~ Archbishop Desmond Tutu 1984

Some of the Founding Fathers

Benjamin Franklin   Alexander Hamilton   Gouverneur Morris   Oliver Ellsworth

Founding Father	Dates	Birthplace	Profession	State Represented
1. Oliver Ellsworth	1745-1807	Connecticut	Lawyer	Connecticut
2. Benjamin Franklin	1706-1790	Massachusetts	Inventor/Statesman	Pennsylvania
3. Elbridge Gerry	1744-1814	Massachusetts	Businessman	Massachusetts
4. Nathaniel Gorman	1738-1796	Massachusetts	Politician	Massachusetts
5. Alexander Hamilton	1755-1804	Br. West Indies	Statesman	New York
6. George Mason	1725-1792	Virginia	Lawyer	Virginia
7. Gouverneur Morris	1752-1816	New York	Statesman	Pennsylvania
8. Edmund Randolph	1753-1813	Virginia	Lawyer	Virginia
9. John Rutledge	1739-1800	South Carolina	Lawyer	South Carolina
10. Roger Sherman	1721-1793	Massachusetts	Businessman	Connecticut
11. James Wilson	1742-1798	Scotland	Lawyer	Pennsylvania

PROFILES OF SOME NON-PRESIDENT FOUNDING FATHERS IMPORTANT TO THE FRAMING OF THE U. S. CONSTITUTION & THE BILL OF RIGHTS

During the fledging years of America's evolution and revolution – from colonialism to nationhood – a cadre of outstanding leaders emerged. Many of these men served as delegates to the various historical conventions, and or, carried out other influential political roles. Historians have dubbed these men, the Founding Fathers.[1] George Washington, John Adams, Thomas Jefferson, James Madison and James Monroe stand out among the Founding Fathers, and are well-known because each assumed the U.S. presidency. However, there were many others, though less well-known, who greatly helped to determine the political and social future foundation and direction of the new nation. A glimpse at the drama that unfolded in Philadelphia during four, hot-sweltering months in 1787, is representative of their importance.

On stage were a total of 55 men: most of them were fairly young, averaging 42 years old; three-fourths of them served in Congress; most played prominent roles in their states; some participated in the Revolution; some were wealthy, but most were not.[2] They met in Independence Hall. They represented 12 of 13 states – Rhode Island sent no delegates. They met to amend and improve the Articles of Confederation – the first constitution of the new nation, America.[3] These men, the Founding Fathers, worked tirelessly from May 14th through September 17th, sweating over the creation of the United States Constitution! This august meeting was called the Constitutional Convention. George Washington presided.[4]

Prior to the Philadelphia conclave, a number of meetings concerned about the Article's shortcomings were held. Most significant among them were the 1785 Virginia-Maryland talks at Mount Vernon and the summits at Annapolis in 1786. To this latter meeting, nine states were invited. Only five states sent delegates. This response so profoundly disappointed Alexander Hamilton that he and James Madison spearheaded the drafting of a group report asking Congress to call the Philadelphia convention. Several months passed. Finally the request was granted. However, with the authorization came stipulations: delegates to the convention could only propose amendments to the Articles; not to develop a new constitution. Eventually, though along in the proceedings, the delegates found these directions unfeasible; the Articles had to be scrapped.[5]

The Articles needed replacing, for in order to resolve the core issues of representation and taxation, modifying and amending would not suffice. A central government was called for; the Articles lacked this component. Each state was sovereign as a member of the confederation. A new governmental structure, therefore, had to be created around a centralized government. The creation was the United States Constitution & the Bill of Rights which is called the Great Compromise. Following is a capsule description of the roles some of the

Declaration of Independence, July 4th, 1776.
Engraving by W. L. Ormsby after John Trumbull.
Library of Congress reproduction number: LC-USZ62-5

Founding Fathers played in this epic drama in effecting the Compromise among the states. Their roles were so pivotal, that the political, economic and social course America took can be traced to their actions and inactions. And, basic to all this drama was the compromise they made over the thorny questions and problems posed by the presence of black people and the economic system of slavery![6]

The Founding Father-delegates, confronted with these conundrums, spent the larger part of the convention wrestling and fuming over the logistics of geography, morality and physicality; what to do about the Blacks and slavery, the corollary problem? How to put all the nuts – and – bolts of this new document together around them? And, how to manufacture it in such a way, that compromise could be effected? And finally adding to the Founders' framework was how to incorporate the Enlightenment philosophy of Natural Rights?

The gears started rolling toward defining the government machinery, after Edmund Randolph (VA) introduced the Virginia Plan. This plan, largely devised by James Madison, provided the delegates the basis for discussion on possible ways to strengthen the government. Three branches of government were proposed: legislative, executive and judicial. The legislative component, with two chambers, represented the people, the Senate and the House of Representatives. And it was this branch that generated the majority of the pros and cons among the delegates. To determine who should be counted in formulating the representations of each state, was complicated by the presence of black people and slavery. Further perplexities arose when taxation was factored in the equation. Finding ways to accommodate the disparities – North and South, slave and non-slave, small states and large states – posed a tall order in trying to bring about equity.[7] The House would be organized this way.

Representing the small states, who felt the Virginia Plan favored the large states, Elbridge Gerry (MA) proposed the New Jersey Plan; it called for all states to have equal representation, regardless of size. Again another deadlock arose. This prompted Roger Sherman (CT) to present a compromise. His plan called for equal representation of each state in one chamber and proportioned representation of each state in the other. Would the latter be figured through taxation of property or the population? Using property as the basis proved not as workable as population. But it too became a sticking point – how do you count the slaves? The North protested counting them along with white people. This would give the South a decided advantage, since most of the slaves populated southern states. And then too, if they were counted, they would probably want congressional representation![8]

Madison discussed the slave qualities: in some respects they were persons; "in other respects they were property. So a formula was finally agreed upon to make them 3/5 of a person to satisfy the North." The North in turn allowed the South to continue to import slaves, but only until 1808. Gouverneur Morris (PA) felt bringing in too many Blacks could ultimately pollute the white man's culture! Also the need to control a demographic and power-shift and to keep the South from padding their numbers, a head tax should be levied on a certain amount of the imported slaves. Gerry added this recommendation, which called for the South to exact another concession from the North: to protect the South's slave property, a fugitive-slave clause was inserted in the Constitution.[9]

A committee was selected to draft the new constitution. John Rutledge (SC), Edmund Randolph (VA), James Wilson (PA), Nathaniel Gorham (MA) and Oliver Ellsworth (CT) worked for 2 weeks on the draft incorporating the three sections of the Constitution that addresses Blacks and slavery: the 3/5, the 1808 slavery trade deadline, and the fugitive-slave clauses in the document. As a believer in Natural Rights, George Mason (VA) found it lacked assurances for individual rights, and so The Bill of Rights (the first ten amendments) was added. And this excluded Blacks because of the 3/5 clause. This, along with the body of the

Benjamin Franklin
Mezzotint by Edward Fisher after Mason Chamberlain.
Library of Congress reproduction number:
LC-USZ62-1434

new Constitution, were approved and signed by 36 of the delegates. Interestingly enough, neither Elbridge Gerry nor George Mason signed.[10] But largely thanks to the presence and the persuasive influence of an aged and ailing Benjamin Franklin (PA), the Constitutional Convention was a success. A success that laid – at the expense of Blacks – the groundwork for the racism that is woven into and pervades throughout the social, economic and political fabric of the American society and the American culture – today.

BACKGROUND
ISSUES & ACTIONS

- **Thirteen Colonies**
- **System of Slavery**
- **Jamestown, Virginia**
- **Middle Passage of the Triangular Trade Route**
- **Age of Enlightenment**
- **Declaration of Independence**
- **Revolutionary War**
- **U.S. Constitution & the Bill of Rights**

From the thirteen English colonies, established along the Atlantic coast in the seventeenth century, the United States of America emerged. The colonies thrived and prospered economically due largely to the system of slavery. All colonies had slaves; however, the bulk of them labored in the southern colonies.

Blacks first appeared in the colonies in 1619. Twenty of them were brought into the settlement of Jamestown in the Virginia Colony. They were technically not slaves, but indentured (binds one to work for another for a certain period of time for pay) servants. The system of slavery gradually evolved in the colonies late in the seventeenth century, when the European market grew its demand for colonial products. As a consequence, the labor needs became commensurate in the colonies. West Africa supplied most of the slaves, who came to America via the Triangular Trade Route on the Middle Passage.

In 1760, King George III began his rule of England. He incurred heavy debts. Increasingly, he pressured the colonies more and more to help bail the empire out of its indebtedness. His actions caused the colonies to protest, leading to their sending an ultimatum to the King. It listed their grievances against him. Among the complaints – in the original draft – was a line charging the King with being responsible for colonial slavery. However, the final draft, known as the Declaration of Independence, did not include this line. The delegate-consensus at the Continental Congress demanded its deletion. The mention of slavery aroused too much of a moral-economic dilemma, not only for the South but for the North as well. Also, it conflicted with the practices of the Colonists, exposing them as hypocrites. Particularly true, since the rebels spouted so much of the Enlightenment rhetoric about Natural Rights: all men are created equal; life, liberty and the pursuit of happiness.

Due to the protracted time and distance between the colonies and the Mother Country, King George III's affirmative reply to the ultimatum contained in the Declaration of Independence, did not reach the Continental Congress soon enough to avert war. The resulting delay led to the outbreak of the Revolutionary War, also known as the War of Independence.

The War broke out in 1775, and the fighting ended at Yorktown in 1781. George Washington commanded the colony troops. He and the Congress – in the beginning – did not allow Blacks to fight. But when Lord Dunmore, the Royal Governor of the colony of Virginia, issued a proclamation inviting them to join the British troops, Washington and Congress lifted the ban. So during the Revolutionary War, there were black men fighting and dying both on the British and the American sides.

The independence America gained by defeating England gave Blacks hope that they, too, would receive the inalienable rights of life, liberty and the pursuit of happiness promised in the Declaration of Independence and be included in "We the People" membership of the Preamble. All the Enlightenment rhetoric excluded them. Their hopes were dashed. They were betrayed… once the Founding Fathers agreed and endorsed The United States Constitution & The Bill of Rights. In fact, what Blacks received was the ultimate insult – they were not even persons – only 3/5 of one! No Rights! And, since The Constitution & The Bill of Rights were placed as the cornerstone of the new nation, this historically racist background, dictates and impacts much of America's political and social policies of today.

THIRTEEN COLONIES

In the seventeenth century, the English established thirteen colonies along the Atlantic coast. The colonies formed the geographical base for the eventual nation of the United States of America. The first settlements were established in Virginia, the leading Southern Colony. North Carolina, South Carolina, and Georgia made up the rest of the Southern Colonies. The two other groups were the Middle Colonies and the New England Colonies. New York, Pennsylvania, New Jersey, Delaware, and Maryland formed the former group, and Massachusetts, New Hampshire, Connecticut, and Rhode Island comprised the latter group.

The colonists varied in backgrounds, but the majority of them represented a religious group. The Pilgrims, Puritans, and Quakers were the most prominent. The geography dictated the type of economy developed in the colonies. But labor was needed in all of them. And all colonies—North and South—held Blacks in bondage.[11] However, an agriculturally-based economy required a massive labor force; hence, the majority of slaves were in the South.

Initially, the workers brought to the colonies were indentured. They were black and white. Their indentured status provided promise of freedom, once their indebtedness ended. The period usually lasted from five to seven years. Once the terms of indentured status were completed, the employer was obligated to give all indentured servants, including Blacks, the land and resources to begin their new life. This gradually changed by the late 1600's, when it became easy to renege on the agreement and use the physical differences and color of Blacks to separate and enslave them.[12] The slave trade flourished, bringing untold numbers out of Africa. A system of slavery was born in America.

THE SYSTEM OF SLAVERY

Slavery in the United States did not begin here. It stemmed from ancient times. But the U.S. system differed in two distinctive ways: 1) the slaves had no legal rights; and 2) eventually, the slave population became exclusively black.[13] The success of southern agriculture fostered and perpetuated the system.

Most of the slave states stretched along a fertile band of flatlands. Cotton, rice, sugar cane, tobacco, indigo, and hemp grew and thrived. Most of the slaves worked in the fields planting, cultivating, and harvesting the crops. Fewer numbers tended the masters' households, and others worked as masons, carpenters, blacksmiths, seamstresses, and other forms of skilled labor.

The Africans came from many different tribes, speaking different languages, and practicing different customs and traditions. The Whites used these differences when placing them in groups, so Blacks could not communicate and possibly organize and rebel against the masters. These measures, in the beginning, were pivotal for control. Religion and the indoctrination from the teachings of Christianity and the Bible later served as an even more controlling method.[14] However, in the end, the slaves used these circumstances to create their own communication system. The Negro Spiritual was chief among the slave songs. The codes developed became an essential part of the success of the Underground Railroad and the Abolition Movement.[15]

Slavery left its mark. Even today, issues and actions faced by our nation most often are shaped by the social-political attitudes and traditions stemming from the immoral roots of racism.[16] Its by-products – segregation and discrimination – perpetuated against black people, caused them to inherit countless societal problems manifested from forced ghettoization, over the generations: dysfunctional families; high crime and incarceration rates; substandard educational achievement; perilous levels of unemployment and underemployment; extensive poverty; inordinate poor physical and mental health.

JAMESTOWN, VIRGINIA

Jamestown, a 1607 settlement on the James River, was the first successful English site in the United States. It survived a shaky start, and began to thrive with the import of indentured workers. Blacks first appeared in Jamestown, in 1619, a year prior to the pilgrims' arrival on the Mayflower, and their landing at Plymouth Rock in Massachusetts Colony. There were twenty Blacks who came off a Dutch ship that dropped anchor in the harbor. It is believed they were a part of looted cargo taken from a Spanish vessel bound for the West Indies. Records show they had Spanish names.[17] The Blacks were purchased by the Virginians and made indentured servants. Records also revealed that these Blacks served out their terms, becoming free and then establishing their own households. In fact, it is from the union of Isabella and Antony that the first black child born in the U.S. came from Jamestown. His name was William Tucker.[18]

THE MIDDLE PASSAGE

The Middle Passage is the term used to describe the second leg of the Triangular Trade Route between Africa and the Americas. For the millions of branded and chained Africans, the Middle Passage loomed as one of the most horrific exploits inflicted on any human beings.[19] It was a nightmare of inestimable physical and psychological damage for those who survived. Diseases and wanton cruelties claimed countless numbers en route. Millions perished. Those who managed to survive the grueling ordeal, reached their destination, and then were confronted with being sold, like livestock, either on ship or in slave markets in American ports. The journey from start to destination lasted between six and eight weeks.

This inhumanity lasted for nearly 250 years! – from 1619-1865 in the United States.

AGE OF ENLIGHTENMENT

A reformist movement, the Age of Enlightenment began in Western Europe around the 1600's, but reached its most influential stage during the eighteenth century. It is this period when the Thirteen English Colonies transformed themselves into a nation – The United States of America. Under the leadership of the Founding Fathers, ideas of governance from Enlightenment philosophers were appropriated, forming the social/political bases for the new nation.[20]

This period in history is also called the Age of Reasoning because the philosophers emphasized the employment of reason as the best method of learning truth. They relied heavily on the scientific method. These thinkers believed that it could be applied to study the nature of man. So they theorized about such issues as education, law, philosophy and politics. They attacked tyranny, social injustice, superstition and ignorance. Many of these ideas, when incorporated, led to both the French and the American Revolutions.

Two of the Enlightenment thinkers who most influenced the Americans were Englishman John Locke and Frenchman Montesquieu. In the drafting of the Declaration of Independence Locke's belief that men must unite to protect the lives, liberty and property is one of its cornerstones. And in the Preamble of the Constitution the Montesquieu's Natural Rights Laws are referenced. These two documents exemplify the tenet of Enlightenment that by man's use of his reasoning powers, a perfect social/political state can be realized.

DECLARATION OF INDEPENDENCE

For the first half of the eighteenth century, during the Age of Enlightenment, England waged war against France. Their conflict in America was called the French and Indian War. In 1763, the War finally ended in an English victory. Just prior to the end of the war, King George III took over the crown of England.

The debts he garnered, plus those he inherited from fighting the war, all but depleted England's resources and funds. He needed to recover them. The King turned to the colonies. The applied pressure grew overwhelmingly. Colonists—Black and White—organized in protest against the taxation and oppression. They called for liberty and freedom from King George III's tyranny and ruling that allowed them no representation, a reflection of the social/political philosophies of Enlightenment.

The colonies united. In 1774, the First Continental Congress met. Colonists sent a document of grievances to the King, asking him to rescind the acts being used to oppress them. The colonists agreed to raise a militia and prepare for war if George did not comply. He did not. The Revolutionary War broke out. A Second Continental Congress convened in May, 1775. The colonies declared their independence. A notice was given to the King. This was the Declaration of Independence. Thomas Jefferson wrote it, with assistance from Benjamin Franklin and John Adams. Jefferson included a passage condemning slavery. However, it was stricken. The majority of the delegates forced its removal[21] because it conflicted with the practices of the colonies, exposing them as hypocrites – showing their duplicity.

THE REVOLUTIONARY WAR (1775-1781)

In1775, at the onset of the Revolutionary War, most colonies barred Blacks from enlisting in the militia, despite their involvement and activism that led to war. Many had served as Minute Men in Massachusetts. They distinguished themselves at Concord, Lexington, and Bunker Hill. More than a hundred fought. But at the urging of southern planters, George Washington and the Continental Congress voiced their opposition to Blacks participating in the war.[22]

However, by January 1777, Washington's and the Congress' hands were forced. Lord Dunmore, the royal governor of Virginia, welcomed the services of hundreds of slaves to fight for England and issued a proclamation promising them freedom—and for those wanting to go to Africa, they could have their own country in Sierra Leone on the West Coast![23] The Blacks helped boost the British fighting force numbers and helped them gain success in the field. The colonists were struggling. Washington and the Congress had to reverse themselves. Recruitment of Blacks received approval. Some northern legislatures passed measures accepting freedmen and slave enlistments. In 1779, the Congress urged southerners to follow suit; the idea was met with reluctance. Very few Blacks served in southern units.

Blacks proved their mettle. They made valiant and valuable contributions toward the colonists' success in defeating the British and bringing birth to a new nation—the United States of America.

THE UNITED STATES CONSTITUTION & THE BILL OF RIGHTS

Blacks hoped that their fighting and shedding blood in the Revolutionary War would bring them freedom and liberty, too. But when the Founding Fathers met, drafted, and adopted the United States Constitution and the Bill of Rights, the Blacks' exclusion was clear and defined. Article I, Section 2 in sentence 3, read:

> Representatives and direct taxes shall be
> apportioned among the several states which may be
> included within this Union, according to their respective
> Numbers, which shall be determined by adding to the
> Whole Number of free Persons, including those bound to
> service for a term of years, and excluding Indians not
> taxed, three fifths of all other Persons.*

The Constitution is called the Great Compromise, a compromise made at the expense of Black *people*: a people brought against their will, a people enslaved, a people greatly essential to the economic development of the country, and a people who fought and died, so those Founding Fathers had a free nation over which they could preside. The Constitution – the ultimate paradox and betrayal. Its Preamble uses phrases such as "We the People," "establish justice, ensure domestic tranquility…secure the Blessings of Liberty to ourselves and our posterity."[24] Yet, by making Blacks only 3/5 of a person,* the Constitution determined that all those glorified goals emanating ironically from the Enlightenment Natural Rights were not meant to include them!

Some historians blame this 3/5 compromise on the South. But James Madison's notes describing the discussions leading to the adoption of the final draft of the Constitution went beyond economics. Rather, the 3/5 compromise was an exposé of a belief system that Blacks were inferior and less than human, an attitude that most Whites, North and South, shared.[25]

This historical racist background dictates today our American political and social policies.

* Three-fifths of a person was a euphemism for Blacks and Black slaves in particular.

BACKGROUND
Analytical Summary:
EFFECTS ON BLACKS

- **Were Established by England**
- **All Colonies Used Slaves**
- **First Blacks were Indentured**
- **Majority of Slaves Came From the West African Coast by this Route**
- **A Line on Slavery in the Original Draft was Deleted**
- **Blacks Fought on Both Sides**
- **Blacks had no Rights**

In human society, our attitudes stem from our experiential thoughts. These thoughts form our behaviors. A human phenomenon; an evolutionary process. It was just such a social-political course America followed in creating the axis of Black-White attitudes and behaviors. Starting at the Thirteen English Colonies, a review of American history background makes this point indelible. The majority of slaves came from the West African Coast on the Middle Passage slave route. The more the colonies reaped increased riches from their human cargo, the more colonial attitudes and behaviors changed toward black people, from acceptance as human beings to inferior subhuman creatures.

The American social-political course got its inception in 1619 at Jamestown, Virginia. It took roots when the first Africans were brought ashore as indentured servants: Antony, Isabella and eighteen other Africans. Initially their color and race seemed not to alter the colonial attitude toward indentured peoples. The incumbent agreements of their servitude were honored same as their white counterparts. But, gradually the economy changed things. Agriculture emerged as the economic bulwark of the fledging colonies, particularly the Southern Colonies. Agriculture ruled. It boomed and thrived. As a result, labor demands intensified. By the beginning of the eighteenth century, the indentured labor system no longer sufficed. Indentured agreements dictated worker-release upon completion of the five or seven-year term. Thus retaining and maintaining an adequate worker-corp became an ever-increasing problem for the employer; workers left faster than they could be replaced. Adding further to the dilemma was the running away of both black and white servants. Plantation owners struggled, perplexed. A new strategy had to be devised. And it was – slavery!

The white run-aways could meld into the general population; Blacks could not. Their physical appearance – color and race – made for the creation of a continuous and on-going labor supply. Through the color-coded and race-based system of slavery – no work agreements had to be honored, no payments had to made, and no humanity had to be respected. This deleterious attitudinal behavior evolved toward black people, and seeped into the American psyche forming the bases of American racism because slavery existed in all of the colonies.

By the time the Founding Fathers led the Thirteen Colonies into nationhood, the degrading, exploitive slave system permeated and dictated nearly all their actions paramount to the issues of governance. Morality was set aside along with the lofty Natural Rights goals Blacks had hoped for. It was no match against the greed and profit-driven leaders. A hierarchy of superiority-inferiority of human worth became firmly entrenched with Blacks assigned the lower role in the colonists' quest to free themselves from England. All the major endeavors of the Founding Fathers reflected racist attitudes and behaviors: the original draft of the Declaration of Independence contained a line denouncing the immorality of slavery, it was deleted from the final document; Blacks fought on both sides in the Revolutionary War, they earned no freedom; in the framing of the U.S. Constitution & the Bill of Rights, Blacks were denied their rights. All these actions took on the hood of color and the mantle of race, overtly and covertly, a blatant denial of the Enlightenment rhetoric the rebel colonists so vociferously spouted.

These political pacesetters' – the Founding Fathers – thoughts, attitudes and behaviors stemmed from the outgrowth of the slave system. An economic system so inhumane and degrading – that it defiled the American psyche. They have kept Blacks ever-struggling to exercise fully their guaranteed, constitutional rights as American citizens.

BACKGROUND END NOTES

1. *The World Book, Volume U-V.* (Chicago: Field Enterprise Corporation, 1974) 126-130.

2. *We The People: The Citizen and The Constitution,* (Calabasas, California Center for Civic Education, 1995) 61.

3. _____, 62.

4. _____, 61.

5. Francis D. Adams and Barry Sanders, *Alienable Rights: The Exclusion of African Americans in a White Man's Land, 1619-2000,* (New York: Harper Collins, 2003) 54-57.

6. _____, 58.

7. *We The People,* 68-69.

8. Adams, 57-61.

9. Linda R. Monk, *The Words We Live By,* (New York: The Stonesong Press, 2003) 30.

10. *We The People,* 63.

11. James Oliver Horton and Lois E. Horton, *Slavery and the Making of America.* (New York: Oxford Press, Inc., 2005), 27.

12. John Hope Franklin, *From Slavery to Freedom* (New York: Vintage Books, 1969) 56-59.

13. _____, "Servitude and Slavery in the Southern Colonies." Chapter VI. "Experimenting in the Middle Colonies." Chapter VII. "Puritan Masters." Chapter VIII.

14. Adams, 56.

15. Arthur C. Jones, *Wade in the Water* (New York: Orbis Books, 1993). Also see Wyatt Tee Walker, *Somebody's Calling My Name* (Valley Forge, PA: Judson Press, 1979) Chapter 4. Also see Appendix.

16. Matthew T. Mellon, *Early American Views on Negro Slavery* (New York: The New American Library, 1969) Introduction v-xiii.

17. C. Eric Lincoln, *The Negro Pilgrimage in America* (New York: Bantam Books, 1967) 11. Also see Horton, 27.

18. _____, 11.

19. Horton, "The Middle Passage an Eyewitness Account." 22-23.

20. John A. Garraty and Peter Gay, editors. *The Columbia History of the World* (New York: Harper & Row, Publishers, Inc., 1972) "Society and Politics, " 692-707.

21. Horton, "The Middle Passage an Eyewitness Account." 56.

22. _____, Original Draft and Caption, 57. Also Editors of *Time, The Making of America* (New York: Time Inc., 2005) "The Peculiar Institution."

23. _____, 59.

24. Monk, 11-17. Also see Adams, Chapter 3, "The Dark Side of the Constitution," 50-78.

25. Adams, 96-105. Also see *Time*, 83.

PANEL 2

Nation Building

1789~1825

President Profiles

George Washington Term: 1789 - 1797	John Adams Term: 1797 - 1801	Thomas Jefferson Term: 1801-1809

James Madison
Term: 1809-1817

James Monroe
Term: 1817-1825

President	Date	Birthplace	College	Profession	Party
1. George Washington	1732-1799	Virginia	None	Planter	None
2. John Adams	1735-1826	Massachusetts	Harvard	Lawyer	Federalist
3. Thomas Jefferson	1743-1826	Virginia	William & Mary	Planter/Lawyer	Democratic-Republican
4. James Madison	1751-1836	Virginia	Princeton	Lawyer	Democratic-Republican
5. James Monroe	1758-1831	Virginia	William & Mary	Lawyer	Democratic-Republican

Our first five presidents were called the Revolutionary Presidents. George Washington, John Adams, Thomas Jefferson, James Madison and James Monroe all were born before there was a United States of America, and they grew up as citizens of English colonies. They predated and lived through the revolution and the Revolutionary War that freed the colonies from the Mother Country. And because of their pivotal roles in establishing the new nation, they also are considered members of the Founding Fathers.

Slavery stamped the social, political, and economic culture of the *13* colonies. By virtue of the Founding Fathers' being born and bred in the leading slave colony of Virginia, each enjoyed a comfortable life made possible by the black slaves. Adams, a New Englander from the Massachusetts colony, grew up in a

30

culture not anchored by slavery; although slavery existed there it was not the driving economic force.

George Washington was a son of a moderately successful Virginia planter.[1] His cash crop was tobacco. Washington's father had 3 children by his first wife; George was the oldest of six children that the father had by his second wife. When George was eleven, his father died. It was Lawrence, the older of his half brothers, who became his surrogate father.[2]

From birth, Washington was attended by slaves on Ferry Farm (later to become Mount Vernon), located nearly 40 miles from the Potomac River. His education was rudimentary, common in plantation society. He was tutored by private school masters. Having a good foundation in mathematics, particularly in geometry, greatly aided him in his occupation as a surveyor.

In 1752, Washington fought with the British, successfully defeating France in the French and Indian War. This military experience ultimately prepared him for his future role as commander of the Continental Army. Here he subsequently led the colonies to victory and to independence from England in the Revolutionary War (1775-1781).

In 1759, following the French and Indian War, Washington married Martha Custis, the richest widow of the colony.[3] This union elevated his social status through her wealth. She added 6,000 acres to his 5,000 and combined her 150 slaves with his 49. He settled down to the gentry-life. He prospered as a tobacco planter, a broker and land-speculator, as well as a surveyor. He also engaged in politics. Prior to the Revolution, he had served in the Virginia House of Burgesses. This role led to his being a delegate to the First and Second Continental Congress, and to his military leadership during the War of Independence. After this, he figured into the framing of the U.S. Constitution, and to his unanimous election as the first President of the new nation – the United States of America.

John Adams had quite a different background than George Washington. Growing up in Massachusetts, he had no association with the slave culture. He descended from Puritan farmers[4] who were intellectuals and who valued education. His father, who taught John to read at an early age, was a farmer and leather craftsman. As a pillar of his community, he served in the militia, and as a constable, a tax collector, and a deacon of the church. This example fueled his famous son's devotion to public service.

John Adams was bright. His superior intellect made learning easy; he was particularly outstanding in math. His family provided him, and his two younger brothers, with a well-rounded education. In the beginning, formal instruction did not appeal to him, mainly because he felt not to have been challenged by his teachers. But his father found a new teacher, under whose tutelage Adams earnestly plunged into the world of knowledge, and in 1751 he entered Harvard. His years flourished with his "growing curiosity, a love of books and fondness for study," he later wrote in his autobiography.[5] Graduating in 1755 with a Bachelor of Arts degree, he went on to study law in Worchester. As the result of his passing the bar (1758), he became a lawyer.

After Adams was admitted to the Massachusetts bar, he steadily built a successful law practice in Boston. He gained prominence with his celebrated defense of John Hancock, a signer of the Declaration of Independence, and as a most chancy counsel for the British soldiers charged with perpetrating the Boston Massacre. He parlayed his legal successes into the political arena, as a member of the Continental Congress, and as a diplomat, where he served as a member of the commission to France; later he was America's first minister to England. Upon his return to the U.S. in 1788, he served as George Washington's Vice President, and in 1796 was elected as the second President of the United States.

Thomas Jefferson, like George Washington, ascended from a culture of slavery. However, unlike Washington, his background was one of southern aristocracy.

His father was a prosperous tobacco planter; his mother was a daughter of one of Virginia's first families and a descendant of English and Scottish nobility.[6] Jefferson was one of ten children. He and his siblings enjoyed the spoils of the family's gentry-life that was under-girded by the slave labor.

Young Jefferson's education was entrusted to tutors, from whom he acquired a background in Latin, Greek, and French. After his father died in 1757—when Jefferson was 14—his education was taken over by a minister, whom Jefferson referred to as "a correct classical scholar." Under his guidance, Jefferson mastered several languages and received an introduction to natural philosophy and geology. It was this intellectual environment that nurtured his thirst for learning. It led to his becoming a man with a range of remarkable skills and accomplishments: an adept writer, lawyer, farmer, naturalist, architect, musician, linguist, classicist, philosopher, scientist, geographer, surveyor, botanist, ethnologist, and paleontologist. He is the Renaissance man of the American Presidents.

Moving beyond home tutoring, at seventeen, Jefferson entered the College of William and Mary (VA). Here he met and became a companion of George Wythe – one of Virginia's leading jurists. Upon Jefferson's graduation (1762), he apprenticed law with Wythe, and received his admittance to the bar in 1767. This association enabled Jefferson to rub elbows with the colony's leading politicians. After two years, following his becoming a lawyer, he was elected to the House of Burgesses.[7] Thus Jefferson began his entrance into politics… big time.

When the colonies' relations with England continued to deteriorate, Jefferson favored resistance to the edicts of King George III. He often spoke for the growing group of radicals. An eloquent protest against royal policy that he drafted, was rejected as too bold by hesitant delegates to the Virginia Convention. (It had been convened to select representatives to the First Continental Congress.) However, when his essay – "A Summary View of Rights of British America" – appeared in pamphlet form, it hit the colonies and Europe with dynamite force, and Jefferson became a major spokesperson for the resistance movement. In the summer of 1775, when he served as a delegate to the Second Continental Congress, his participation was temporarily interrupted by the death of his mother and the illness of his ailing wife; in December he left Philadelphia, the site of the Congress, and returned to Virginia. He remained at his Monticello home until May of 1776. Within a month of his return to Philadelphia, Richard Henry Lee, of Virginia, proposed that the colonies declare their political connection to the British crown "totally dissolved."[8] Lee's proposal received approval from the delegation. And Jefferson, along with John Adams, Benjamin Franklin, Roger Sherman of Connecticut, and Robert Livingston of New York, formed the committee to draft the formal Declaration of Independence.[9]

The committee deferred to Jefferson to write the draft. His reputation as a skilled writer and a strong advocate of the resistance cause made him the logical author. From June 8, 1776 to June 28, 1776, he worked tirelessly on it: polishing, changing and rewriting. Adams and Franklin added amendments. The committee submitted the document to the Congress on June 28, 1776. Jefferson's original draft contained more than 1,800 words. Over 460 words were expunged. Ironically, among them were the references that condemned slavery! After considerable discussion and deliberation, the Declaration was issued on July 2, and made public two days later – July 4, 1776.

With his major task completed, Jefferson returned to Virginia. He subsequently succeeded Patrick Henry as its wartime governor in 1779. Then in May of 1784, after the War ended, and he served as a delegate to the Continental Congress, Jefferson was sent to France to assist Franklin and Adams in preparing consular treaties. A year later he succeeded Franklin as minister to France, a post he held until October 1789. Upon his return to the new nation, he became the Secretary of State in Washington's cabinet. He subsequently became Vice President in the John Adams' administration. This finally led to his presidency in 1800.

Like Washington and Jefferson, **James Madison** came from a Virginia-planter background. He was the first born of seven children. Besides being a prosperous tobacco planter, his father served as a justice of the peace. He imparted to young James the obligation, as a member of the planter class, to assume community service. His mother taught him, early, to read and write. An apt student, he began his formal education at eleven. In 1769, he entered the College of New Jersey (later Princeton University). A dedicated student, he studied diligently. Madison was heavily influenced by the political philosophers, John Locke, David Hume, and Baron de Montesquieu and their thought which provided the foundation for the Period of Enlightenment. He later applied the philosophies in formatting the U.S. Constitution, of which he is called the Father.[10]

Madison received his bachelor's degree in 1771. At one point he entertained the idea of becoming a minister. After awhile, he vetoed it. Then he turned to law, which he found boring. Although he obtained a legal background, he was not admitted to the bar. Madison had always suffered from fragile health. His intense study weakened him for a time. But when the Revolution came, he found it to be a healing tonic. He plunged into the struggle. His scholarship and dedication to public service made him one of the most insightful and pivotal of the Founding Fathers. Because of his political acumen and statesmanship, Madison gained the highest office of the new nation. In 1808, he was elected the fourth President of the United States.

James Monroe, as the last of the Revolutionary Presidents, though younger than his predecessors, shared a patriotic background. His father was known to have joined George Washington and other Virginians in calling for a boycott of British goods in 1766.[11] This was in protest against the colonial policies of King George III. Few details are recorded about Monroe's childhood; however, information shows us the father was moderately prosperous as a planter and carpenter. He provided well for James and his four siblings. After his father died when young Monroe was 16, he inherited the entire estate and assumed the responsibility for the welfare of his younger brothers. Despite these demands, his education did not suffer. He became quite astute in Latin and math while attending a boys' academy. At 16 he entered the College of William and Mary. His study was interrupted by the Revolution. He dropped out. He joined the Continental Army in 1777. Monroe never returned to college to earn his degree, although he did read the law with Thomas Jefferson.

After the Revolutionary War, Monroe built a political career. From being a member of the Virginia Assembly, he was selected to membership in the Continental Congress. He held a myriad of state and federal offices. Chief among them was his appointment by Washington as Minister to France; later Jefferson appointed him Minister to Great Britain. These steps led to his position of Secretary of State under Jefferson, and then his presidency in 1816.

Washington, Adams, Jefferson, Madison and Monroe unfortunately failed to recognize or envision the ensuing damage from the belief that Blacks were inferior. These Revolutionary Presidents continued to hold the same attitude toward Africans as colonial America had held in the past. This belief is attested to by their acceptance, their endorsement, and their enforcement of the U.S. Constitution with its assertion of Blacks being 3/5 of a person as well as its inclusion of fugitive slave sections. Jefferson had provided the wording to condemn slavery in the original wording in the Declaration of Independence. When that wording was eliminated, it was the beginning of a choice these men made for America: to struggle between right and wrong, between what is right for all people or what is right for their pockets. In addition, the 1790 Naturalization Law pointedly denied Blacks their citizenship. Furthermore, the Founding Fathers' very candid writings about Blacks reflected white supremacy views, beliefs and behaviors. These attitudes set the stage and bases for the continuing racial dilemmas that plagues the institutions of American society today.[12]

NATION BUILDING ISSUES & ACTIONS

- **Ratification of the U.S. Constitution & The Bill of Rights**
- **Four Presidents as Slave Owners**
- **Louisiana Purchase 1803**
- **Slave Trade Ban 1808**
- **Invention of Cotton Gin 1793**
- **Compromise of 1820**

The ratification of the United States Constitution & The Bill of Rights set the political and social course for America. They authorized and directed how presidents carry out their duties in the enforcement of the laws of the land. When the Founding Fathers drafted the document it was a compromise; a compromise agreed upon at the expense of black people. The 3/5 clause designated Blacks – in a euphemistic manner – to be not a whole person. This was racism. That racist stigma still lingers over America – the legacy of slavery.

Slavery existed in all the colonies, and it continued when they became states. At this time, as it was before independence, most of the slavery was in the agricultural South. Many of the southern planters grew wealthy from the system, particularly those from Virginia. By virtue of their wealth, they amassed vast political influence and political power. It therefore follows, that four of the new nation's first five presidents, hailed from Virginia gentry. Their privileged lifestyle – George Washington, Thomas Jefferson, James Madison and James Monroe – was the courtesy of the slaves they owned. John Adams, a New Englander, owned no slaves.

In 1803, the new nation doubled in size. President Thomas Jefferson got an offer from the French ruler, Napoleon Bonaparte – one he could not refuse: he could buy 800,000 square miles of western lands for 15 million dollars! Jefferson authorized Secretary of State James Monroe to make the buy. The buy became known as the Louisiana Purchase. This acquisition presented a formidable dilemma. At the center many questions arose concerning the role of slavery and black people, such as: How much expansion of slavery? How will the spreading be controlled? And what areas should be allowed to have it? Several developments complicated the situation.

During the late 1700's, the federal government began encouraging industrial growth. It fostered new manufacturing methods. Eli Whitney's 1793 invention of the cotton gin revolutionized the processing of cotton. Cotton became King. Demands spurred the southern planters to increase and expand the acreage, and labor needs accompanied the phenomenon. More workers, more slaves! Then, due to the mandate decreed by the U.S. Constitution banning the Transatlantic Slave Trade beginning in1808, meeting the labor urgency posed a further problem, temporarily. Ingenuity created another domestic industry: slave breeding, selling and trading – another rung was added to the ladder of degradation of black people.

These developments led to political intervention, because freesoilers did not want slavery spilling out of control into the new lands of the Louisiana Purchase. The balance between slave states and non-slave states was threatened. To deal with this issue, Congress enacted the Compromise of 1820. The balance was maintained by admitting Missouri as a slave state and Maine as a free state. Unfortunately, this legislation proved to be only a stop gap....

RATIFICATION OF THE U.S. CONSTITUTION AND THE BILL OF RIGHTS

The Articles of Confederation formed the first government plan of the new nation. It proved ineffective. The Constitution and the Bill of Rights were drafted as its replacement. To be operational, the Constitution had to be ratified by nine states. New Hampshire made it official in June 1788. Fully ratified, it took effect, as the law of the land with the convening of the new Congress in March 1789. The new nation, through its delegates, authorized and approved an unfair and racially biased government.

FOUR PRESIDENTS AS SLAVE OWNERS

Virginia developed into one of the leading states of the new nation. Its prosperous economy and political leadership destined it to be the logical source for presidential material. All Virginians, George Washington, Thomas Jefferson, James Madison, and James Monroe fulfilled the destiny. They enjoyed a gentleman's life of wealth and comfort. These amenities came by virtue of slave labor and a Constitution that endorsed black inferiority.

LOUISIANA PURCHASE

During Thomas Jefferson's tenure, Napoleon reigned in France. Louisiana Territory belonged to the French. By taking this land back from Spain, the French caused American merchants concern about shipping on the Mississippi River and deposit rights at New Orleans. Jefferson decided he needed to buy New Orleans. Early in 1808, he sent James Monroe to Paris to negotiate.

Napoleon wanted to conquer the world. He subjected France to enormous debt. His warring cost heavily in troops and money. He was in need of money to carry on his campaign with England. To the surprise of Monroe, Napoleon offered to sell all of Louisiana including New Orleans for 15 million dollars!

Without hesitation, Jefferson authorized its purchase, doubling the size of the new nation. It eventually became the center of conflict over the expansion of slavery and the accompanying sectionalism rancor.[13]

SLAVE TRADE BAN 1808

"Article I, Section 9, Sentence 1: (The United States Constitution) The migration or Importation of such persons as any of the states...think proper to admit, shall not be prohibited by the Congress prior to the year one thousand eight hundred and eight...."

As in Article I, Section 2, sentence 3 of the Constitution,[14] the above section deals also with the North-South compromise over determining each state's representation in the U.S. House of Representatives. And, as in the former Section, the Founding Fathers affected the compromise without using the words: slave or slavery. The phrase "migration and importation of such persons…" uses the words without designating who the "persons" are. In essence, it meant the South could count imported slaves as 3/5 of a person until 1808—for the next twenty years—until the ban of the Atlantic slave trade became law. Then the North would not have to contend with an unfair, and an uneven, growth of southerners in the House, because of the Atlantic slave trade.

This, however, barely dented the slave business. Slaves were still smuggled in illegally from Africa until the close of the Civil War. In addition, the South created a very lucrative and thriving domestic slave breeding and selling business, further dehumanizing black people.[15]

THE COTTON GIN

Eli Whitney invented the cotton gin in 1793. It greatly increased the efficiency of processing cotton and of slave productivity, as well as furthering the need for adding more slaves. The invention of the cotton gin made Cotton King and further perpetuated the system of slavery and its accompanying ills for both black people and for the country as a whole.[16]

THE COMPROMISE OF 1820

The Compromise of 1820 was also called the Missouri Compromise. When in 1819, Missouri applied for statehood, northern politicians objected. Its admission would upset the free state – slave state balance (Missouri was slaveholding), and it would bring slavery into the northern part of the Louisiana Territory. It also posed the question as to what would happen when additional states were carved from the West and the North territories.

Maine's application for statehood supplied the solution. Maine came in free; Missouri entered slave, retaining the balance. However, the Compromise of 1820 proved only to be a stopgap. The acquisition and expansion of more land and territory, subsequently nullified the Compromise.[17]

NATION BUILDING
Analytical Summary:
EFFECTS ON BLACKS

- **Blacks 3/5 of a Person**
- **John Adams Owned No Slaves**
- **Conflict Over Slavery Expansion**
- **Establishment of Domestic Slave Breeding and Selling**
- **More Slaves Needed**
- **Balance Number of Slave and Free States**

Presidential Oath of Office

"I do solemnly swear (or affirm) that I will faithfully execute the Office of President of the United States, and will to the best of my ability, preserve, protect and defend the Constitution of the United States."

They set the precedent: Presidents Washington, Adams, Jefferson, Madison and Monroe. They presided over a brand new nation and a government conceived from the Enlightenment philosophy. This governance philosophy centered around the Natural Rights of Man concept. It drew its political power from "We the People." A people identified in the U.S. Constitution under Article 1, Section 2, thusly: "Whole number of free persons, including those bound to Service for Term of Year, and excluding Indians not taxed, three-fifths of all other Persons." The latter group euphemistically infers the three-fifths to be Blacks. Other than this benign inference, Blacks get no specific mention. Yet, with the Founding Fathers largely being lawyers, worded this controversy over Blacks, as being property or people, led to the three-fifths compromise-premise in the Constitution allowing the 3/5 issue open to interpretation. So when Washington,

Adams, Jefferson, Madison and Monroe swore to preserve, protect and defend the Constitution, it implied that they need not concern themselves with Blacks. After all, Blacks held no "We the People" membership enumerated in the Preamble. But this could not have been further from the truth.

These presidents ever-found Blacks to be a concern, ranging from political to personal issues. The fact that four of them – Washington, Jefferson, Madison and Monroe – owned slaves, they were forced to be concerned. They led a gentry-life supported by a domestic slave breeding system. Slavery also supplied the glue unifying the young nation's thriving economy. Therefore, virtually all of its political, social and economic viability was dependent on Blacks as slaves. Hence the presidents continually sought answers to questions spawned by the presence of Blacks and the accompanying issue of slavery.

What to do about the role of slavery due to the vast lands acquired through the Louisiana Purchase? How to enforce the Constitutionally decreed Slave Trade Ban of 1808? And then, as a consequence, how to maintain a labor supply? Particularly pressing since the revolutionizing technology of the cotton gin. What about the balance act of free states to slave status? Then there were the free Blacks; who were only quasi-free? Many had inherited their status, perhaps from their indentured forbearers.

The course of action the Presidents took on these problem issues was pure irony. These men of the Enlightenment Age set the precedent that made America racist, the antithesis of the philosophy they so eloquently proclaimed in their inaugural addresses. Washington, Adams, Jefferson, Madison, and Monroe fostered a social, political, and economic system in America that caused black people to continue to not be free, to have no rights, to be denied the fruits of their labor; and to be degraded and dehumanized. Unfortunately the approach each president took foreshadowed little chance of America fulfilling the promises for the Enlightenment philosophy which was to foster the rights of man.

NATION BUILDING END NOTES

1. Michael Beschloss, *American Heritage Illustrated History of the Presidents: More Than Two Centuries of American Leadership*, (New York: Crown Publishers, 2000) 17.

2. William A. Degregorio, *The Complete Book of U.S. Presidents*, (New York: Wings Books, 1996) 2.

3. _____, 4.

4. Beschloss, 35.

5. Degregorio, 23.

6. Beschloss, 49.

7. _____, 50.

8. Editors of *Time,* "The Making of America: Life, Liberty and the Pursuit of a Nation," (New York: Time Books, 2005) 57.

9. Degregorio, 43, 44.

10. Beschloss, 65.

11. Degregorio, 74.

12. Adams, Chapter 3. "The Dark Side of the Constitution," 50-78. Also *Time*, 82-85.

13. _____, Chapter 4. "The Founding Fathers at Home," 79-108.

14. *Time*, "How the West was Won," 106-115.

15. Franklin, "The Domestic Slave Trade," 175-182.

16. Meier, 48.

17. Adams, 136-141.

\

President Profiles

John Quincy Adams	Andrew Jackson	Martin Van Buren	William Henry Harrison	John Tyler	James K. Polk	Zachary Taylor
Term: 1825-1829	Term: 1829-1837	Term: 1837-1841	Term: 1841-1841	Term: 1841-1845	Term: 1845-1849	Term: 1849-1850

President	Date	Birthplace	College	Profession	Party
6. John Quincy Adams	1767-1848	Massachusetts	Harvard	Lawyer	Democratic/ Republic
7. Andrew Jackson	1767-1845	South Carolina	None	Lawyer	Democrat
8. Martin Van Buren	1782-1862	New York	None	Lawyer	Democrat
9. William Henry Harrison	1773-1841	Virginia	Hampden-Sydney	Soldier	Whig
10. John Tyler	1790-1862	Virginia	William and Mary	Lawyer	Whig
11. James K. Polk	1795-1849	North Carolina	N. Carolina University	Lawyer	Democrat
12. Zachary Taylor	1784-1850	Virginia	None	Soldier	Whig

John Quincy Adams, Andrew Jackson, Martin Van Buren, William Henry Harrison, John Tyler, James K. Polk and Zachary Taylor grew up when Blacks in general, and slaves in particular, meant little more than a commodity. The precedent set by their predecessor Revolutionary Presidents, along with their own backgrounds, shaped their social-political attitudes towards all Blacks.

John Quincy Adams was the son of the second U.S. President. Like his father, he had no association with the slave culture. In fact, his formative years growing up were spent largely outside the United States. Born in Massachusetts, young John Quincy, like his father, received an extraordinary education. However, he bettered his father's education. From age 10 to 17, he lived and was educated in

Europe, when senior Adams held various assignments in France, the Netherlands and Britain.[1] By the time John Quincy returned to the U.S. in 1785, he had mastered Latin, Greek, French, Dutch, and to a lesser extent, Spanish. Within two years after entering Harvard, he graduated Phi Beta Kappa and second in the class of 1787. During the next two years, Adams studied law leading to his admittance to the Massachusetts bar in1790.

Adams did not pursue law as a career. He parlayed his youth experiences in Europe into representing the U.S. in the diplomatic field. He served as minister to the Netherlands, Prussia, Russia, and Great Britain. Because of this stellar background, President James Monroe appointed Adams as his Secretary of State, where he distinguished himself to be among the most gifted and accomplished Secretaries of State. He served from 1817-1825.[2] This was the phenomenal background John Quincy Adams brought to the White House upon his election in 1824.

Andrew Jackson brought a starkly different background to the White House than did his predecessor, John Quincy Adams.[3] Jackson had frontier roots. He was of Scotch-Irish ancestry and was the only American-born child of his immigrant parents. (He had two older brothers who were born in Ireland.) Jackson's parents settled in a region straddled between North and South Carolina. Andrew's father died just prior to Jackson's birth. By the time he was 14, his mother died; Andrew was left as an orphan. However, he had two uncles. He lived alternately between the two of them. Before her death, Jackson's mother saw to his getting a rudimentary education, although he was not a good student. Yet, after a period of time pursuing unwholesome activities, he settled down and spent two years studying law. In September 1787, Jackson was admitted to the North Carolina bar. Here he practiced law when the northern section of North Carolina entered the Union as Tennessee. And it was also here that he started his political life, interspersed with military exploits.[4]

Jackson had first tasted the military at age 13. He and his older brother, Robert, joined the Continental Army during the American Revolution; he served as a messenger. In 1812, the young nation was at war with Britain again. As a governor-appointed major general of the U.S. Tennessee Volunteers, he led raw recruits in battle with such sterling brilliance in Natchez, Mississippi, that his men nicknamed him "Old Hickory." By May of 1814, Jackson became a Major General in the regular U.S. Army.

Once again his military prowess shone: first in the invasion of Florida leading to the capture of Pensacola, and then on to the Battle of New Orleans. This decisive victory over crack (elite) British troops officially ended the War of 1812. At war's end in 1816, General Andrew – Old Hickory – Jackson emerged as a national hero. However, his military exploits did not stop with the defeat of the British. He went on to engage in brutal warfare against the Seminole Indians. His hatred of them and other tribal groups of the Cherokee Nation carried over into his Indian policies during his two-term administration as President.[5] His contempt toward Blacks was equally as deep.

Capitalizing on his military fame, Jackson gained political stature. He served in the U.S. Congress representing Tennessee, both in the House and the Senate. Riding his military and political successes, Jackson garnered prominence in the Democratic Party, which eventually led to his presidency in 1828.

Whereas Andrew Jackson was the first American-born in his family, **Martin Van Buren** was the first President born an American citizen. All the preceding presidents were born prior to the Declaration of Independence, and thus they were British subjects. Van Buren differed from Jackson also in his geographic background, having been born and raised in New York. Of Dutch ancestry, his great grandfather emigrated in 1631 from the Netherlands to the Upper Hudson region as an indentured servant. Van Buren's father was a farmer and tavern keeper. Although he owned a few slaves,[6] the future President never owned any.

Van Buren grew up in a household that spoke Dutch. His family, although not destitute, was relatively poor. He was one of eight children. His father scuffled to make a decent living for his large brood. At an early age, young Martin helped by working in the tavern and delivering produce from the farm after school. His education consisted of the basics he learned at a dreary, poorly-equipped village schoolhouse. Later he briefly studied Latin at an academy. However, his formal education ended before he reached 14; still he excelled in composition and speaking. And, a prominent attorney took him on as a law apprentice. He thrived. In 1803, he was admitted to the New York bar at age 21.

After his admission to the bar, Van Buren joined his brother in a law practice. He also engaged in politics, receiving his first appointment to public office in 1808. His political acumen led him up the political ladder. He climbed up first to local, and then to state and federal offices. Following a brief tenure as governor of New York, Van Buren served as Secretary of State during Andrew Jackson's first presidential term. He then became Jackson's Vice President during the second term. Through the close support and association with Andrew Jackson, Van Buren gained party (Democratic) endorsement and was elected the eighth President of the United States.

William Henry Harrison, the ninth President, came from a background of aristocracy, similar in inherited public service that was John Quincy Adams'. But Harrison's lineage was even more august. His great grandfather had emigrated from England to the Virginia colony in 1632 where he served on Virginia's council and subsequently became one of the largest landowners in the colony. A succession of Harrison's grandfathers served in the Virginia House of Burgesses. Benjamin Harrison V, his father, signed the Declaration of Independence, and was the official draftsman of congressional dispatches that were sent to General George Washington in the field during the Revolutionary War.[7]

This was the political atmosphere that young Harrison grew up in during the American Revolution; he was also the last President born of a British subject. Despite their early life being disrupted by the Revolutionary War, his family recovered to regain its planter-prosperity, undergirded by slave labor. Tutor-based, his early education gave him the fundamentals. And, at age 14, after having decided on a medical career, he enrolled in Hampden-Sydney College for a premed course of study. Classical languages, geography, history, mathematics and rhetoric formed the list of studies. He especially liked military history; however, he stuck with his hopes of being a doctor. In 1790, he enrolled at the University of Pennsylvania Medical School in Philadelphia. Shortly after Harrison's arrival, his father died. His was a short stay at the school. He ran out of money, and he abandoned the idea of being a doctor; he joined the U.S. Army.

Harrison became a professional soldier (1791-1798 and 1812-1814) during which time he rose from ensign to major general. He fought in the Northwest Territory Indian Wars and in the War of 1812. Between stints in war, Harrison forged a political path as an official in various capacities in the Northwest Territory, and in Ohio. His military successes enhanced his climb to be a prominent Whig. And in 1836, he became the party's presidential nominee, but lost to Martin Van Buren. However, when Harrison ran again four years later, he was victorious. He became the ninth President of the United States.

William Henry Harrison did not last long as President. He died one month after his March 4, 1841 inaugural address. His death, from pneumonia, was due to his lengthy speech outdoors in a brisk March wind; Harrison wore no hat, gloves nor overcoat. Following the inauguration, he was caught in a downpour while strolling back to the White House. He was drenched. All this proved fatal to the 68-year-old, newly-elected President.[8]

John Tyler was Harrison's Vice President. Because of Harrison's sudden death, Tyler, unexpectedly became president. He, like his predecessor, was born and bred in Virginia. His father, who had served as governor of Virginia (1809-1811), was a prosperous planter who owned 40 slaves. There was a close bond between young Tyler and his father. This came about when his mother died; he was 7 years old. He was taught to play the fiddle by his father; they enjoyed lively musical sessions together. At 12, Tyler entered the preparatory school at William and Mary. He later progressed to the college level and received his degree graduating in 1807, at the age of 17. In 1809, he was admitted to the Virginia State bar. He studied law successfully in Richmond in the office of Edmond Randolph, the first U.S. Attorney General.

Save for a brief stint with the state militia during the War of 1812, Tyler carved out a long, distinguished political career before taking the reins of the presidency. As a Jeffersonian Republican, he was elected to the Virginia State House. Later he served in the U.S. Congress, both as a U. S. Representative and a U.S. Senator. It was after he left the State Legislature, that Tyler changed his party affiliation to the Whigs. They tapped him in 1840 to be William Henry Harrison's running mate under the slogan: "Tippecanoe and Tyler, too." Because Harrison was the first U. S. President to die in office, John Tyler set the precedent of succession of how a Vice President assumes the Presidency.[9]

During this period of Westward Expansion, like the Presidents before him – Andrew Jackson, William Henry Harrison and John Tyler – **James K. Polk** came from a southern plantation background. His father was a prosperous planter, surveyor and land speculator. He owned thousands of acres of land in North Carolina and middle Tennessee, along with large numbers of slaves. Although he never held political office, he was a Jeffersonian Republican, a staunch supporter and friend of Andrew Jackson. Both of them were native-Carolinians, who had become Tennesseans.

James' family moved to Tennessee from North Carolina when he was 10 years old. Here his grandfather lived, having purchased extensive amounts of land.

Much of the area was virgin territory and had to be cleared. Polk toiled unendingly, helping the family prepare the land for the new home. Until he was 17, his basic education was informal. His formal instruction began when he enrolled in a Presbyterian school. He studied diligently and made fine progress. In 1816, he entered as a sophomore at the University of North Carolina. His excellence in debate and public speaking inspired him to have a career in politics. After graduating with honors, he studied law with a prominent attorney. In 1820, he was admitted to the bar, and the same year he became a clerk in the Tennessee State Senate. This job opened the political door for Polk.

Polk possessed a driving work ethic. This gained him a reputation as an industrious Jacksonian Democrat. While in Washington representing Tennessee in the U.S. Congress, he earned the leadership role of Speaker of the House of Representatives. His career in politics flourished under the Jackson and Van Buren administrations; however, when the Whigs took over the Presidency during the Harrison-Tyler tenure, Polk's rise was temporarily forestalled. But, in the 1844 run-for-the-Presidency, he beat out two other candidates. As a stalwart steward of Manifest Destiny, who had Andrew Jackson's strong backing, James Polk furthered the fight to spread slavery by becoming the eleventh U.S. President.[10]

Zachary Taylor assumed the presidential mantel after James K. Polk. Although both were southerners and slave owners, they differed in their views about spreading slavery into the newly-expanded lands. Taylor opposed it. He also differed from Polk in background. Taylor's lineage was one of aristocracy, being a direct descendant of a Pilgrim leader who arrived on the Mayflower. His forefathers later settled in Virginia to establish a dynasty of prominent planters and public officials. Taylor shared the same great-grandfather as James Madison, the fourth U.S. President.

Zachary Taylor's father served in the Continental Army during the Revolutionary War. He was a lieutenant colonel, who distinguished himself in battles at White Plains and Brandywine. After the war, he moved young Zachary and his seven siblings to Kentucky, on the edge of the western frontier. The elder Taylor owned more than 10,000 acres of land in various parts of Kentucky. Slave labor made the Taylor family lands productive and prosperous.

At the time when Taylor was growing up, his family and other settlers of this frontier area lived under constant threat of Indian attacks. He became, as a result, an unusually gifted marksman, and a rugged individualist. Receiving only a basic tutored education, he never went to college; instead, his ambition and attraction to the military led to his army career. He was a military officer from 1808-1848, where he rose from first lieutenant to major general. The War of 1812, the Black Hawk and Second Seminole War – wars against Indians – and the Mexican-American War brought him fame.[11] He was affectionately nicknamed by his men as, "Old Rough and Ready."

At the end of James Polk's presidency, the Democrats had lots of dissention in the party. Divergent views on the slave question, abolition and sectionalism precipitated much of the discord. With this wedge dividing the party, the Whigs reclaimed the White House, riding in on the coattails of the national hero, Zachary Taylor – "Old Rough and Ready."

As was the turmoil that surrounded the Zachary Taylor election, so was the atmosphere characterizing the period of Westward Expansion. Its growing pains spawned chaos and tumult. The presidents of the era could not handle wisely the slavery problem, the core of the foment. The question pervaded all discussions: What to do about slavery and Blacks? All these presidents' actions – or inactions – exacerbated a continually deteriorating situation. They did little to improve anything remotely related to Blacks – or Indians and Mexicans, for that matter.

- **John Quincy Adams** used citizenship regulations to deny Blacks jobs as ship captains or employment in postal areas;[12]
- **Jackson** militarily enforced removal of the Cherokee Nation, simultaneously divesting them of their land, and eliminating a refuge for runaway slaves;
- **Tyler** detested anti-slavery societies and tried desperately to abolish them;[13]
- **Harrison's** sudden death short circuited any plans to spread slavery in the added lands;
- **Van Buren** hoped that deportation and colonization of Blacks would solve the problem;
- **Polk** pushed expansionism, provoking the Mexican-American War. Also Polk's agenda called for spreading the slave system onto conquered Mexican lands;
- Although **Taylor** opposed spreading the infamous system, he paradoxically increased his personal slave enterprise in Louisiana and Florida.

This was an unfortunate time; a time that further entrenched the new nation into the mire of racism. This legacy, forwarded by the founding fathers, was the blueprint followed by the Westward Expansion Presidents: Blacks as human beings were inferior; and Blacks as slaves were a commodity. But then, adding fuel to the fire, was the Manifest Destiny mantra, "All this is providential, God is on our side condoning this behavior…" The lack of vision and foresight that characterized the Revolutionary Presidents also crippled Adams, Jackson, Van Buren, Tyler, Polk and Taylor in their decision-making, their policies and their political actions.

WESTWARD EXPANSION
ISSUES & ACTIONS

- **Five Slaveowner Presidents**
- **Indian Removal Act**
- **Manifest Destiny**
- **Texas Annexation**
- **Mexican American War**
- **Gold Rush**
- **Slave Revolts**

During the era of Westward Expansion, the new nation's political power continued to be held by southerners, slave-holding southerners. It was from this cadre that five of the next seven U.S. presidents came: Andrew Jackson, William Henry Harrison, John Tyler, James K. Polk and Zachary Taylor. Taylor was the only one of this group not seeking the expansion of slavery. The other two presidents of this period – northerners John Quincy Adams and James Van Buren – also did not politically push for broadening the slave system.

Andrew Jackson sought to curb Indians' harboring of runaway slaves. He held intense disdain for both groups. By urging Congress to pass the Indian Removal Act, and by passing innumerable treaties, Jackson succeeded in eventually divesting the Cherokee Nation – the Cherokee, the Creek, the Chickasaw, the Choctaw and the Seminole – of its eastern lands. Lands Jackson referred to as having only "retarded improvement." And in doing so, he deprived runaway slaves of their refuge, plus he enabled the land-grabbing Whites to gobble-up choice Indian land in Georgia, Alabama, Mississippi, and parts of Florida, South Carolina and Tennessee.

In 1845, John L. O'Sullivan, a New York journalist, articulated a rationalization as to America's right to overspread and possess the whole of the continent. He proclaimed it was its Manifest Destiny, a Providential inheritance. "God was on our side" mandated America to fulfill a divine mission, to take the lands and to develop the white man's culture; its being superior to that of Native Americans and Mexicans who occupied the lands. This mantra further justified slavery. The Texas Annexation of 1845 and the exploitive vanquishing of the Mexicans in the Mexican American War (1846-1848) led the administrations of Tyler, Polk and Taylor to enforce the Manifest Destiny doctrine.

Hunger and greed for gold received a massive impetus with the January 1848 discovery in California. Within six months, Pacific coastal towns were all but deserted due to the surge to dig in the Sierras. By the end of 1848, news spread to the East; and during the next year, the 49ers, over 80,000, swarmed from all parts of the U.S. and throughout the world. Men of all stripes. Blacks – runaway slaves, freemen and mountain men, in particular – joined the rush!

During the 1820's, 1830's and 1840's, slave revolts were occurring with inordinate frequency. Fear and suspicion gripped Whites. Jack Bowler, Denmark Vesey and Nat Turner led uprisings that continued to chill the nation. Fugitive-slave laws and ordinances passed in ever-increasing ferocity and frenzy. Blacks – free and slave – suffered under the onslaught of the white backlash.

FIVE SLAVEOWNER PRESIDENTS

Andrew Jackson, William Henry Harrison, John Tyler, James Polk and Zachary Taylor owned slaves. These five, plus the four founding father Presidents, brought the total to nine of our country's first twelve Presidents who practiced slavery. It is not difficult to understand why little or no progress was made during this period in eradicating the system and improving conditions for black people. Rather the contrary took place: more land, more slavery.

INDIAN REMOVAL ACT

From the time Europeans first set foot on American soil, they held as their prime objective to take and to control Indian land. As the new nation grew, its greed was commensurate. Early on, Thomas Jefferson backed Congress in removing members of the Cherokee Nation in Georgia to lesser lands. But it took Andrew Jackson's heartless and relentless drive to force them completely from their ancestral lands in Georgia, South Carolina, Alabama, and upper Florida. The Cherokees, the Chickasaws, the Choctaws, the Creeks, and some of the Seminoles fell prey under the 1830 Indian Removal Act. This was no piecemeal operation. Jackson ordered the U.S. Military to root them out of their homes and relocate them thousands of miles beyond the Mississippi River. This western territory is known as Oklahoma today. This cruel, inhumane act, known as the "Trail of Tears," exacted its toll. Nearly one fourth of those who embarked on the massive evacuation perished, a near genocide.

Jackson held contempt toward Blacks and Indians. He believed Blacks were subhuman; his views of Indians were not much higher. His disdain became manifest as more and more runaway slaves found refuge among the Indians. Some Blacks, by intermarrying members of the Cherokee Nation, gained tribal membership. Yet, ironically, other Blacks just exchanged masters, a white one for an Indian one. However, regardless of what kind of relationship existed between Blacks and Indians, Andrew Jackson, as president, exercised his power to remedy the situation. He pushed Congress to pass the Indian Removal Act and defied a U.S. Supreme Court ruling that decreed the Act illegal. He boasted that he commanded the military, and thus the court could not enforce its decision, rendering it invalid.

So Jackson, in carrying out his mission of expelling the Cherokee Nation from their lands, gained double satisfaction: it opened choice land for white occupation and exploitation, and it eliminated a refuge and sanctuary for runaway slaves.

The Indian Removal Act proved only a harbinger of things to come for Indians and Blacks under subsequent presidential actions.[14]

MANIFEST DESTINY

The mantra "God is on our side" shaped the actions and policies of Whites in their quest for more and more land. By the 1830's, this took on a religious zeal. The belief brought on the feeling that God, the republic, and the democracy alike, demanded the American duty to press on west, to settle, to civilize, and to democratize all the lands from the Atlantic to the Pacific, between Canada and Mexico! John L. O'Sullivan, an eastern journalist, articulated this concept through the term "Manifest Destiny."[15]

The Presidents – Jackson, Van Buren, Tyler, Polk and Taylor – plus the Congress, latched onto the theme by the 1840's. "This continent was intended by Providence as a vast theatre on which to work out the grand experiment of Republican Government, under the auspices of the Anglo-Saxon race," the words spoken by a congressman addressing the House.[16] His sentiments signaled a further rocky political and social road for Indians and Blacks.

TEXAS ANNEXATION

Spanish control of Mexico began in 1519 with the arrival of Hernando Cortes, a Spanish Conquistador, and his ultimate conquest of Montezuma and the Aztec Empire. Subsequent Spanish colonization and domination lasted until their overthrow in 1821. Mexico gained its independence. However, shortly before their defeat, the Spanish issued a land grant in 1820 to an American named Moses Austin. By doing so, they hoped the Americans could bring about development of the northern sector, of which Texas was a part. The practice of granting free land to Americans continued under the newly-formed Mexican government. But in order to get the grant, the grantee was to agree to certain restrictions, among which was a ban on slavery. Americans paid no attention; they brought slaves into Texas anyway.

This violation, along with others by the Americans, angered the Mexican government officials. They, at the same time, were displeased with the native people of the area, who were called Tejaños. The Tejaños colluded with the Americans to separate from Mexico. Their rebellion sparked a war. Inspired by the rally cry of "Remember the Alamo," the Americans and Tejaños defeated Mexico and gained their freedom in 1836. This made Texas an independent state – The Lone Star State.

The American government coveted Texas. Presidents Tyler and Polk saw a Texas Annexation as furthering Manifest Destiny, and as a means of spreading slavery. Bitter arguments ensued in Congress between the North and South over adding Texas to the United States. The pro-Texas faction won out, and Texas joined the Union as a slave state in December, 1845.

MEXICAN AMERICAN WAR

President Polk led the action that brought Texas into the Union. He purposely agitated Mexico by sending American troops across the border. This action brought on war with Mexico. It broke out on May 13, 1846, after his deliberate provocation.[17] With superior resources and power, the United States eventually defeated Mexico in February of 1848. With the signing of the Treaty of Guadalupe Hidalgo,[18] more than 525,000 square miles of territory were added to the nation. California, Nevada, Utah, Arizona, and parts of Wyoming, Colorado and New Mexico comprised the new land acquisition. This expansion intensified the quarrels over slavery, thus increasing Congressional compromises and legislation over the issue.

CALIFORNIA GOLD RUSH

On February 3, 1848, the Mexican American War ended with the signed Guadalupe Hidalgo Treaty. Just days prior, the epic gold discovery occurred at Sutters' Mill, California.[19] It set off a global frenzy. A surge of goldseekers flooded the San Francisco area in 1849. The Forty-niners, as they were called, changed this sleepy little town into a city of over 25,000 in no time. The Gold Rush brought Blacks, too. Both free and runaway Blacks saw opportunity. They hoped for a chance to stake a claim and to strike it rich. But like the majority of the 49er's, their dreams were just that – dreams, unfulfilled. But unlike the unsuccessful Whites, Blacks failed usually for different reasons. However, they stemmed mostly from the very familiar scenario – *Racism*.

Whites from the North and the South brought their hateful attitudes toward Blacks to California with them. When black seekers managed to stake a claim, all too frequently, they were jumped, frightened away, beaten and even murdered. Not deterred, they held on to their dreams, finding other avenues to ply their skills – both black men and black women. They established laundries, barbershops, hotels, restaurants and other types of service businesses. Once again they overcame the odds.

SLAVE REVOLTS

Even before George Washington found slave behavior an annoyance and a disruption, revolts accompanied slavery. Slaves rebelled when being taken from Africa, boarding the ships, on board the ships, on the high seas, and on to the plantations. Contrary to the rationalizations, myths, and legends of the "happy slave," the revolts, uprisings, and conspiracies initiated and carried out by Blacks refute this.

Some of the more prominent slaves who led revolts were Gabriel Prosser, Jack Bowler, Denmark Vesey and Nat Turner. Although ill-fated and unsuccessful, these episodes of bloodletting and mayhem caused fear and unrest among the slave owners and other Whites.[20] Therefore policies and procedures were strengthened during this time to restrict and control Blacks.

WESTWARD EXPANSION
Analytical Summary:
EFFECTS ON BLACKS

- **John Q. Adams and James Van Buren had No Slaves**
- **Slaves Lose Refuge**
- **Administrations Urged Expansion in Texas and Mexican Territory**
- **Blacks Among 49ers**
- **Slaves Increase Fight for Freedom**

The attitudes of disdain and superiority by Whites towards Blacks established in Eighteenth Century America continued to intensify during the Westward Expansion Era. The presidential pattern of slave-holding men in the office followed their predecessors. Greed for more and more land grew commensurately along with Manifest Destiny mania. America was in a frenzy; at the same time, Black reaction gained strength as they sought ways to overcome racism.

Despite the 1808 Slave Trade Ban that came to pass – slavery did not abate. Instead, slaves were still smuggled in from Africa and a bustling domestic slave trade thrived. The slave-catching industry added even more strife to black life, both in the North and in the South. Cotton was King and analogous businesses made many northern and southern Whites wealthy. Among those benefiting from the slave labor were five of the seven presidents – Andrew Jackson, William Henry Harrison, John Tyler, James Polk and Zachary Taylor. So they had vested interests in keeping a slave economy and Blacks in bondage. When the Indian Removal Act displaced the Cherokee Nation, the Texas Annexation added more southern land, and the provoked war-victory over Mexico widened the land grab even more. The greed and the graft, spurred by Manifest Destiny, caused the incumbent presidents little pause in acting in favor of exploitation.

The era of Western Expansion showcased unfettered American agreed. Wrapped in the veneer of Manifest Destiny, the presidents used any wanton means possible to gobble up Mexican lands, to destroy Native American societies and to expand black bondage. As dark as times were for Blacks, signs of light flickered: national morality was sinking, but black resolve was rising.

Many Blacks, free and slave, grew steadily overwrought with the degradation and exploitation. Some fled west to California, joining the gold-seeking 49ers. Some in the South exploded into rioting. The majority of those Blacks who followed the Gold Rush and dreamed of striking it rich, failed. But they did not give up, even though the gold eluded them. They found other avenues of opportunity. Being opportunists, both black men and black women, parlayed their skills and ingenuity successfully into other business pursuits. Meantime, in the South, slave revolts spread. Jack Bowler, Denmark Vesey and Nat Turner were in the vanguard. Although their exploits failed, all was not in vain. Other Blacks and their white allies gave the federal government, and subsequent presidents, notice that slavery and black oppression must cease!

WESTWARD EXPANSION END NOTES

1. De Gregorio, 92.

2. _____,94-96. Also see Beschloss, 92, 93.

3. _____,106-108.

4. _____,109-110.

5. The Cherokee Nation was composed of five southeastern tribal groups: the Cherokee, the Choctaw, the Chickasaw, the Creek and Seminole. Jackson, as president, carried out his contempt toward the Indians by militarily ordering their removal from their ancestral lands in Georgia, Alabama, South Carolina, and parts of Florida. The Indian Removal Act of 1830 gave him the authority to banish them to the territory now known as Oklahoma. The Indian journey in which one out of four died was called "The Trail of Tears."

6. The colony of New York was initially settled by the Dutch. Slavery was prevalent. Sojourner Truth, the ex-slave abolitionist, was in bondage in New York. Her first language was Dutch.

7. De Gregorio, 137-138.

8. _____, "Death In Office," 145.

9. Beschloss, "His Accidency," 132-133.

10. De Gregorio, 166-168.

11. _____, 178-180.

12. Adams, 146.

13. _____, 148.

14. Paul Johnson, *A History of the American People* (New York: Harper Collins, 1999) 351.

15. _____, 371-372.

16. _____, 373-376.

17. _____, 376, 377.

18. _____, 381.

19. _____, 384-387.

20. Lincoln, "Slave Revolts," 26-31.

Slavery & Sectionalism

1850~1861

President Profiles

Millard Fillmore
Term: 1850-1853

Franklin Pierce
Term: 1853-1857

James Buchanan
Term: 1857-1861

President	Date	Birthplace	College	Profession	Party
13. Millard Fillmore	1800-1874	New York	None	Lawyer	Whig
14. Franklin Pierce	1804-1869	Hew Hampshire	Bowdoin	Lawyer	Democrat
15. James Buchanan	1791-1868	Pennsylvania	Dickinson	Lawyer	Democrat

It was during one of the most tumultuous and terrifying periods in American history, that the national leadership was the most inept and weakest. Millard Fillmore, Franklin Pierce and James Buchanan occupied the White House.[1] These presidents so compromised the nation's moral currency, until it reached heights of irretrievable civility over the question: what to do about slavery and the black people?

Paradoxically, all three of these men were born, and grew up in the North. Yet, they sympathized with the South.[2] Pejoratively, they were called "dough faces," by some of their northern contemporaries.

Millard Fillmore hailed from humble beginnings. He grew up on a New York farm, where his family lived in a log cabin. His youth was rugged. The elder Fillmore had made flawed decisions. He lost the property and became a tenant farmer. Millard, as the second oldest of nine siblings, was forced to bear his share of the farming chores early: clearing fields, plowing, harvesting and chopping wood.[3]

Until he was 17, Fillmore received an informal, basic education in reading, writing and arithmetic. At 19, he enrolled in an academy that was set up in his small community near Buffalo, New York. Fillmore was an eager student. Recognizing his son's zeal for learning, his father, in 1819, arranged for him to study law in the office of the county judge. During this tenure, a dispute arose between him and the judge – he wanted Fillmore to evict poor families off the magistrate's tenant farms. Finding this highly distasteful, the aspiring lawyer quit.[4] Before resuming his law studies, he accepted a teaching job. He later went on to complete all the legal requirements to pass the New York bar in 1823.

Fillmore plunged intensively into politics in 1824. As an Anti-Mason, he supported John Quincy Adams for president. From this involvement, he made great strides in New York state politics as an Assemblyman to the U.S. Congress as a U.S. Representative. He belonged to the Whig party. Previously his clout had led to the establishing of a strong wing of the party in Western New York. This activity provided the stepping stones to his being chosen as Zachary Taylor's running mate in 1848. Incredulously, Fillmore never met Taylor until after their successful election. And, as Vice President, he was virtually ignored by the administration. As strange as that was, things became even more bizarre: Taylor died suddenly on July 9, 1850, as a result of a gastro-intestinal upset from the shock of eating cherries and drinking massive amounts of ice water in the summer heat. Fillmore assumed the presidency at noon the following day![5] Needless to say, as the thirteenth U.S. President, Millard Fillmore inherited a White House rife with problems. Problems ostensibly stemmed from slavery and sectionalism. Unfortunately, under his watch, the national political picture grew more bleak. Upon leaving the presidency, Fillmore closed the door on the Whig party from ever having anyone represent it in that office again. His poor performance led to the voters putting the Democrats in charge. Franklin Pierce carried their banner. He took over the presidency after his successful election in 1852.

A New Englander, **Franklin Pierce's** ancestry in America began with a great-grandfather who emigrated from England and settled in Massachusetts in 1634. Succeeding generations lived in the colony until after the Revolutionary War. Pierce's father moved to New Hampshire, and here Franklin Pierce was born. He was one of eight children.

Since his father figured prominently in the state political circles, young Pierce benefited. He grew up on a large estate. Receiving a well-rounded education through his attendance at a number of prestigious academies and Bowdoin College, Pierce cultivated a great interest in John Locke and the Enlightenment Philosophy.[6] He became an accomplished political debater, earning him recognition on campus; and at the 1824 Bowdoin commencement, he delivered an outstanding speech on "Intellectual Character." He was quite bright and upon graduation, he studied law successfully. In September of 1827, he was admitted to the New Hampshire bar.

As was often the case, when one passed the bar, a political career frequently ensued. Pierce followed this path. He started as a member of the New Hampshire Legislature. From 1833 -1842 he served in the U.S. Congress, first as a representative and later as a senator. His political pursuits were briefly interrupted. In 1846 the Mexican-American War erupted. Pierce immediately enlisted, serving until the war's end in 1848. The same year, he resigned from the army, once again returning to politics. His stature grew in the Democratic Party, and in 1852 he became its presidential nominee. Franklin Pierce won the election over the Whig candidate. He entered the White House vowing to preserve the system of slavery, as a constitutional right.[7] During his one term as the 14th President, Pierce performed poorly. The Northern Democrats did not endorse him for a second term because of his sympathetic policies towards the South. Instead, they picked another northerner, James Buchanan from Pennsylvania.[8]

James Buchanan was the oldest of eight children of an Irish emigrant. His father came to America in 1783 and settled in Pennsylvania. Here James was born, in a log cabin. His father prospered as a merchant and farmer. Buchanan and his siblings thus grew up in comfortable surroundings. His education began with the learning of the fundamentals at common schools. It was furthered at an academy where he excelled in Greek and Latin. He entered Dickinson College as a junior in 1807. After his graduation in 1809, he applied himself diligently to studying law. He passed the Pennsylvania bar in 1812.

Intermittently, between a short stint of military service during the War of 1812, and his membership in the Pennsylvania House of Representatives, Buchanan practiced law. It was his success in the profession that led to his political career. Besides serving in the state house, he went to Washington. He represented Pennsylvania in the U.S. Congress; he was U.S. Minister to Russia, an Andrew Jackson appointee. Under James Polk, he served as Secretary of State. During the Pierce administration, he was Minister to Great Britain. His diplomatic work boosted his party popularity, so when the Democrats sought a replacement for Pierce, Buchanan got the nod as their presidential nominee in 1856.[9] He won to become the 15th U.S. President. His selection met with resounding approval in the South because he sympathized with them in keeping the system of slavery.

SLAVERY & SECTIONALISM
ISSUES & ACTIONS

- **Compromise of 1850/Fugitive Slave Laws**
- **Underground Railroad**
- **Uncle Tom's Cabin**
- **Abolition Movement**
- **Kansas-Nebraska Act**
- **Dred Scott Decision**
- **Formation of Republican Party (GOP)**
- **"Dough Faces"**

Millard Fillmore, Franklin Pierce and James Buchanan combined to make the domestically bad situation of the nation into an insurmountable one. Each appeased, compromised and endorsed policies, laws and actions, so horrific, that Blacks plunged deeper into human degradation:

- Aggressively enforced the 1850 Fugitive Slave Law
- Pushed popular sovereignty of 1854 Kansas-Nebraska Act
- Supported the 1857 U.S. Supreme Court Dred Scott Decision

The enactment of the Compromise of 1850 grew out of the disagreement over slavery. It created sectionalism, a struggle between the North and South. A Fugitive Slave Law was a component of the Compromise. It (the Fugitive Slave Law) received intensive and rigorous enforcement as a desperate response to the Underground Railroad, the Abolition Movement, the stir from the Harriet Beecher Stowe book, *Uncle Tom's Cabin*, and slave insurrections of various kinds.

The short-lived effectiveness of the Compromise forced Congress to supplant it with the Kansas-Nebraska Act in 1854. More problems abounded. The U.S.

Supreme Court entered the fray by handing down the Dred Scott Decision, further inflaming the various factions wrangling over slavery and sectionalism. Chief Justice Roger Taney ruled Blacks had no rights that Whites had to respect because "they were not citizens. They were property."

Tensions over slavery split the Whig Party, resulting in the 1856 organizing of the Republican Party, or the Grand Old Party (GOP). Presidents Fillmore, Pierce and Buchanan, as northern sympathizers of the South, carried the tag of "dough faces" by the way they allowed themselves to be shaped politically by others like a piece of dough.

COMPROMISE OF 1850 / FUGITIVE SLAVE LAWS

To ease sectional tensions between the North and the South, lawmakers crafted the Compromise of 1850, the heart of which aimed to mollify relations over the slave question. It was comprised of five separate bills: 1) admitting California as a free state; 2) taking away Texas' claim to eastern New Mexico Territory with a ten million dollar reparation; 3) granting popular sovereignty to the New Mexico and Utah Territories; 4) abolishing the slave trade – not slavery – in the nation's capital, Washington, D.C.; and 5) enforcing the Fugitive Slave Law more severely and more strictly. This wreaked immeasurable fear and terror on all Blacks - in the North, in the South - free or slave. Whites increased slave patrols and fostered a thriving industry for professional slave catchers. No Black was safe. Large bounties or rewards paid by the government encouraged all Whites to join the hunt. The effectiveness of the Compromise of 1850 lasted briefly. It soon became obvious that neither section, North nor South, could be reconciled. The free soilers – those who wanted no slavery in the territories – and the advocates for slavery fought fiercely throughout, presaging the Civil War.[10]

THE UNDERGROUND RAILROAD

The Underground Railroad was not an actual steel and steam railroad that ran underground. It was an ingenious system devised to enable slave escapes into the North and Canada. The language of railroading served as the means of communication. The operators used terms such as "conductors," "agents," "depots" and "way-stations" – all lingo that explained the workings of the secret network. They employed a myriad of escape modes for the runaway slaves. Such modes included using paths and river crossings through the woods, fields and swamps. Slaves also rode on boats, ships, trains, horse and buggy and wagons as transport traversing from place to place on the road to the "Promised Land."

The flight to freedom started long before the Underground Railroad name was attached to it. A society of Philadelphia Quakers in the 1700's carried out ways for liberating fugitive slaves. They were motivated by their belief in human decency. Slavery violated this.

The Underground Railroad, so secretive, so clandestine and so complicated; its full story remains untold. How many were involved? How many fled from bondage? Where and to what extent were all of the stations in operation? How long did it run? There are lots of unanswered questions.[11]

However, it is well known that it was not Whites giving all the assistance, and Blacks being only the receivers. Many Blacks were pivotal in the operation of the system. Harriet Tubman,[12] William Stills,[13] Frederick Douglass,[14] and countless ordinary freed and non-freed Blacks risked their lives. They were inspired and encouraged by the Negro Spirituals that were created from the African oral tradition and European Christianity.

The Underground Railroad stands as a testament to the human spirit dedicated to goodwill and brotherhood.

UNCLE TOM'S CABIN

The appearance of *Uncle Tom's Cabin* in 1852 stirred further intersectional furor. Harriet Beecher Stowe's novel sent shock waves through the nation.[15] It sold more than 300,000 copies in its first year. Dramatized in Northern theatres, it inspired countless thousands to take up the banner of abolition. The South, and its leaders, vociferously initiated a campaign denying the truth of the story told in the book. But, the damage was done. As a result, the outrage over the brutality of slavery spread. The Abolition Movement ignited in the North. Southerners reeled from the clamor. The Southern clergy countered by invoking the argument of proslavery: through the ages, the church had sanctioned slavery as a means of converting the heathen to Christian civilization. Other institutions joined in the battle – the colleges, the legislatures, the Southern press – and struck with a vengeance defending slavery. Of course, at the center of it all was economics. Where would the South be without free slave labor, or the North without the profits from the raw materials produced by the slaves?

THE ABOLITION MOVEMENT

Manifest Destiny spawned divergent views, in the South and in the North. The South saw Manifest Destiny as a means of perpetuating their slave-holding economics; the North saw in it an empire of liberty – a common man's purview. From this philosophy, the anti-slavery, or abolition movement, gained strength in the North. However, the abolition mission did not include large numbers. To many Northerners, slavery was regarded as a Southern problem, one that did not concern them; yet, on the other hand, there was a segment of the population that advocated absolute freedom, immediately, for Blacks. A coalition of Northern and Southern Whites and Blacks waged a relentless campaign.[16] William Lloyd Garrison, Wendell Phillips, Frederick Douglass, Sojourner Truth, the Grimke sisters and the Tappan brothers represented the vanguard. Untold numbers took up the abolitionist calling to end slavery.

73

Abolitionists formed channels of communication to spread their message. Among them were orations, newspapers, religious endeavors and organization infiltration. But, perhaps the most daring and epic were the clandestine exploits carried out by the direct action of the Underground Railroad.

KANSAS-NEBRASKA ACT

The sectional truce brought about by the 1850 Compromise no longer satisfied either side of the slave question. New legislation was needed; hence, the passage of the Kansas-Nebraska Act in 1854 nullified the 1850 Compromise. It called for popular sovereignty, letting the question of slavery be decided by the territorial legislatures, ultimately by the settlers. This provision was designated to win southern support, but the antislavery people furiously attacked the bill, causing long and bitter debate in Congress. However, President Pierce favored and signed it. It became law. Civil unrest broke out all over Kansas. The fighting between the two factions was gruesome. Kansas became known as "Bloody Kansas."[17] This may have hastened the Civil War.

DRED SCOTT DECISION

The Dred Scott Decision was handed down by the U.S. Supreme Court in 1857. It favored the South.[18] This case dealt with the status of a slave who had left a slave-holding state and moved to a free state (the Mason-Dixon Line separated the slave-holding and the free states). Such was Dred Scott's situation. He had been a slave in Missouri, a slave state. However, he accompanied his owner, Dr. James Emerson, an Army surgeon, into the free states of Wisconsin and Illinois in 1834, for a new military assignment. Emerson returned to Missouri and brought Scott back with him. When Emerson died, Emerson's widow became Scott's new owner. Since Scott had lived in the North, it qualified him to sue Emerson's widow for his freedom because of the northern free-state policy. Originally, the

Missouri's State Supreme Court judge ruled in Scott's favor. However, Dr. Emerson's widow appealed to the U.S. Supreme Court for a reversal.

After the widow's appeal was filed, President Buchanan improperly intervened by urging the Associate Justice Robert Grier, a fellow Pennsylvanian, to provide the Northern vote. That vote supported Maryland slave owner Chief Justice Roger Taney's majority opinion to nationalize slavery. Taney used the 3/5 Clause of the Constitution to support his decision. This led to the infamous Dred Scott Decision which reflected the negative and immoral attitude of America toward black people. Taney first stated that Blacks, free or slave, were "beings of an inferior order," who "had no rights which the white man was bound to respect." He further declared that Scott could not bring suit in federal court because "Negroes are not citizens, but property!" The Dred Scott U.S. Supreme Court ruling subsequently became the law that nationalized slavery.

FORMATION OF THE REPUBLICAN PARTY (GOP)

The formation of the Republican Party, sometimes referred to as The Grand Old Party (GOP) as a new political party, resulted by virtue of schisms. The Whig Party split, as did the Democratic Party, over slavery. Their disputes came to a head over the Kansas-Nebraska Act.[19] The anti-slavery factions of both parties joined forces with a group of freesoilers. Alan E. Bovay, an abolitionist activist, brought the anti-slavery groups together. They declared themselves a political party in 1854: the Republican Party. The GOP entered its first candidate in the 1856 presidential race. James Buchanan, a non-controversial Democrat, won that election, primarily because of the GOP's narrow anti-slavery platform. Broadening the platform beyond anti-slavery, the Republicans ran another candidate in 1860. This time he won: Abraham Lincoln became the first Republican to be elected U.S. President because the Democratic Party had split over the slavery issue.

"DOUGHFACES"

"Doughfaces" was a derogatory name given to northerners who sympathized with the southerners' point of view, their causes and their interests.[20] William Lloyd Garrison, the rabid abolitionist, described them "as pliant as a piece of dough as ever was handled." He specifically pointed to Presidents Fillmore, Pierce and Buchanan as appeasers of the South.

SLAVERY & SECTIONALISM
Analytical Summary:
EFFECTS ON BLACKS

- **Fugitive Slave Law Caused Stronger Enforcement**
- **Ingenious System Devised to Help Slaves Escape in the South**
- **A Novel that Further Stirred Furor Over Slavery**
- **Anti-slavery Crusade**
- **Nullified Compromise of 1850**
- **Resulted Split Over Slavery**
- **Northerners Who Were Southern Sympathizers**

During the era of the tumultuous Slavery/Sectionalism revolt, black people could not look to the White House for any support. Presidents Millard Fillmore, Franklin Pierce and James Buchanan, all northerners, sympathized with the South (they were nicknamed "dough faces"). They backed the issues that would preserve slavery and would continue black oppression. They presided over the government that amped-up policies and enacted laws that inflamed the sectionalism. At the same time, Blacks and their white abolition-allies stepped up their campaign to counter the federal status quo stance and the pro-slave policies.

Fillmore and Pierce did what they could to back pro-slave legislation such as the slave-catching ordinances that were created, when the Compromise of 1850 called for stronger enforcement of the Fugitive Slave Laws. Buchanan interceded illegally in the Dred Scott Decision and pushed to aid the pro-slavers in their quest to spread slavery into Kansas by supporting the Kansas Nebraska Act. On the other hand, those committed to abolish the pernicious practices and policies of slavery, were just as zealous. The organization of the Republican Party (the GOP) and Harriet Beecher Stowe's book – later a drama – "Uncle Tom's Cabin" sparked furors. They energized the Abolition Movement. Blacks were very active and involved, too: Harriet Tubman's Underground Railroad exploits, Frederick Douglass' firebrand eloquence and slave insurrections of various kinds were some of the strategies they marshaled to further the anti-slavery battle.

The nation's moral authority was on trial. But Presidents Fillmore, Pierce and Buchanan failed to meet the challenge. Countering their ineptitude and filling the leadership void were men and women, black and white – imbued with moral convictions – took the mantel. Because of their courage and fortitude, questions about slavery and the status of black people were on the way to be answered.

SLAVERY & SECTIONALISM END NOTES

1. James Taranto, editor. *Presidential Leadership* (New York: Free Press, 2005) Appendix I. Table 3: Rating of Presidents … Failure - 36. Fillmore; 38 Pierce; 40 Buchanan, 259. (Ratings based on 40 Presidents).

2. James M. McPherson, editor. *To the Best of My Ability* (New York: D.K. Publishing, 2004) 98.

3. DeGregorio, 188.

4. _____, 189.

5. _____, 191.

6. [See Glossary for Enlightenment Period]_____, 198,199.

7. McPherson, Franklin Pierce 1852 Inaugural Address: Inset quote, 363.

8. DeGregorio, 215.

9. _____, 214, 215.

10. Adams, "The Rise of Interregional Tension," 156-166.

11. Meier, Part II Chapter 11, 112-117.

12. Kate Clifford Larson, *Harriet Tubman: Bound for the Promised Land* (New York: Ballantine Books 2005) Portrait of the most famous conductor of the Underground Railroad.

13. Franklin, 39, 42.

14. _____, "Frederick Douglass: writes narrative," 202; anti-slavery activities, 237.

15. Adams, *Uncle Tom's Cabin*, 115-116.

16. Franklin, 246, 249-253.

17. Horton, 156-157.

18. _____, 157-159. Also see Adams, 164-166.

19. Adams, 166.

20. McPherson, 68, 114, 360.

PANEL 5

Civil War

1861~1865

President Profile

Abraham Lincoln
Term: 1861-1865

President	Date	Birthplace	College	Profession	Party
16. Abraham Lincoln	1809-1865	Kentucky	None	Lawyer	Republican

Abraham Lincoln, as the 16th U.S. President, entered the presidency faced with unprecedented odds.[1] The ineptness of his predecessors, Presidents Fillmore, Pierce and Buchanan, left America literally imploding. America was staggering under conflagration in Kansas and Missouri over the sectional slavery battle. Lincoln was something of an anomaly. Compared to the three former presidents who were easterners, who had brought outstanding political credentials and experience to the White House, Abe was a homespun, self-taught lawyer from the Midwest. Yet, it was he who parlayed wisdom, acumen and vision, to rescue and to save the Union.

Lincoln was a child of the frontier. Though he was born in Kentucky, his family moved to Indiana in 1816, when he was seven. Despite being a little boy, he always worked hard doing farm chores, carrying and gathering wood, hoeing the vegetables and lugging buckets of water, when the family lived in Kentucky. After they moved, he helped his father build a log cabin. This was home for the rest of his childhood. As a frontier youth, Abe did his share of clearing, plowing and planting. His father even hired him out to neighboring farms. By the age of 17, he used his homemade flatboat to ferry produce down the Mississippi River to New Orleans. The money he earned, he gave to his father. Four years later, the family moved again. This time, they settled into another log cabin, in Illinois. However, Lincoln continued to work on the river and became independent of the family.[2]

Both of Lincoln's parents were illiterate. His mother died when he was nine years old. His father remarried. The stepmother was kind to him and encouraged him to learn to read and write. By his own admission, Lincoln estimated that all together, he had about one year of formal education. The crude frontier schoolhouses opened only sporadically, only whenever a literate person happened to pass through. Always eager to learn, Lincoln read about any and everything he could get his hands on. He was a voracious reader. He regularly read the family Bible, and borrowed books at every chance he could. Lincoln's persistence in self-education paid off. He became quite an engaging speaker. People of New Salem, Illinois – the town where he settled – urged him to run for the state legislature.

Lincoln announced his candidacy. But at about the same time, in 1832, the Black Hawk War broke out between the U.S. and the Sax/Fox Indian tribes. They fought over settlements of Whites on their lands. Lincoln enlisted for military duty.[4] The war was short-lived. Lincoln saw no action. Returning to Salem, he lost his bid for office because the war had interrupted his campaigning. But he started learning law. In 1836, he was admitted to the bar. Almost simultaneously, he was elected this time to the state legislature. He served three terms. Then he went to Washington to represent Illinois in Congress in 1847-1849. He grew unhappy with President Polk's underhandedness in starting war with Mexico. Lincoln declined to run for a second term. He returned to Illinois and resumed his law practice, very successfully. However, he continued involvement in politics. In 1858, he made a bid for the U.S. Senate. His famous debates against Stephen Douglas over the spread of slavery brought him praise and recognition.[5] Yet he lost the bid for U.S. Senate. When the new Republican Party was organized, Lincoln joined. And in 1860, the Republicans picked him as their nominee. He defeated three other presidential contenders and became the 16th U.S. President.

83

CIVIL WAR
ISSUES & ACTIONS

- **The Confederacy**
- **Resources of the North and the South**
- **Colored Troops**
- **Emancipation Proclamation**
- **New York City Draft Riots**
- **Appomattox**
- **Lincoln's Assassination**

Upon Lincoln's election, South Carolina seceded from the Union and subsequently led ten other southern states in forming the Confederacy, in February, 1861. The Civil War, between the North and the South, started with the firing on Fort Sumter, South Carolina on April 12 by the Confederacy. From the beginning the North had superior resources.

Many myths have surrounded "Honest Abe," as he is called. Lincoln was shrewd and possessed political guile. The yarn about his going to war to free the slaves – untrue. He very emphatically declared that fighting the Civil War was to save the Union.[6] And further, if by chances Blacks were freed, so be it. Lincoln's attitude toward black people reflected that of majority Whites: Blacks are inferior to Whites. Projecting this further – the Emancipation Proclamation freed no slaves.[7] It was another example of his duplicity. Touted as "the Great Emancipator," to the contrary, he was also referred to as "the Reluctant Emancipator." However, whatever the view, it is apparent that Abraham Lincoln proved his mettle in meeting and confronting the nation's problems in an epic way. He saved America – and as a by-product, unshackled black Americans.

Midway, as victories turned the war in favor of the Union, Lincoln issued the Emancipation Proclamation. It actually freed no slaves. But, the Proclamation permitted Blacks to join the military, a right denied them in the beginning. Colored troops made up ten percent of the Union Army.

In the summer of 1863, Lincoln instituted the first federal draft. It met with opposition; there were riots, and New York City had the worst ones. Prime targets were Blacks.

On April 9, 1865, the war ended with General Robert E. Lee's surrender to General Ulysses S. Grant at Appomattox, Virginia. Five days later the President was shot. Lincoln died on April 15th from a bullet fired by John Wilkes Booth, a Confederate sympathizer, who feared that Lincoln's Reconstruction policy would give Blacks citizenship.

THE CONFEDERACY

Lincoln's election brought southern bitterness. Southerners viewed this as an abolitionist victory because the new Republican Party stood for the abolishing of slavery. The South threatened from time to time to leave the Union starting even before the Constitution was ratified.[8] This time it happened. South Carolina led the secession in December, 1860. By the time President Buchanan's term ended, ten other states followed, establishing the Confederate States of America.[9] The Confederacy elected Jefferson Davis president and made Montgomery, Alabama, the capitol.

The Confederacy claimed the arsenal at Fort Sumter, South Carolina, because it was located within the Confederacy's border. Confederate troops fired on it to provoke a war. This provocation led to Lincoln's declaration of war against the Confederacy; thus began the Civil War, on April 12, 1861.

Not all slaveholding states seceded. Missouri, Kentucky, West Virginia, Maryland and Delaware remained in the Union, fighting on the North's side.[10]

RESOURCES OF THE NORTH AND SOUTH [11]

	North (Union)	South (Confederacy)
Population	23 states, with population of 22 million	11 states, with population of 9 million (including 3.5 million slaves)
Industry	85% of nation's factories; 90% of its skilled workers	15% of nation's factories; 10% of its skilled workers
Transportation	22,000 miles of railroads; large merchant marine; naval supremacy	9,000 miles of railroads; few large merchant ships and naval vessels
Finances	Control of 70% of nation's wealth	Control of 30% of nation's wealth
Military Forces	Few experienced officers; soldiers poorly prepared for army life (many of them former city dwellers and factory workers)	Superior military leadership; good soldiers

COLORED TROOPS

Training of black soldiers started immediately after the Emancipation Proclamation provision declared them the right. They were designated as the United States Colored Troops (USCT)[12] and made up one-tenth of the Union Army. At the start, most served under white officers; however, by war's end, nearly 75 Blacks held officers' commissions. The same pay was not granted to Blacks until a year later in 1864 after the Emancipation Proclamation permitted them to fight. When captured by the South, they were rarely treated as prisoners-of-war. If they were not killed, they were made slaves. At the battle of Fort Pillow, Tennessee, black soldiers fell prey to this policy. The Confederate General in charge was Nathan Bedford Forrest, who became the organizer of the Ku Klux Klan.

By the end of the War, more than 200,000 Blacks served in the Union Army and the Navy. One of the white captains remarked about their performance. He said, "Their conduct was heroic; no troops could be more daring and more determined." Another officer cited their exploits at the battle of Milliken's Bend. His remarks were, "So they fought and died, defending the cause that we revere. They met death coolly, bravely; nor rashly did they expose themselves, but all were steady and obedient to orders."

The Congressional Medal of Honor, created during the Civil War as the nation's highest military award for valor in combat against an armed enemy, was awarded to twenty-two black soldiers during the Civil War.

EMANCIPATION PROCLAMATION

Because the nicknames of "the Great Emancipator" and "Honest Abe" are applied to Abraham Lincoln, a review of the Emancipation Proclamation (EP) is in order. Questions arise as to the validity and accuracy of such acclamation. How much of Lincoln's action was inadvertent? How much was intentional?

Background: Lincoln's issuance of the EP came about at the urging of some of his cabinet members, and some of the party-activists. His hesitancy and delay has deemed some historians to dub him as "the Reluctant Emancipator"... In addition, concerns arose about his duplicity in the drafting of the document (EP). How genuine was Honest Abe? His eloquent phrasing and political shrewdness mislead: no slaves were freed! Why weren't they? Let us examine the second paragraph of the Proclamation through this excerpt:

"That on the first day of January, A.D. 1863, all persons held as slaves within any state or designated part of a state the people whereof shall then be in rebellion against the United States shall be then, thence forward and forever free; and the executive government of the United States, including the military and naval authority thereof, will recognize and maintain the freedom of such

persons and will do no act or acts to repress such persons, or any of them, in
any efforts they may make for their actual freedom."

On the surface, the EP is very forthright. But, examine further, carefully. The key phrase is, "any state or designated part of a state … in rebellion against the United States …" These states in rebellion are the eleven southern slaveholding states that seceded from the Union. They formed the Confederacy, had their own constitution, and their own government. They were no longer under the jurisdiction of the United States, and the U.S. President. Without legal authority, Lincoln's Proclamation had no validity; he could not free those slaves. Yet, where he did have legal authority, Lincoln either inadvertently, or intentionally, failed to address an analogous situation that existed in the slaveholding border states (Kentucky, West Virginia, Missouri, Delaware and Maryland) that fought for the Union. As a consequence, these slaves remained in bondage, resulting in no slaves being emancipated by Lincoln's Emancipation Proclamation. The document had spin – and it was brilliant, political psychology... However, in the seventh paragraph it means what it says.

In paragraph seven, Lincoln continues his shrewdness: permitting Blacks the right to serve in the military without specifying them by name. It reads…

> *"And I further declare and make known that such persons*
> *of suitable condition will be received into the armed service*
> *of the United States to garrison forts, positions, stations, and*
> *other places, and to man vessels of all sorts in said service."*

Black men were permitted the right to serve in the military,[13] even though Lincoln does not specifically refer to them as black people; instead, calling them "such persons."

NEW YORK CITY DRAFT RIOTS

Lincoln's imposing of the first federal draft in the nation's history, led to the New York City (NYC) Draft Riots. One of the worst riots in American History, broke out in NYC on Monday, July 13, 1863.[14] For four days, layered with elements of religious, racial, ethnic and class conflict, rioters – largely poor Irish Catholics – looted, set fires, slaughtered, lynched and committed other unspeakable heinous atrocities against black citizens. Black businesses, homes, churches and other facilities were destroyed. Countless numbers of children perished when the black orphanage was torched. Blacks fled the city, their community literally obliterated. The official toll counted 105 dead; but it is believed, that most certainly, more than 500 died!

All this came about through the agitation of southern sympathizers. New York City had long traded with the South. Some New York politicians made inflaming speeches, calling the Civil War "a rich man's war and a poor man's fight." They emphasized its unfairness: Men could opt out of any conscription, if they provided a substitute, or paid a $300 exemption. Most working men barely earned that amount in a year. Mostly Irish Catholics made up NYC's poor, of the million people living in Lower Manhattan's squalid, fetid pigsty. They would be the ones to do the fighting; their families would be forced onto charity rolls. Riled by agitators, who told them this was a government that would send them, "to die for slaves, who would replace them, at even lower wages, on the docks, and in the factories," they unleashed their fury upon nearly every Black in sight – young, old, children, adults, middle class or poor. It did not matter. The rioting raged out of control, until Lincoln called out federal troops to quell the blood-letting.

APPOMATTOX

At Appomattox Court House, Virginia, on Sunday April 9, 1865, two of the greatest Civil War generals – Ulysses S. Grant of the Union and Robert E. Lee of the Confederacy – met in a farmhouse.[15]

It was a war so bloody, and so costly in human terms, that it holds the distinction of being the worst war fought in American History. Nearly a million men were killed or wounded. Deaths, including those from disease, totaled 529,332. Disease killed more men than bullets. Over 68,000 of the killed and wounded were Black!

Cost of the Civil War	Union	Confederacy
Troops Killed in Battle	110,000	95,000
Troops Dead from Illness	250,000	165,000
Troops Wounded	275,000	100,000
Estimated Wartime Expenditures	$3 billion	$2 billion (plus cost of freed slaves)

The terms offered by Grant were accepted by Lee, and the Civil War officially ended – and so did slavery.

LINCOLN'S ASSASSINATION

Two days following the Appomattox surrender, Abraham Lincoln addressed the nation. He understood that the solving of postwar and post emancipation problems would not be easy. A new government needed shaping in the South, and that overcoming its "disorganized and discordant elements" presented a formidable task. He continued, "that literate Blacks, and black veterans would be extended the vote. Dark days loomed ahead …." His words were prophetic, for seated in the audience, that day, was John Wilkes Booth! [16]

Three days later, Lincoln was shot – by John Wilkes Booth. On the evening of April 14, 1865, Lincoln and his wife Mary went to the Washington, D.C. Ford Theater, to see the play, *Our American Cousin.* A few minutes after ten, a shot rang out! Booth had sneaked into the presidential box and shot Lincoln in the head.

Booth was a Confederate sympathizer, who along with his conspirators, plotted to kill not only the president, but other Union officials as well. Lincoln was the only one they succeeded in killing. He did not die immediately. The next morning around seven a.m., on April 15th, Lincoln passed away. His death marked the first assassination of a U.S. President.[17]

CIVIL WAR
Analytical Summary:
EFFECTS ON BLACKS

- **South Left Union, Reacted to Lincoln Being Elected, Formed Own Government**
- **South Fired on Fort-Sumter - Led to Civil War, North had More Resources**
- **Emancipation Proclamation Permitted Blacks to Fight**
- **Emancipation Proclamation Freed No Slaves**
- **Riots Reacted to Lincoln's Instituted Draft**
- **Confederate General Robert E. Lee Surrendered, North Won and Slavery Ended**
- **Lincoln First President Killed in Office**

For American black people, the Civil War Era was both telling and defining. It supplied some of the answers to the perennial national questions about Blacks and the disgrace of slavery. From 1619 onward they could not find nor could they get answers to such basic questions as: What does it take to be an American? When will any president show some moral authority? What concrete social and political actions will rectify the injustices? And what kind of guarantees will there be to protect and defend Blacks?

When Abraham Lincoln's election to the presidency triggered the southern states' defection, serendipity entered. But in order for Blacks to get answers, it took a bloodbath and an almost near-national extinction.

By firing on Fort Sumter in 1861, the Confederacy (the eleven seceded southern states) determined in waging war against the Union that it would keep and maintain "the southern way of life" – a lifestyle dedicated to continue having the four million slaves as the economy with free labor – unyielding and relentless. Despite the North holding the upper-hand in resources and logistics, the South would not be deterred.

President Lincoln was just as determined to preserve the Union as the South was to separate it. Even though Lincoln swore that freeing the slaves was not his reason for fighting the Civil War, many of his actions – both deliberate and inadvertent – Blacks still factored heavily into his practices and policies: the instituting of the draft, the dispatching of federal troops to New York City to quell Whites' attacks on Blacks, issuing the executive order – the Emancipation Proclamation authorizing Colored Troops to fight for the Union – ordering the rebel states to swear to abide by the Thirteenth Amendment before gaining admittance back into the union, brought hope. At last Blacks would finally get telling responses and definitive actions from a president who asserted some moral authority.

Confederate General Robert E. Lee surrendered to Union General Ulysses S. Grant at Appomattox on April 9, 1865. The war ended. Six days later President Lincoln's life ended, cut short by an assassin's bullet. As a result, it will forever remain unknown what further he would have done, or might have done to answer more questions regarding Blacks' place in American society. Regardless, Abraham Lincoln saved America; and his actions thus enabled black people to be counted as a whole person.

CIVIL WAR END NOTES

1. McPherson, 118.

2. Beschloss, 189.

3. DeGregorio, 228.

4. _____, 230.

5. _____, 231.

6. _____, 239.

7. _____, 127, 128.

8. Horton, 183.

9. Adams, 193.

10. Meier, 130.

11. Lincoln, "The Negro in the Union Army", 59 – 61.

12. Horton, 174.

13. Barnet Schecter, *The Devil's Own Work* (New York: Walker Publishing, 2005).

14. Adams, 196.

15. Horton, 207.

16. Beschloss, 207.

17. Meier, 128.

Reconstruction

1865 ~ 1877

President Profiles

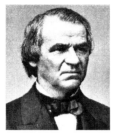

Andrew Johnson
Term: 1865-1869

Ulysses S. Grant
Term: 1869-1877

President	Date	Birthplace	College	Profession	Party
17. Andrew Johnson	1808-1875	North Carolina	None	Tailor	National Union
18. Ulysses S. Grant	1822-1885	Ohio	West Point	Soldier	Republican

The Andrew Johnson and Ulysses S. Grant administrations rank among the weakest in American history.[1] Following on the heels of Abraham Lincoln's brilliant leadership in rescuing the Union, and eventually abolishing slavery, their ineptitude glares even more.

Andrew Johnson was southern-born and bred. The older son of a North Carolina handyman-father, and a tavern-maid mother, he grew up in poverty. His father died when he was three years old.[2] The family circumstances sank deeper into poverty. Taking in washing and sewing, his mother managed to eke-out a living for young Andrew and his brother. Forced to help with the family needs, Johnson was apprenticed to a tailor at 14 years old. He never received a formal education. However, reading to the illiterate apprentices was a custom of the day. So it was with Johnson. Some of the subjects read to Johnson were the U. S. Constitution, American History from books, and politics from the local paper. This lasted for six years. A disagreement with his master led to the young tailor's running away from home fleeing to South Carolina. When he returned home, a year later, he was unable to resume his apprenticeship. He moved to

Tennessee, gaining relative success in the tailoring business. In the meantime, his mother remarried, but her living conditions did not improve. Therefore, Johnson returned to North Carolina, and brought his poverty-stricken mother, stepfather and younger brother to Tennessee, to take care of them.

While in Tennessee, Johnson married. His bride was the 16 year old daughter of a Scottish shoemaker. Johnson was fortunate that his bride was literate. She encouraged and taught him to read and write.[3] They studied together. He trained himself to be a rather accomplished public speaker by engaging in debates with students from a nearby college. This talent brought attention and praise. He began parlaying his way into politics.

Andrew Jackson greatly influenced Johnson. Like Jackson, he championed the causes of the common (white) people.[4] In fact – possibly resonating from his background of a poor White – Johnson held deep contempt for the planter class aristocracy, and for northern Whites. This contempt was exceeded only by his hatred of Blacks! Something of a paradox: despite Johnson's disdain of the slave-owning planter class, he – through his political success – became a slave-owner.

Johnson established an outstanding political career in Tennessee.[5] He was foremost, a Democrat. He represented his state in the U. S. House of Representatives, and also in the U. S. Senate, and later as governor. He influenced the eastern section of Tennessee to stay in the Union when the Confederacy formed. He drew President Lincoln's attention, and during the first years of the Civil War, he was appointed and served as Military Governor over that district. Then, when Lincoln sought re-election, he selected Johnson as his running mate, hoping his presence would mitigate the South's return to the Union.

Quite in contrast to Andrew Johnson's growing up days, **Ulysses S. Grant**, an Ohioan, had a comfortable childhood.[6] The eldest of six children, he lived with his family in a village, a short distance from Cincinnati. His father owned a successful tannery, and a farm. Grant was shy. He disliked working in the tannery around people. But, he enjoyed the farm, and working with horses. His outstanding talent with the horses developed into superior horsemanship. Having received a well-rounded education at private academies, Grant in 1839, received an appointment to the U. S. Military Academy at West Point, New York, through his father's insistence. Grant disliked the military, and the prospect of army life, but stayed in the Academy in deference to his father's wishes.   In general an average student, he did excel in math and horsemanship. However, upon his graduation with the rank of second lieutenant, in 1843, he was assigned to the Fourth U.S. Infantry Regiment. War loomed between America and Mexico. When it broke out, Grant's outfit became fully engaged. They took part in capturing Mexico City in 1847. Having distinguished himself, Grant received praise and a promotion for his military skill, bravery and leadership.

After the Mexican American War ended in 1848, Grant married. Shortly afterward, a son was born to him and his wife. The military was rough on him and his young family. His pay was so low, that he could barely support his dependents. He became depressed. He began to drink. For the good of his family, and himself, Grant resigned his commission. But, his ventures in civilian life netted little success; he suffered business failures, one upon another. Then the Civil War erupted in 1861, and President Lincoln called for volunteers to fight the Union cause. At 39 years old, Grant answered the call.[7]

He assumed the rank of colonel, and was assigned to the Illinois Volunteers. His Academy training served him well. Lincoln promoted him to brigadier general, the reward for Grant's superb display of strong military and command qualities. At Vicksburg, Mississippi during the 1862-1863 campaign, he so distinguished himself in leading his men to victory over the South, that Lincoln put him in command of all the Union forces.[8] Grant led the North to victory over the South. Then, in the end, he accepted the surrender of the South at Appomattox in April, 1865, from the Confederate General Robert E. Lee. Grant became a national hero which led to his becoming the eighteenth President of the United States.

As Presidents, Johnson and Grant entered the White House with very different attitudes and expectations for Blacks, and for the reconstruction of the fractured nation, but in the end the results were the same: Blacks did not fair well under neither Johnson nor Grant. Johnson's assumption to the presidency followed Lincoln's assassination. Johnson was not suited for the office. At this critical juncture in our nation – reconstruction and unification – vision, diplomacy and openness were needed. These attributes were woefully lacking in Andrew Johnson. His ascendancy to the presidency could not have come at a worst time.[9] This void in skillful leadership negated any chance of his partnering with Congress to solve the nation's pressing problems of Reconstruction. This was apparent in his not consulting Congress when he accepted the Confederate states back into the Union while Congress was on its April—December vacation. His pugnaciously surly manner, and divisive pettiness, forced the hand of the Radical Republicans to rescue the Blacks and the nation from Johnson's decisions for a while.

In the beginning, Grant showed promise. He was very definitive in his goals: to solidify black suffrage in the South; to persuade southerners to accept a racially mixed society; and to gain support in the North for moderate Republican Reconstruction policies.[10] But, his efforts were fraught with conflict and discord – coming from various factions. White southerners wanted to return to the ways of the Ante Bellum South. White northerners wanted to leave Blacks physically, and politically, in the hands of the southerners. And, Blacks wanted to rewrite the social-political contract. Even though they initially were so hopeful, Blacks saw by the end of Grant's tenure the Reconstruction gains eroding and slipping away. Grant was unable to assert the decisive and stalwart leadership he displayed during the Civil War. Blacks paid the price, as did the nation.

RECONSTRUCTION ISSUES & ACTIONS

- **Andrew Johnson's Presidential Assumption**
- **Black Codes**
- **Freedmen's Bureau**
- **Radical Republicans**
- **Military Protection**
- **Black Officials**
- **Civil War Amendments**
- **Johnson Impeachment**
- **Ku Klux Klan**
- **Ulysses S. Grant Elected**

Following Abraham Lincoln's assassination, Andrew Johnson, as the vice president, assumed the presidency. He inherited Lincoln's Reconstruction plans. These plans called for leniency toward the South. However, Johnson's actions and policies made it even easier than Lincoln's plan for the re-admittance of the Confederate states into the Union. With the states' return, the newly-freed slaves, without resources, found themselves once again, still at the mercy of their former masters. Mistreatment prevailed. Black Codes, harsh laws based on the old Slave Codes, were instituted.

Johnson and the southerners' actions riled Congress. Great changes came about spearheaded by the Radical Republicans. Congress' impeachment of Johnson led to the enactment of laws and policies which insured that Blacks could retain their newly- gained civil rights. These policies included actions such as military protection, installment of black office holders (but Whites kept the power), advocacy of the Freedmen's Bureau, and Civil Rights Acts, later ratified, as Civil War Amendments.[11] These measures, temporarily, restored black rights.

Ulysses S. Grant's election gave hope to Blacks during his first term. However, his leadership skills as the Civil War general did not transfer into his second term; corruption surrounded him in his administration, and conditions further deteriorated for Blacks in the South. The hope for Blacks faded by the end of Grant's presidency with the proliferation of white supremacy groups such as the Ku Klux Klan.

JOHNSON'S PRESIDENTIAL ASSUMPTION

In 1864, when Lincoln ran for his second term, he changed his running mate. He dropped the northerner of the first term for a southerner. His hope was to ease politically the transition of bringing the South back into the Union at the end of the War. He chose Andrew Johnson from Tennessee.

Johnson was a U.S. Senator at the time of the secession, but the part of Tennessee under his leadership did not join the Confederacy. As senator, he supported keeping the Union together and adhering to the Constitution. Yet, at the same time, he felt keeping slavery came under states' rights as stated in the Tenth Amendment. Johnson's stance impressed Lincoln. Johnson, also, belonged to a group of Union-loyal Democrats who joined Republicans in 1864 to form the National Union Party. As Vice President, he assumed the presidency on April 15, 1865 – a day after Lincoln was shot.

BLACK CODES

When Congress was on vacation, Johnson took office. He immediately began implementing his own Reconstruction Plan without Congress' approval. On May 29, 1865, he issued a proclamation of amnesty to the South. He pardoned white southern men who would take the loyalty oath to uphold the U. S. Constitution.

However, the chief Confederacy leaders were not permitted to take the oath. Johnson appointed provisional governors, who then set up state governments, and arranged for Congressional elections.

By the time Congress reconvened in December, each new southern state legislatures had enacted laws consigning Blacks to a second-class status. Johnson accepted this. These laws, based on the old slave codes, were called Black Codes.[12] They represented the work of an unrepentant, and vengeful South. The Black Codes imposed all sorts of restrictions on Blacks' civil rights: Blacks could marry only non-whites; they could not hold public office; they could work at only certain jobs; they could buy or acquire land only under certain conditions; their children could not be educated under the new public school system; they could not vote; nor could they be a witness in court unless it concerned other Blacks. These were but a few of the laws that made a mockery out of all the bloodshed to rid the nation of slavery.

FREEDMEN'S BUREAU

The government, in March 1865, established the Bureau of Refugees, Freedmen, and Abandoned. Departments were set up throughout the Union-occupied South. The Bureau furnished aid and relief to Blacks, and poor Whites. Their needs were immediate. The Bureau provided the destitute with clothing, food, housing and fuel. It relieved suffering by establishing medical staffs and setting up hospitals. Freedmen courts were organized to service those who sought protection in their freedom to choose their own employer and to receive a fair wage. Legal marriages were registered. Also, at this time, many Blacks took new names denoting their new status; for example, Freeman, Freedmen, Peoples and Persons.

During the years of the Bureau's existence, perhaps its most remarkable achievements were in the field of education. The agency organized and super-vised various types of facilities and institutions in fostering black education and training. Some of the most prominent historical black colleges and universities of today, that received aid and inspiration from the Freedmen's Bureau, are Fisk University, Howard University, Atlanta University and Hampton University.[13]

RADICAL REPUBLICANS

The Congressional members of the Republican Party that favored a "hard peace" for the defeated South were called the Radical Republicans.[14] Thaddeus Stevens of Pennsylvania and Benjamin Butler from Massachusetts led those in the House; Charles Sumner of Massachusetts, and Benjamin Wade from Ohio led those in the Senate. This group, early on, showed their displeasure over Lincoln's proposed Reconstruction Plan, deeming it too lenient. Then when Andrew Johnson assumed the presidency, after Lincoln's death, Johnson received even more, pointed disdain for his excessively lenient actions.

Congress went on recess shortly after Johnson took office. In its absence, he made it easy for the reconstructed states to re-enter the Union. The Radicals were incensed. From then on, it became a power struggle: the Republicans versus Johnson. Congress passed laws; Johnson vetoed them; Congress overrode them. This tumult continued throughout Johnson's reign. But fortunately for Blacks, the Radical Republican-led Congress prevailed.

MILITARY PROTECTION

Johnson's contrary actions incited Congress. The legislators became more determined than ever to deal with Johnson and the South. They passed a series of Reconstruction Acts in March 1867. Johnson vetoed them. Johnson's vetoes were overridden. Congress triumphed. These Acts ended southern control in the former rebel areas and restored Blacks' civil rights and provided military protection for them.

The South was divided into five military districts. Soldiers were sent in to keep law and order; many Blacks were included among the troops. Each district was governed by a Union general. The governors convened constitutional conventions. Every adult male – including Blacks – could vote to select the delegates. However, former Confederate officials were ineligible. Each constitution had to accept the 14th Amendment, black male suffrage, and the right of Blacks to hold office. Upon the approval of Congress, the state could re-enter the Union. By 1870, all Southern states were back in the Union.

Thanks to the Radical Reconstruction, with its military protection, for the first time in American history, Blacks had civil rights.

BLACK OFFICIALS

Under the new state constitutions, Blacks were elected and appointed to political offices and positions – in the "New South."[15] The Reconstruction legislatures made it possible for Blacks – and poor Whites – to participate in the political process. They eliminated the infamous Black Codes, and they raised the standard of living for common people by providing free public school education, public services and social welfare.

The black officials came from varied backgrounds. Some were illiterate; some were self-educated; a few had managed to obtain a college education. Besides being elected to state offices, a number of them served in the U.S. Congress. Mississippi sent two Blacks to the Senate: Blanche K. Bruce and Hiram R. Revels. Between 1869 and 1880, twenty-three Blacks served in the U.S. House of Representatives.

Hiram R. Revels proved himself to be competent. He served from 1875 to 1881 during which time he introduced much progressive legislation. Those bills dealing with veteran pensions were adopted. However, those he brought up dealing with Indian problems, Chinese immigration and racial segregation in the military were considered too radical by Congress to address.

A considerable number of the black representatives were either state politicians or war heroes. Robert Smalls of South Carolina, Alonzo Ransier, also of South Carolina, and John T. Lynch of Mississippi, had all distinguished themselves as political leaders and war heroes.

During the Radical Reconstruction Period, Blacks never politically ruled in the South, contrary to the beliefs of disgruntled Whites who were threatened by the Blacks' new rights. Blacks never held real power. Whites were always in control of the southern state governments. From the time when white men of the North (carpetbaggers) formed a Republican coalition with southern white men (scalawags), Whites held the political leadership, and the political power positions. They depended on black voters to keep the Republican Party in office. Whites never lost control at any time – not during, nor after, Reconstruction.

CIVIL WAR AMENDMENTS

The Civil War Amendments were made possible because of ARTICLE V in the U.S. Constitution, which deals with the amending process. This feature became very important during Reconstruction toward making Blacks, American citizens.

Amendment 13 abolished slavery in 1865, changing slave status from property to a person; Amendment 14, in 1867, defined citizenship; this clarification gave them eligibility entitling all Blacks to receive civil rights as stated in the Constitution. Amendment 15, in 1870, cleared them (black males) to exercise their civil rights through suffrage, the right to vote. Because these Amendments were added to the Constitution as the result of the fighting of the Civil War, they are called the Civil War Amendments.[16]

JOHNSON IMPEACHMENT

All during Andrew Johnson's presidency, Johnson "locked horns" with Congress. Determined to limit his powers, Congress passed a number of bills; the most decisive one was the Tenure Act in 1867. This Act prevented Johnson from removing any official from his cabinet without the approval of Congress. Johnson defied this by firing one of his cabinet members. So, in February 1868, as a result of Johnson's actions, Congress exercised its powers of impeachment granted it in the Constitution by provision of ARTICLE I, Section 2, and Section 3.[17]

The House of Representatives on the 24th of February, 1868, by a vote of 126 to 47, impeached Johnson; they adopted 11 articles against him. The most important articles were the first and eleventh. They charged that Johnson violated the Tenure Act, in dismissing an official without Congress' consent, and that he conspired against Congress and the Constitution for not enforcing the Reconstruction Acts, and that he was disrespectful of Congress.

On March 13, 1868, the impeachment trial began. The Senate was the court; the Chief Justice of the U.S. Supreme Court, presided. The trial lasted three months, closing on the 16th of May. A conviction required a 2/3 vote from the senators. The vote, to convict Johnson of the charges, failed by one vote! Johnson was found not guilty, allowing him to remain president until the end of his term.

Andrew Johnson was the first U.S. President impeached. William J. Clinton was the second. He, too, was found not guilty.

THE KU KLUX KLAN

The Ku Klux Klan first appeared in the South after the Civil War.[18] It started as a social group for Confederate veterans in 1865. It was founded in Pulaski, Tennessee, headed by Nathan Bedford Forrest, a former Confederate general. Even as a social group, the members dedicated themselves to a political agenda:

the re-establishment of white supremacy, and the overthrow of the Congressional-backed state governments. The Klan spread rapidly throughout the South. They swore to use any means to prevent Blacks from exercising their freedom and their civil rights.

The Klan, and many other white supremacy groups, stirred up hate and fomented riots against Blacks at the slightest pretext or provocation. Hooded and robed, these night riders waged a reign of terror and violence. They burned crosses; they beat, tarred and feathered; they mutilated, threatened, tortured and lynched Blacks and their white sympathizers. This was the Klan's marquee. At election time, they rode in conspicuous caravans, and sat at polling places with loaded guns on their laps intimidating Blacks, in order to prevent their voting. Forrest became disenchanted with the Klan behavior, and he disavowed their actions.

When states failed to end the terror and violence, Congress passed laws in 1870 and 1871 to suppress some of the white supremacist activities through the enforcement of the Fourteenth and Fifteenth Amendments. It was only a matter of time that Reconstruction would come to an end. This happened with the election of Rutherford B. Hayes, in 1876. Fulfilling his election promises to the Southern Democrats, Hayes helped the southern political leaders by pulling out the federal troops that were protecting the Blacks and their rights. This led to Blacks losing their enfranchisement. Whites took full control of the state governments. Having accomplished their mission, the Ku Klux Klan disbanded, temporarily. It resurfaced again, with even greater ferocity, in the early 1900's.

GRANT'S PRESIDENCY

When Ulysses S. Grant entered the White House following Johnson's toxic years, he brought a breath of fresh air. The struggle for power between Andrew Johnson and the Radical Republicans had added more turmoil to an already-fractious nation. Having gained stature as a Civil War hero, Grant inspired hope among many people, black and white. He proclaimed that his primary goal was to restore unity to the nation by fostering harmony between the North and the South, and to a mixed-society.

He tried to fulfill his promise. During his first term, Grant seemed in control.[19] His proctoring of the Fifteenth Amendment's ratification that assured Black civil rights, looked good. But, after a while, it became apparent that his centrist efforts had little chance to succeed. Once Congress permitted the southern states to rejoin the Union, he was bombarded, on all sides, with trouble. And Grant was unable to transfer the leadership he displayed in the War to the attending problems in governing the reconstituted nation that was rife with sectional and racial antagonisms.

The re-admitted South began to systematically deprive and defraud the Blacks. Only two months after Georgia rejoined the Union, it expelled the black members of the state legislature. In other southern states, terrorist groups rampaged. They used various tactics of intimidation, violence and disenfranchisement to suppress Blacks. This reign of terror ran rampant throughout parts of Tennessee, Alabama, Mississippi and South Carolina. In Louisiana, more than two hundred black plantation workers were murdered. In 1871, Grant did suspend the writ of habeas corpus in parts of South Carolina, for a time making it easier to arrest some of the white supremacists. He also sent federal troops to try to quell some of the violence. But, by the end of his first term and into the remainder of his administration, Grant was so besieged with problems beyond the South, he was rendered indecisive and incompetent; he could not act.

In the North, where suffrage was begrudgingly extended to Blacks through the Fifteenth Amendment, disinterest prevailed. In many instances northern Whites wanted to get on with their business – and to let the South deal with solving the "black problem."

Added to these woes, the nation suffered an economic downturn, the Panic of 1873. Eastern banks failed. Hit by this financial panic were bankers, manufacturers and farmers of the South and the West. And, simultaneously, all sorts of scandals of corrupt administrative behaviors began erupting. Some of Grant's cabinet members took pay-offs and bribes, and embezzled government funds. Grant found leading the Country far different from leading the military during the Civil War. His strong leadership during the Civil War did not translate into his presidency. Unfortunately, Grant's political ineptitude during his closing years in office became his legacy. This was reflected in his inability to carry out his promises to a Reconstructed Nation, including Blacks.

RECONSTRUCTION
Analytical Summary:
EFFECTS ON BLACKS

- **With Abraham Lincoln's Death, as Vice President Johnson, the Constitution Designated Him as President**
- **Harsh Laws Based on Slave Codes**
- **Congressmen Who Led Action and Legislation for Freedmen**
- **Federal Agency Aid to Freedmen**
- **Five Districts in the South**
- **Federal and State Positions Held; Whites Kept the Power**
- **Constitutional Rights**
- **Led to Enactment of Pro-black Laws**
- **One of Many White Supremacy Groups**
- **Black Rights Deteriorate**

Presidents Andrew Johnson and Ulysses S. Grant were the bookends to the Reconstruction Era. They were the alpha and omega of the most promising period for Blacks in America – up until this time. The Civil War ended. The first of the Civil War Amendments abolished slavery. President Lincoln's assassination thrust Johnson into the presidency. And he immediately proclaimed to act on behalf of the newly-emancipated slaves. They believed him; he lied.

Shortly after Johnson took office, Congress took its six months recess. The congressmen returned to their respective districts. They left with the intent of dealing with the business of Reconstruction upon their reconvening in December. In the congressmen's absence, the new president proceeded with his duplicitous and dastardly acts. He granted amnesty, widely and freely among the rebel states! His political gesture brought these states, one by one, back into the Union. And these rebel states brought back, on their return, some of the same oppressive practices used against Blacks during slavery. Only the names changed from Slave Codes to Black Codes.

Once the congressmen came back to Washington and learned of Johnson's double dealings, a contingent of them expressed gross indignation. The group led by the Radical Republicans proceeded, forthwith, to counter Johnson's anti-black and illegal racist actions. Ways were devised and laws passed to restore and protect the rights Blacks had just gained: the Johnson-eliminated Freedmen's Bureau was reactivated providing needed services; five military districts were established for their protection; the enacted Civil Rights Acts were ratified into the 14th and 15th Amendments; and Blacks' rights to hold political offices were fostered – although Blacks never displaced white control nor white political power. However, many of those social and political questions about Blacks and slavery that hovered over America since 1619 were answered – and implemented.

Johnson's impeachment triggered this moral surge, an element sparingly in-corporated previously. This flame of liberty burned brightly, but only for a brief time. By the time Ulysses S. Grant assumed the presidency, it started to dim. The national focus changed. The North turned its attention toward other issues having little or nothing to do with the welfare of Black people. Most of their advocates had grown tired, old or died. Thus the goodwill they received postwar was but a glimmer – an opening for a vengeful South to show it had regained its power. It re-emerged!

Despite Grant's good-intentions, his ineptness could not match the resurgent power of the white supremacy groups. Under such hate groups as the Ku Klux Klan, the South was well on its way toward reclaiming "the southern-way of life." Coupled with northern indifference and federal neglect, black Americans' flame of hope was all but doused. And Reconstruction ended.

However, the era of Reconstruction was redemptive for America, even though briefly. Its moral thrust was a break through. It enabled black people to be constitutionally free, to be citizens and to taste some of the Enlightenment tenets proclaimed in the Declaration of Independence, the U.S. Constitution & the Bill of Rights. The 3/5 of a person no longer applied. The social-political parts of American life began to include black people.

RECONSTRUCTION END NOTES

1. Taranto, Ranking based on 40 presidents by Scholarly field: Grant 29th; Johnson 37th.

2. DeGregorio, 243.

3. _____, 249.

4. Beschloss, 210.

5. DeGregorio, 250-251.

6. Beschloss, 221.

7. _____, 222.

8. _____, 224.

9. Adams, 204.

10. _____, 207.

11. Franklin, "The Black Codes," 187-190.

12. Lincoln, 68. All during the Jim Crow Era when black people were prohibited from enrolling in the southern white colleges, these segregated schools produced the majority of the black leadership. Since the civil rights laws of the 1960's, the black colleges, by law, desegregated, but the majority still maintain a largely black student body.

13. Franklin, 304-305. Also see Adams, Alienable Rights, 193-207.

14. Since Blanche K. Bruce and Hiram R. Revels served in the U.S. Senate during Reconstruction, only three other Blacks have been elected and served: Edward W. Brooke III (R. Mass.) 1966 – 1978; Carole Mosely Braun (D. Ill.); Barak Obama (C. Ill.) 2006 – 2008. Since Reconstruction, many Blacks served in the U.S. House of Representatives beginning in 1929 with Oscar Stanton De Priest (R. Ill.) 1929 - 1934. No blacks served as governor during Reconstruction. Two black Americans have been elected state governors: Douglas Wilder (D. Va.) 1989 – 1993, and Deval Patrick (D. Mass.) 2006 – present. A third black governor is David Paterson of New York (D). He ascended to the governorship in 2008. This occurred when the elected governor resigned due to scandal. Paterson had been the lieutenant-governor; thus he inherited the vacated office.

15. See note #10.

16. Johnson, 504.

17. Johnson, 506-507.

18. Adams, 207 - 224. A well-articulated narrative describing Grant's struggle, and ultimate failure, in trying to protect Blacks and their newly-won rights.

19. The Civil War Amendments – 13, 14, 15 – did little in effecting full rights for Blacks, at the time of ratification. Although slavery, in its traditional form was outlawed, the sharecropping system claimed its place trapping many southern Blacks for generations. Just as the 13th took a different form in implementation, such was true with the interpretation of citizenship and voting rights for black people. It took another hundred years, during the Civil Rights Movement of the 1960's, before the Civil War Amendments became actuated, and black people received some semblance of their rights, as guaranteed under the United States Constitution & the Bill of Rights. Also see Monk, 206-232.

PANEL 7

National Transformation

1877 ~1885

President Profiles

Rutherford B. Hayes
Term: 1877-1881

James A. Garfield
Term: 1881-1881

Chester A. Arthur
Term: 1881-1885

President	Date	Birthplace	College	Profession	Party
19. Rutherford B. Hayes	1822-1893	Ohio	Kenyon	Lawyer	Republican
20. James A. Garfield	1831-1881	Ohio	Williams	Lawyer	Republican
21. Chester A. Arthur	1829-1886	Vermont	Union	Lawyer	Republican

In the throes of Western Expansion, America was a young, growing nation – not even a century old. It is during this time that Rutherford B. Hayes and James A. Garfield were growing up in their formative years in Ohio, and Chester A. Arthur was doing likewise in upstate New York.

Rutherford B. Hayes and **James A. Garfield** shared many other background similarities besides being Ohioans.[1] Each came from a family of five children. And, while both future presidents were very young, their fathers died. Hence, they were raised by their mothers. Despite coming from a single parent household, they enjoyed a relatively comfortable childhood and young adult life. Both were studious; both were well-educated. Hayes' college preparation was gained in private school. At age 20, he graduated at the head of his Kenyon College (Ohio) class. The following year in 1843, he entered Harvard Law School, emerging two years later with his law degree. Upon his admission to the bar, Hayes distinguished himself as an outstanding criminal lawyer in Cincinnati. Numbered prominently among his many successes were black civil rights cases.[2]

Unlike Hayes, who took an uninterrupted path to his college education, Garfield did not.[3] With an appetite whetted for adventure that he acquired from reading endless books of heroic exploits, Garfield left home – he became a sailor. But, his sailing days were short-lived. He contracted malaria. Returning home, and after his recuperation, he resumed his education. In 1851, at 20 years old, he began college. He succeeded, outstandingly. Upon graduation, within three years, he went from student, to college professor, and then upward to college president. Garfield was a scholar.

Chester A. Arthur was born in Vermont, but spent his growing-up days in and around upstate New York. His father, an Irish immigrant teacher-preacher, moved a lot, fulfilling various assignments. However, young Arthur, despite being one of nine children, and making frequent moves with his family, managed to garner a good education. A college graduate at 17, he went on to be a successful lawyer which included defending many Blacks in fighting civil rights cases.[4]

Hayes, Garfield and Arthur were of age when the Civil War erupted in 1861. Both Hayes and Garfield fought on the Union side. They served as generals in the army. Arthur did not fight in the War. He spent that time as the New York Inspector General of the militia, a civilian position.[5] After the Civil War ended, each man returned to civilian-life and became prominent in the politics of the Republican Party.

NATIONAL TRANSFORMATION ISSUES & ACTIONS

- **Hayes' Election**
- **Withdrawal of Federal Troops**
- **Jim Crow**
- **Indian Wars**
- **Buffalo Soldiers**
- **Immigration**
- **Exodusters**

The administrations of Rutherford B. Hayes, James Garfield and Chester A. Arthur occurred during an era of drastic change and upheaval. The Civil War and Reconstruction left America in shambles. It was in the throes of attempting to redefine and transform itself. Strife pervaded the economic, social and political systems. These presidents assumed the reins of a severely weakened executive branch and a disarrayed legislative branch. Overall, America was a mess: sectional bitterness, widespread corruption and the unraveling of black civil rights, plus the accompanying ills of industrialism.

Hayes entered the presidency under a cloud that never lifted.[6] He dealt with an unwieldy congress his one term. Garfield had a shortened term; he died of wounds from an assassin's bullet.[7] As his vice president, Chester A. Arthur became president. He was the fourth person to be made president due to the predecessor's death.

Rutherford B. Hayes' election in 1876 ended Reconstruction. It had limped along for sometime. Ulysses S. Grant presided, during his last term, when the nation focused on issues having little to do with Blacks' rights or black concerns.

Hayes held this mindset. His and the Republican Party's objective was staying in power, at any cost. And that cost came through a clandestine deal. The Federal troops, who provided Blacks protection, were withdrawn. Blacks, bereft of any federal support, fell into the clutches of a very vengeful South.

The insidious system of Jim Crow pervaded, unabated. The many gains garnered under Reconstruction by Blacks all but disappeared in general. However, there still existed a glimmer of hope. Unfortunately it came at the expense of the Indians of the West. The federal government waged war against them determined to take their land and make it available for white development. In this campaign, black military contingents were trained and commandeered; they became pivotal in the success of the enforcement of the operation. They were the Buffalo Soldiers. Their role was bittersweet.

In addition to the national focus on the development of the West, industrialism in the northeast was becoming paramount. And a new labor force was born: European immigrants. They flooded the cities, doubling and tripling their sizes. With this influx of white newcomers, once more black people got shafted. At the same time black workers and black labor in the South became so egregious in their treatment, many fled north. Kansas became a more welcoming destination. Those refugees were called the Exodusters. They found some solace in garnering land through the Homestead Act.[8]

HAYES' ELECTION

Reconstruction was all but dead by the time Hayes took office. All it needed was the final nail in its coffin. Hayes provided it. His election was tainted. His Democratic opponent won the popular vote and led the electoral college, but nineteen votes were in dispute: Eighteen from the Republican-controlled states of Louisiana, Florida, South Carolina, and one from Oregon. A commission was appointed to resolve the controversy over the disputed votes. The commission determined that the votes should go to Hayes, giving him the Presidency. Southern

Democrats charged it to be a stolen election, and threatened rebellion. Hayes then made a deal with the Southern Democrats: he promised to withdraw Federal troops, to rebuild the southern economic system and to appoint southern Democrats to his cabinet. As a result of this capitulation, chances for Blacks to claim first class citizenship ended.[9]

WITHDRAWAL OF FEDERAL TROOPS

Federal troops went to the South, as a part of the Reconstruction Acts, passed by Congress in1867 and 1868. This legislation called for dividing the unreconstructed southern rebel states into five military districts. The troops' duties and responsibilities were to preserve, to protect and to enforce the laws in the districts. Laws designed to enfranchise, mainly, the newly-freed Blacks.

The Federal troops remained in the South until 1877 when Rutherford B. Hayes became President in a disputed 1876 election. Hayes got the presidency by brokering a deal with Southern Democrats, where he promised the South "home rule." This meant Whites were free to treat Blacks in any way they wanted, without federal government interference. And to achieve this, Hayes began withdrawing the troops 14 days after his inauguration! One by one, the Republican-backed southern state governments collapsed, only to be succeeded by anti-black, state governments. Hayes' actions dismantled Reconstruction – and Blacks' hopes, at the same time.

"JIM CROW"

Democrats returned to power in the South. They devised ways to circumvent the 14th and 15th Amendments. Along with violence, and intimidation of Blacks, a form of segregation, called Jim Crow, reinstated with a vengeance white supremacy and white rule.[10] Blacks no longer had support: they were completely deprived of their political and civil rights by the southerners, the North was weary of black issues, and the old anti-slave leaders were aging or dead. Blacks were left naked to the brutality of the Southern Jim Crow onslaught – a new Black Code! The original Jim Crow was a stereotypical character played by white entertainer Thomas "Daddy" Rice on the minstrel stage. The term Jim Crow came to identify the southern system of legal racial segregation.[11]

INDIAN WARS

During the Nation's transformation, the government's attention veered toward Indians and their lands. Renewed vigor emanated from all quarters to finish the quest that was interrupted by the Civil War. Blacks were brought into the Western crusade. Buffalo Soldiers – black infantry and cavalry units – helped supply military muscle in driving the Indians off their lands onto reservations. The thirty-year span from 1860 to 1890 of the Indian Wars proved to be the final piece to Manifest Destiny.[12]

BUFFALO SOLDIERS

In 1866, Congress authorized the formation of the Buffalo Soldiers.[13] The term "Buffalo Soldiers" was a name given by the Indians. Some say because of the hair resemblance, others say because of their strength, and tenacity in fighting – perhaps, both.

The Buffalo Soldiers were divided between the infantry and the cavalry: the 24th and 25th Infantry and the 9th and 10th Cavalry. Until the Indian Wars concluded, the Buffalo Soldiers performed almost entirely west of the Mississippi River on the frontier. In fact, the 9th and 10th units made up over 20% of the U.S. Cavalry in the West. All officers were white.

The contributions of the Buffalo Soldiers were inestimable in the winning of the West. Duties they performed: engaging in expeditions against the Indians, guarding strategic points, building roads, hunting horse thieves, building and repairing military posts, erecting telephone lines, and being escorts and guards.

Between the end of the Indian Wars in the 1890's and the disbandment of the Buffalo Soldiers in 1913, they defended the frontier, fought against the Spanish at San Juan, Cuba, in the Spanish American War, and against Pancho Villa in the skirmishes with Mexico.[14]

IMMIGRATION

A national phenomenon of industrialization brought in a tide of European immigrants. Between 1880 and 1900, nine million immigrants entered the country, the largest number of new arrivals, in part, in any twenty-year period of American history.[15] Growth in iron, steel, mining, and lumber industries plus major developments in manufacturing required millions of laborers. The government directed its attention from the plights of southern Blacks toward Northern capitalism, Big Business – and the pursuits toward building an industrial empire. The few Blacks who went north found problems in competing against the ethnic European immigrants in the cities.[16]

THE EXODUSTERS

During the period of unrest and turmoil for Blacks, particularly in the South, a black migration took place. In 1879-1880, Southern Blacks poured into Kansas. They were called the exodusters.[17] They came largely from Mississippi, Kentucky and Louisiana, in answering a call from the state of Kansas. It was a frontier movement. Largely leaderless, this influx created problems by upsetting the societal and economic conditions. Many suffered. A few of these migrants succeeded economically. Gradually the anomaly faded from public notice and the exodusters melded into the Kansas scene or they moved to neighboring states. Robert G. Athearn, a historian, concluded that "The Republicans, without issues of consequence in 1880, gave the flight national importance in the hope that it would gain votes for them, and at the same time, reduce the South's population and representation in Congress."[18]

NATIONAL TRANSFORMATION
Analytical Summary:
EFFECTS ON BLACKS

- **End of Reconstruction**
- **Blacks at Mercy of the South**
- **Led to loss of Civil Rights**
- **Final Campaign to Take the Rest of Indian Land**
- **Used to Enforce Government Indian Removal Policy**
- **Northern Attention Turned Away From Blacks Toward Industrialism and the New Labor Force**
- **Blacks Fled the South to Kansas**

Transformation: *the act or process in changing a condition, a character or nature in form or appearance. Synonym: Metamorphosis*

Reconstruction altered the black-white dynamic of the nation. The 1877 – 1885 era was thus dubbed National Transformation. To understand the transformation, an examination of black-related issues and the actions the presidents took in dealing with them (issues) is needed. As advocates of white superiority, Presidents Rutherford B. Hayes and Chester A. Arthur had to apply different or modified approaches to the same types of social and political issues paramount throughout American history, that kept Blacks in an inferior position.

The 1876 Rutherford B. Hayes election demanded administrative changes and actions. With southern states back in the Union by virtue of his selling-out to them, Hayes was forced to act on their behalf. These actions usurped Blacks' newly-gained status and rights. First he withdrew the federal troops, closing the five military districts: this removed Blacks social-political protection, opening up wider avenues for Whites to utilize additional heinous practices, initiated through the system of Jim Crow. Then there were the northern industrialists, whose greed he had to assuage. Never satisfied, they continuously applied pressure on the federal government and the presidents – Hayes and Arthur – to feed their ravenous appetites for power and money. Directly or indirectly, all sections of the country hinged their political power on economic control. And as throughout America before, economics always involved black people and/or their labor. Only at this time, the nature and the conditions of the economy grew exponentially more complex.

Manifest Destiny was still on the agenda; it had not been fully realized. Indians stood in the way. Their western lands needed to be taken and to be secured. Wars were waged against them for the land. Again, Blacks figured in the national scheme. The government recruited and trained them into a military force called the Buffalo Soldiers. Their job: supply the labor in the quest of divesting the Indians of the rest of their lands. That they did – and well.

In the meantime, in the North nascent industrialism cried for labor – but not black free labor. It would have to be paid for – not a desired practice to be cultivated because for over two hundred years Whites got their labor virtually free. So industrial tycoons did not want that headache, but still wanted cheap labor. They turned to immigration for the answer. Thousands, tens of thousands of immigrants flooded the American shores coming form Europe to Ellis Island and from Asia into Angel Island. In the meantime, the South tried to cope with surplus black labor. It called for another strategy: migration. Kansas and places West had to absorb the overflow.

These multiplicity of issues and problems called for transformation. Only this time all of the power was not in the hands of the presidents and white advocates. By virtue of Reconstruction, black people gained empowerment. The Civil War

Amendments provided constitutional support, the educational and economic knowledge received through the Freedmen's Bureau and the priceless experience derived from political participation metamorphosed into a rising black voice. Some Blacks took advantage of the Homestead Act staking claims and establishing viable communities in the West. However the majority of Blacks remained in the South. Despite white supremacy oppression, and Jim Crow restrictions, they persevered as had their slave ancestors.

Although transformation is evolutionary and continuous, this period in America stands out as epic for Black people. As a people free from bondage, they amassed a strength and a determination of social and political resolve, empowering them to establish their rightful place in America.

NATIONAL TRANSFORMATION END NOTES

1. Beschloss, 232, 263.

2. DeGregorio, 282.

3. _____, 296.

4. _____, 310.

5. Beschloss, 272.

6. Franklin, 332.

7. McPherson, 152.

8. The Homestead Act of 1862 gave 160 acres of public land to any person over 21 years of age, citizen or one seeking citizenship; the law required that a person live on it for five years and improve the land during that period. This law aimed to promote the settling of the West.

9. Franklin, 332.

10. Horton, 227.

11. Jim Crow refers to practices, institutions, or laws that promote segregation of Blacks from Whites. The term comes from the name of a song sung by Thomas Rice, a white performer (1808 - 60) in a black-faced minstrel show.

12. Dee Brown, *Bury My Heart at Wounded Knee* (New York: Holt, Rinehart &Winston. 1973) xi-xii "Introduction:… the thirty-year span between 1860 and 1890 . . . It was an incredible era of violence, greed, audacity …. During this time the culture and civilization of the American Indian was [virtually] destroyed…" The Indian Wars became the last piece in the Manifest Destiny puzzle.

13. Donnie D. Good, *The Buffalo Soldier* (Tulsa, Oklahoma: Thomas Gilcrease Institute of American History, 1970).

14. William Loren Katz, *The Black West* (New York: Simon & Schuster, 1996) Chapter 8.

15. Pamela Reeves, *Ellis Island* (New York: Dorset Press, 1991).

16. Lincoln, 84.

17. Nell Irvin Painter, *Exodusters* (Lawrence: University Press of Kansas, 1986).

18. Robert G. Athearn, *In Search of Canaan* (Lawrence: Regents Press of Kansas, 1978) 155.

PANEL 8

Populism & Industrialism
1885 ~ 1897

President Profiles

Grover Cleveland
Terms: 1885-1889
1893 - 1897

Benjamin Harrison
Term: 1889-1893

President	Date	Birthplace	College	Profession	Party
22. Grover Cleveland	1837-1908	New Jersey	None	Lawyer	Democrat
23. Benjamin Harrison	1833-1901	Ohio	Miami (Ohio)	Lawyer	Republican
24. Grover Cleveland	1837-1908	New Jersey	None	Lawyer	Democrat

The United States struggled to stay united during the growing years of Grover Cleveland, in New York,[1] and Benjamin Harrison, in Ohio.[2] During the formative years, the nation experienced the growing pains from Western Expansion; sectional strife over slavery; and finally, the nation-splitting Civil War between the states. Of these events, the Civil War had the most effect on Cleveland's and Harrison's lives and impacted them differently.

Grover Cleveland was born in New Jersey into a family of nine children. It was a hard life because he went to work early to help support his family. His itinerate Presbyterian minister father made little money, and moved frequently in and around New Jersey and New York. His father died when Cleveland was 16 years old.[3] At 17, he left home. His uncle, from Buffalo, N.Y., took him in. Cleveland became a clerk in a law office, which led to his becoming a lawyer. Despite never attending college, he read his way to being a lawyer. In 1859, he was admitted to the New York state bar and worked in the same firm where he started as a young clerk.

In 1861, the Civil War erupted. Cleveland did not serve. His help was desperately needed to support his mother and the younger children. He paid a substitute to take his place in the Union Army.[4] (This fact was later used against him by his political enemies.) Nevertheless, this did not deter his rise in politics, and his prominence in the Democratic Party. He rose from ward worker, assistant district attorney, sheriff, Mayor of Buffalo, Governor of New York and in 1884, the Democratic nominee for president. He went on to become the first Democratic President since the Civil War.[5] His reputation was one of honesty and not being owned by political factions. This was extremely rare, at the time, when the nefarious Tammany Hall[6] ruled.

Benjamin Harrison – unlike Cleveland's humble beginnings – descended from political aristocracy.[7] His great-grandfather signed the Declaration of Independence; his grandfather, William Henry Harrison, served briefly as a U.S. President; and his father was a two-term U.S. Congressman. The second of ten children, Harrison grew up in very comfortable surroundings on his grandfather's expansive farm where he was born. He received a well-rounded education that culminated with his 1852 graduation from Miami University (Ohio). After reading law with a Cincinnati firm, he was admitted to the bar two years later. He then moved to Indianapolis, Indiana, to practice law. It was also here, that he began a political career with the Republican Party. Harrison held numerous local and state positions.

In 1861, Cleveland's and Harrison's lives were impacted by the Civil War differently. Whereby Cleveland did not join the fray, Harrison recruited and commanded the 70th Regiment of Indiana Volunteers.[8] He was well-respected by his men who affectionately called him "Little Ben" (he stood only five feet six inches). Beginning as a colonel, he molded his regiment into a highly disciplined unit that fought valiantly in many battles for the Union. A fearless commander, he rose to the rank of brigadier general.

Following the War, Harrison returned to law and Republican Party politics. Through high profile positions, he gained national prestige – he had appointments from President Garfield and President Hayes. His high esteem garnered the GOP nomination for president, and the subsequent victory over the incumbent, Grover Cleveland, in 1888.[9]

Grover Cleveland served the only two non-consecutive terms in the U.S. presidential history.[10] Benjamin Harrison was sandwiched in between.

POPULISM & INDUSTRIALISM ISSUES & ACTIONS

- **Populism**
- **Sharecropping**
- **Industrialism**
- **Unions**
- **Booker T. Washington and W.E.B. DuBois**
- **Plessy vs. Ferguson**
- **Cleveland and Harrison Attitude Toward Black People**

After the Civil War, a severe economic depression gripped the nation. Southern white farmers suffered heavily. Long lasting, this economic situation grew so critical by the 1890's, that farm and agricultural groups formed a political-bloc to seek reform. This led to Populism.

The condition of Blacks was even more dire. Blacks were the prime labor source for farming and agriculture. Blacks became surplus labor. Whites, in the South, in order to absorb these black workers, without sacrificing their profits, created a quasi-slave system called sharecropping.

During the Civil War, the Northeast developed a thriving manufacturing industry. It flourished into industrialism after the War. Cheap labor from Europe flooded the country.[11] The immigrant workers suffered from deplorable working conditions, as did the domestic workers. (There were a few Blacks among the latter group.) To improve the poor labor situations, unions were formed.

After Reconstruction, when Blacks were literally cut asunder by the Federal Government, and by their white advocates, they had to develop their own leaders. Among this leader-cadre, Booker T. Washington and W.E.B. DuBois forged to the front. These two men could hardly have been more opposite in their backgrounds, in their viewpoints and in their philosophies, as to how Blacks fit politically, socially and economically in the American scheme.

During this period, the U.S. Supreme Court handed down the Plessy v Ferguson Decision. A ruling so devastating to Blacks that it took over another half century to restore their constitutional rights gained during Reconstruction. (The restoration came about, only after the U.S. Supreme Court ruled in 1954, that segregation was constitutionally illegal.) Cleveland and Harrison took little note of black peoples' plight – who had become the invisible ones.

POPULISM

Populism was a grassroots movement of a farm/agriculture bloc. The economic fallout from the Civil War left the farm and agriculture industries in ruins. The South was particularly hard hit – mainly small farmers. They had their farms foreclosed. The financial tycoons of Wall Street over-charged the struggling farmers and agriculturists, while the federal government steadily raised their taxes, and backed the tycoon money brokers. Populism was primarily a movement of southern Whites. However, for a short time in the beginning, black farmers were allowed to participate. But subsequently, as white supremacists increased their agitation against Blacks, the contempt and hate against Blacks grew more venomous. This led to their exclusion from the movement, and the benefits of the political gains derived through the Populist Party.

SHARECROPPING

The system of sharecropping was the South's answer to the white farmers' economic problems. Reconstruction left them with their regained lands, but without money to develop them. Northern financiers lent them money; however, taking advantage of the southern farmers' dire situation, the money brokers charged them exorbitant rates. Despite there being surplus black labor, the white farmers could not afford to pay them. And on the other hand, Reconstruction left Blacks landless, poor, and virtually homeless. Thus to save the white farmers, and rescue the black workers, the system of sharecropping was devised.

The white farmers hired the Blacks, but charged them money to use the land, the implements, and the supplies that belonged to the white farmers. At the end of the year, if the black workers did not successfully produce enough crops to yield a shared profit, then their indebtedness was increased. And usually, this would continue year after year, until the Blacks were so hopelessly in debt, that they could never pay the white farmers. Hence, the black workers ended up, in essence, working for free for white farmers – making the system of sharecropping another form of slavery.

INDUSTRIALISM

Industrialism developed in the Northeast. The expanded needs and demands for manufactured goods and products – weapons, farm equipment and machinery of all kinds – during the Civil War stimulated the industry. It spurred tremendous economic growth, which in turn, after the War, spawned many new and additional industries, such as steel, petroleum and electrical power. The ways of doing business were transformed, also. Corporate organizing, investment banking and retail practices all morphed into the rise of Big Business.

This Post-Civil War industrial growth in the U.S. brought about a cadre of strong-business leaders. Some admirers called them "captains of industry," while some critics, less enamored, dubbed them "robber barons." Andrew Carnegie (steel), John D. Rockefeller (railroad and oil), J. Pierpont Morgan (investment banking), Cornelius Vanderbilt (railroad), and James B. Duke (tobacco), were tycoons who made their fortunes at this time. They modeled industrialism.

UNIONS

Unions evolved as worker-advocate organizations, when industrialization engulfed the U.S., and an unending urge, and need, pressed every type of industry for workers! Cheap labor flooded the Northeast from Europe, and into California from China. However, there was little migrating during this period to these areas by Blacks from the South. So, in the beginning of union organizing, they did not figure too strongly in the movement. But, it is after the early 1900's, toward the start of WWI, when black labor came into the union picture.

BOOKER T. WASHINGTON AND W.E.B. DUBOIS

Booker T. Washington, an ex-slave, emerged on the post-Civil War scene, as a black leader.[12] His outstanding work as an educator brought him considerable acclaim, particularly among Whites. As the organizer of Tuskegee Institute in Alabama, he espoused industrial education for Blacks, as opposed to an academic education. His political, economic and social philosophies condoned racial accommodation, and racial separation. These views did not please some of the other black leaders. Most vocal among them was W.E.B. DuBois. But Whites overwhelmingly endorsed Washington's stance.

In 1895, at the Cotton States International Exposition, in Atlanta, Georgia, Washington received a resounding reception by white attendees, after his accommodationist speech. "In all things that are purely social, we can be as separate as the five fingers, yet one as the hand, in all things essential to mutual progress." He further underscored his position on black economic development by stating "…I would say, [to Blacks] cast down your buckets where you are … cast it down in agriculture, mechanics, in commerce, in domestic service, and in the professions."

Booker T. Washington's words were construed by Whites to be the sentiments of all Blacks, to be socially and politically separate, from Whites. Within the next year, 1896, the U.S. Supreme Court handed down "the separate, but equal" ruling, Plessy v Ferguson. It declared segregation to be legal, and it denied Blacks the constitutional rights they had won during Reconstruction.

To some students of Black history, they contend that many of Washington's views and philosophies about race were detrimental. They feel his attitude did not then (nor does it now) foster racial equality. And, because he, Washington, was so influential, his words and actions encouraged Whites in furthering the practices of white supremacy and racism.

Booker T. Washington
(photo from the
Library of Congress)

Dr. W.E.B. DuBois
(photo from the
Library of Congress)

W.E.B. Dubois' air of elegance and erudite-thought was just as impressive as the sound of his illustrious name. William Edward Burghardt DuBois loomed large among the more brilliant twentieth century sociologists and thinkers, on the subject of race.[13] Although a contemporary of Booker T. Washington, he could not have been more different in background and philosophy than Washington.

A West Virginia-born ex-slave, Washington taught himself to read and write. Driven by diligence and perseverance, he worked his way through Hampton Institute (W.Va.), furthering his education at this Freedmen's Bureau school established for Black and Indian training. By contrast, DuBois, born three years after emancipation, 1868, began his education at an integrated grammar school in Great Barrington, Massachusetts, his birthplace. This was followed by his attendance at Fisk University in Nashville, Tennessee; it, too, was a school established by the Freedmen's Bureau. Later he went to Harvard University, in Massachusetts. Here he received his Bachelor's degree (1890) and his Ph.D. (1895). In addition, between earning his Harvard degrees, DuBois spent two years of study in Germany, at the University of Berlin.

As a scholar and educator, DuBois widely disseminated his views and his philosophies through historical studies, poetry, novels, lectures, essays, articles and philosophical discussions. On the other hand, Booker T. Washington, as president of Tuskegee Institute, Washington used his position, his oratory and his writings to convey his message. His speech at the 1895 Cotton States Expo, exemplified his beliefs that the most prudent way for Blacks to advance politically, socially and economically in America, was to pacify the white man; in other words: be accommodating.[14] Dubois countered this view with a vociferous voice: "assail white people's ears with protests and demands."

Washington's approach proved to be more effective with Whites, particularly the influential ones such as Presidents Theodore Roosevelt and William Howard Taft; and industrialists Andrew Carnegie and John D. Rockefeller, whom he counted as his friends. Thus, Booker T. Washington was given the mantle by whites, as "the designated black leader."

Washington preached that Blacks should accept their second-class status as a starting point in their ascent to full citizenship. But this could not be attained until they "earned" the white man's trust and approval. He proposed that Blacks: forgo any political involvement, such as voting; that their skills be plied primarily in the industrial trades; and that industrial education and training be paramount in their emergence.[15] And above all, Blacks should be hard working, thrifty and patient.[16]

DuBois found Washington's attitude toward race abhorrent. In his book, *The Souls of Black Folk*, he scathingly attacked Washington's accommodation philosophy. Being one of the founders of the NAACP, and editor of its magazine, *The Crisis*, DuBois used this as a platform to persuade others in opposing the Washingtonian philosophy.

DuBois declared that Washington apologized for white man's injustice toward Blacks, in the North and the South.[17] He stated, "(Washington) does not rightly value the privilege and duty of voting. By doing so, Mr. Washington belittles the emasculating effects of caste distinction." DuBois proclaimed further, "That an industrial education was not the right kind for our promising black youth – 'The Talented Tenth'" – the phrase DuBois coined. "They need to hone their intellect through higher education and develop the sophistication needed, as strong black leaders, to aggressively fight for Negro rights with confidence and even a touch of arrogance."

These two men – Booker T. Washington and W.E.B. DuBois – contributed immeasurably to American history. Their voices, their command and their leadership were what America needed. Regardless of one's viewpoint, Washington's and DuBois' importance among all American leaders, is inestimable.

PLESSY V FERGUSON 1896

In 1892, Homer Plessy filed suit against the East Louisiana Railroad for unlawful jailing as violating his Thirteenth and Fourteenth Amendment rights. Judge John Howard Ferguson presided at the trial. Plessy, a man whose lineage was 7/8 white and 1/8 black, sat in the rail car designated for whites. Louisiana considered him Black.[18] Therefore, he should have sat in the area designated for Blacks. The Northern-born judge initially ruled in Plessy's favor, stating that he did not commit a violation. Later, after discussion with some of the Louisiana lawyers, he reversed the ruling, finding Plessy guilty. So, in 1896, Plessy appealed to the U.S. Supreme Court. The seven-person majority upheld the Louisiana Supreme Court decision of Ferguson. Speaking for the majority, Justice Henry Brown wrote:

"That [the Separate Car Act] does not conflict with the Thirteen Amendment, which abolished slavery … is too clear for argument … A statute which implies merely a legal distinction between the white and colored races – a distinction which is founded in the color of the two races, and which must always exist so long as white men are distinguished from the other race by color – has no tendency to destroy the legal equality of the two races … The object of the [Fourteenth A]mendment was undoubtedly to enforce the absolute equality of the two races before the law, but in the nature of things it could not have been intended to abolish distinctions based upon color, or to enforce social, as distinguished from political equality, or a commingling of the two races upon terms unsatisfactory to either."

The Plessy Decision set the precedent for the constitutionality of separate facilities as long as they were equal. This quickly extended to all other areas of public life. Segregation was made legal!!![19] "Separate but equal" doctrine prevailed in America until struck down in 1954 by the Brown v Board of Education. This ruling declared that the doctrine of "separate but equal" was unattainable and socially – politically damaging to the nation's health.

Cleveland and Harrison Attitude Toward Blacks

Black life grew even worse during both Cleveland's and Harrison's administrations. Conditions, at times, seemed hopeless. The hopelessness was quite apparent with the disenfranchising Plessy v Ferguson ruling, in 1896, which made segregation constitutionally legal! Cleveland addressed none of the issues targeting Blacks. Harrison initially advocated for black civil rights, but lacking influence with Congress, his efforts went nowhere.[20] Blacks were left to languish in a sea of white hate and contempt during the Cleveland-Harrison years.

Even though both men were northerners by background, that fact bore little or no significance in their presidential leadership or decisions as far as abetting Blacks in their social, political, and economic struggles. In fact, it only further affirmed, to Blacks, that geography plays little in who presides over the White House. Blacks learned that the politics of the time dictated the actions and policies of the presidents. And too often, Blacks did not factor positively in the political agenda. It was as though black people were invisible to Cleveland and Harrison.

POPULISM & INDUSTRIALISM
Analytical Summary:
EFFECTS ON BLACKS

- **The Grassroots farm-bloc movement excluded Blacks**
- **An Economic System that Replaced Slavery Throughout the South**
- **Industrialism Spawned Unions that Prevented Blacks from Reaping the Spoils of their Industry**
- **Booker T. Washington Encouraged Blacks to Accommodate Whites; W.E.B. DuBois Opposed this Second-class Philosophy**
- **A U.S. Supreme Court Ruling that Legalized Segregation**
- **The Invisible Ones**

The Civil War left in its wake a ravaged, depleted South. Its once thriving agricultural economy – built on the backs of Blacks – fell into shambles. No longer expansive prosperous plantations, per se; only small yeoman-operated farms dotted the landscape. The farmers struggled. Heavily-mortgaged, debt-ridden and beholden to northern bankers, they launched a grassroots political protest. It grew into Populism, a formidable third party, strongly challenging the Democrats and the Republicans. At its inception the Populist Movement let a few black farmers hold membership. But as white farmers' circumstances grew steadily more dire, so did their venomous attitude spread toward black farmers – Blacks were ousted. And, as for the surplus black worker corp, their plight became even more abysmal, victimized further by Jim Crow.

Blacks organized their own agricultural alliance. However, lacking clout and numbers, success all-but eluded them. And, with Whites having the upper hand, Blacks found themselves, once more in an humiliating and degrading economic system – sharecropping. So mired were they it took on the ramifications of slavery and all the repeat social-political ills. A quagmire. Blacks had begun to believe that Reconstruction would never allow it to happen to them again. Instead, Post Reconstruction transformation exacerbated their rapidly deteriorating conditions.

The Presidents Cleveland and Harrison paid little or no attention to white southerners and paid less to black people; treating them as though they were invisible. Abandoned. The presidents turned federal resources and ingenuity toward the furtherance of northern Big Business – industrialism. The nation was drawing its wealth and power from northern industry. This was the national focus. Both parties, the Democrats and the Republicans, courted the industrial tycoons. Their endorsement insured the political power and control each sought. Consequently, to maintain the titans' support and their demand for labor, it was a political imperative for the Party to satisfy their insatiable need. Immigration supplied the answer. But it brought with it an accompanying problem to address – Unions.

The South had surplus labor. But the workers were black. The tycoons did not want them in the North nor did they want to pay them. Their appearance in the North would complicate matters. So European whites and American poor-whites filled the bill for cheap labor. Working conditions proved so exploitative and intolerable that Unions were organized. They spawn untold mayhem and violence in their endeavor to exact a better working environment from management. Blacks were little affected. Although there were some Blacks in the North, union membership was closed to them. So the federal government was preoccupied only with white union worker-activities. And black working and general living conditions in the South drew no presidential or federal concern.

Thus, as it had been throughout America's short history, Blacks were forced into a survival-mode.

When the U.S. Supreme Court handed down the segregation-legalizing Plessy v Ferguson ruling, Blacks' light plunged deeper. They scrambled for a "Moses." Booker T. Washington and W.E.B. Dubois emerged as the Black voices. They differed widely, philosophically: Washington urged accommodation and separation; "do not offend white people by voting, intruding into white folks' business." DuBois exhorted self-determination and integration; "use the power of the ballot box, using it to exercise your God-given rights".… Whites heartily embraced Washington's message. They anointed him – the designated Black Leader.

During this period of abandonment and betrayal by the presidents and the federal government, Blacks scuffled to organize their own populism. They tried to make a way out of no way – since they were all but invisible to Cleveland and Harrison.

POPULISM & INDUSTRIALISM END NOTES

1.   DeGregorio, 321.

2.   _____, 332.

3.   Beschloss, 281.

4.   Degregorio, 323.

5.   Beschloss, 281.

6.   _____, 282.

7.   _____, 293.

8.   DeGregorio, 334.

9.   Beschloss, 294.

10. McPherson, 164.

11. Ellis, 15.

12. Hodges, "The Age of Booker T. Washington," 257-265. Also Franklin, 390-397.
     Also Booker T. Washington (Autobiography) *Up From Slavery*.

13. Hodges, "Dubois Scholar and Leader," 254-256. Also see W.E.B. DuBois.
     The Souls of Black Folk, his anti-Washington rationale.

14. Franklin, 391.

15. _____, 393.

16. _____, 393.

17. Lincoln, 72. Also see Hodges, 195.

18. Despite Homer Plessy's having more "white-blood" than "black blood," and in appearance
     looked physically like a white man, that "one-drop" of black-blood made him a member of
     the black race in Louisiana.

19. Adams, 235-239.

20. Taranto, 116.

Imperialism & Progressivism

1897 ~1921

President Profiles

| William McKinley
Term: 1897-1901 | Theodore Roosevelt
Term: 1901-1909 | William Howard Taft
Term: 1909-1913 | Woodrow Wilson
Term: 1913-1921 |

President	Date	Birthplace	College	Profession	Party
25. William McKinley	1843-1901	Ohio	Allegheny College	Lawyer	Republican
26. Theodore Roosevelt	1858-1919	New York	Harvard	Author	Republican
27. William Howard Taft	1857-1930	Ohio	Yale	Lawyer	Republican
28. Woodrow Wilson	1856-1924	Virginia	Princeton	Educator	Democrat

William McKinley, Theodore Roosevelt, William Howard Taft and Woodrow Wilson were highly educated and professionally trained in their areas of pursuit. This kind of presidential preparedness they personified has become representative of the ensuing men to occupy the White House. However, their family backgrounds differed in many ways. But they all shared the unsettling times in America as children and young men.[1]

Their growing-up years – of all four men – occurred simultaneously to the shaping and defining of the white attitude toward Blacks. Slavery. The Civil War. Reconstruction. McKinley, Roosevelt and Taft appear not to have come from families who were involved in issues pertaining to improving the political, economic and social conditions of black people. This seems rather ironic about Taft and McKinley, as they both hailed from Ohio.[2] Ohio was a bastion of abolition and Underground Railroad activity. Yet, their families were engaged in other political activism. In fact, when McKinley was eighteen years of age, he entered the Civil War. He fought on the Union side, serving under the later-to-be president, Rutherford B. Hayes.

Theodore Roosevelt came from wealth and privilege.[3] Descendants of 17th century Dutch settlers in Manhattan, New York, some of his family members were land owners and business men who did not advocate for Blacks. However, given their wealth and social status, it is probably fair to presume that most of the domestic and household labor was carried out by black people.

The lone southerner of these four presidents, Woodrow Wilson, was the son of a Presbyterian minister.[4] Paradoxically, his father grew up in Ohio. He moved to Virginia with his Scottish immigrant wife. There they started raising their family. Woodrow, the second child of four children, was born a few years later. While he was very young, his family moved once again. This time they relocated to Georgia. When the Civil War broke out, Woodrow and his family, felt the War first hand. Being a strong southern sympathizer, and believer in the states' rights, his father turned his church into a hospital for wounded Confederate soldiers. In later years, Wilson wrote of his painful memories – memories of the Union soldiers, under General William T. Sherman, laying siege to Georgia. This atmosphere and background factored heavily into Wilson's presidential policies and practices toward Blacks.[5]

Subsequently, McKinley, Roosevelt, Taft and Wilson all became deeply involved in politics, holding various local, state and national offices, before ascending to the presidency. It was during this time that the national contempt toward Blacks led to the U.S. Supreme Court Decision of Plessy v Ferguson; it was a further negative influence on the actions and policies of these presidents toward Blacks.

IMPERIALISM & PROGRESSIVISM
ISSUES & ACTIONS

- **Spanish American War**
- **Progressivism**
- **NAACP and National Urban League**
- **Black Newspapers**
- **World War I**
- **Black Soldiers**
- **Northern Migration**
- **Presidential attitudes & actions toward Blacks**

Presidents Theodore Roosevelt and Woodrow Wilson sought to make America into a world power. Presidents William McKinley and William H. Taft were drawn into the politics of the times; the times when European countries (England, Germany, France, Italy, Portugal, Belgium and the Netherlands) carved up Africa and Asia, imperialistically building empires. America adopted similar imperialistic policies which led it into entanglements, skirmishes and wars also. Most notable are the Spanish American War and World War I. During these forays, Blacks were heavily involved and served in the military in segregated units.[6]

On the domestic front, progressivism held sway from 1901-1917. Roosevelt brought it to the White House. His chief concern was that Big Business was running the country, and their control needed curbing. Progressives stood for a liberal approach toward social, political and economic reform. However, Blacks' plight grew steadily worse.[7] Reform applied only to Whites.[8]

Due to the fallout from the Plessy ruling legitimizing segregation, Blacks found themselves increasingly oppressed. The organizations, the National Association for the Advancement of Colored People (NAACP), and the National

Urban League (NUL), emerged as bulwarks in the struggle. Also, Black Newspapers sprang up throughout the country. They contributed immeasurably in waging the civil rights battle.

Following WWI, thousands of Blacks fled from a de jure segregated South. Their trek to a de facto segregated North was called the Northern Migration, which led to their urban ghettoizing of Blacks in many northeastern cities.

Throughout this period, these adverse and oppressive developments continued. They characterized the struggle Blacks waged in a segregated America. (Blacks were bereft of constitutional support until the Brown Decision was issued in 1954.) Presidents McKinley, Roosevelt, Taft and Wilson's negative attitudes and actions toward black people defied belief.

SPANISH AMERICAN WAR

American expansionists had coveted Cuba before the Civil War, but the war dwindled their interests. However, after Reconstruction ended, and the nation's attention turned toward spreading capitalism, and being a world power, their interests were rekindled. Americans established business interests on the island, despite the fact Cuba belonged to Spain. Off and on, Cubans staged uprisings against Spain, in an effort to gain their independence. In 1895, a revolution broke out. Neither the Spanish nor the Cuban rebels were strong enough to win. Fighting continued, unresolved, until 1898, when America got involved.

American newspapers agitated for war in Cuba to force the Spanish out of the Western Hemisphere. Exaggerated accounts of Spanish oppression being perpetrated on the Cuban people were printed and widely circulated. Many incensed Americans began demanding action. Some felt the U.S. should acquire naval and military bases in Cuba, and become an imperial power like the Europeans. So when the American battleship *Maine* blew up in Havana harbor, under mysterious circumstances, cries of "Remember the Maine" rang-out.[9] President McKinley's

149

hand was forced. He sent notes to Spain, demanding that the Spanish government grant Cuba independence. Spain refused to assent to the ultimatum. America and Cuba declared war on each other. The war began on April 25, 1898, and lasted until August 13, 1898, with America winning freedom for Cuba and making protectorates of other Spanish holdings such as the islands of Puerto Rico and the Dominican Republic.

At the time the Spanish American war began, Theodore Roosevelt, an expansionist, was Undersecretary of the Navy in McKinley's cabinet. He resigned his position as Undersecretary of the Navy, joined the military and went to Cuba. There he led a cavalry regiment called the "Rough Riders." Although the war was primarily one of naval combat, Blacks fought with Roosevelt on land in Cuba. The army had four all-black units, and Congress authorized the addition of ten more units. All officers were white above the rank of second lieutenant. As per usual, Blacks distinguished themselves despite their second-class citizenship. They fought with particular valor in Cuba at San Juan Hill, Las Guasimas and El Cañey.

Once again, Blacks contributed to America's success. The part they played in fighting the "splendid little war" – the name given to the Spanish American War – furthered America's quest – the quest to be a world power.

PROGRESSIVISM

The years from 1897 to 1917 have been called by some historians the Progressive era. The majority of progressives were white, middle-class city dwellers from the Northeast and the Midwest. Theodore Roosevelt brought progressivism to the White House. Roosevelt and the Progressives were reformists. Their objective was to improve and change the political, economic and social climate of America by curbing the power of the business tycoons and improving the working and living conditions of the workers. During this era, national changes and achievements were made – but primarily all for Whites' benefit. Things were just the contrary for Blacks because so many of their gains made during Reconstruction were eroded badly during this period of Progressivism.

NAACP AND THE NATIONAL URBAN LEAGUE

In the years leading up to the First World War, Blacks had two prominent civil rights organizations that led the fight against the oppression and injustice being perpetrated upon them: The National Association for the Advancement of Colored People (NAACP), and the National Urban League. Organized in 1909, the NAACP attacked the legal barriers to black equality and constitutional rights.[10] They sought enforcement of all the applicable federal amendments. Their approach was/is to use the courts.

The National Urban League, organized in 1911, specifically dealt/deals with the problems of urban Blacks. Their pressing concerns were aroused when thousands of migrants from the rural South crowded into the cities. Racial prejudice, poor housing, job discrimination and other such torments confronted them at nearly every turn. So the League devoted its efforts for improvements through the job training and employment opportunities. It used the approach of persuading white employers and businesses to train and hire Blacks.

Both the NAACP and the League are interracial. Both organizations are still active today. They are still fighting some of the same problems that led to their initial reasons for forming.

BLACK NEWSPAPERS

The Black Newspapers – the Black Press – became a very vital medium in providing not only information, but they bolstered the morale of the black community. This was sorely needed as the Whites pushed Blacks farther and farther away into their own oppressed, separate world. Black newspapers sprang up throughout the nation. They were the conduit of a people yearning to express their voice. The newspapers brought solidarity and community to black people.

Some of the more famous newspapers were *The Chicago Defender, Baltimore Afro-American, The Pittsburg Courier, The Kansas City Call,* and *The Los Angeles Sentinel.* [11]

WORLD WAR I

There had been no general war in Europe since the early 1800's, during the Napoleonic era. But by the late 1800's, tensions began to build up. European countries were competing over wealth and world supremacy. The most dramatic quests took place in ravaging Africa, and pillaging it of its lands and resources. This imperialism developed into nationalism. Imperialism and nationalism caused European relations to turn ugly. Alliances formed. Military buildups occurred. Skirmishes broke out. Finally, on June 28, 1914, the assassination of the heir to the Austro-Hungarian Empire stirred up the various enemy alliances. By August 1914, a full-blown war ensued – WWI started.

At the outset, the United States avoided getting involved. Americans viewed it as an European war. During his first term, Woodrow Wilson promised to keep America out of war. But things changed drastically by his second term. America sympathized with England, France and their allies. This brought German wrath. Germany promised Mexican officials, that if they would side with the Germans, they could get back their lost territories taken by the U.S. in the Mexican American War. In addition, German subs began attacking American shipping in mid- March, 1917. Wilson and his cabinet agreed that the time for retaliation had come. So he sent a message to Congress in early April, asking for a declaration of war. Congress complied. America officially entered WWI on April 6, 1917. Wilson said America was entering "to save the world for democracy." Once again, Blacks did their patriotic duty. Some volunteered and others were conscripted. But all of the men fought in segregated units commanded almost entirely by white officers. World War I ended with Germany surrendering on November 11, 1918.

BLACK SOLDIERS

During this period of imperialism, America fought in two notable wars, the Spanish American War and World War I. Black soldiers, despite formidable barriers of wanton discrimination from their own country – America – they served with valor.

In the Spanish-American War of 1898, Blacks participated through service in various military areas, in Cuba and in the homeland. However, it was the four units of the Buffalo Soldiers, who fought the Indian Wars in the western U.S., and who saw combat in Cuba. Even before the war was declared, there were at least thirty Blacks aboard the *Maine* when it blew up; twenty were killed. But in the battles with the Spanish in Cuba, some eye witnesses claimed, had it not been for the bravery and intervention at Las Guasimas and San Juan Hill of the Ninth and Tenth cavalries, Theodore Roosevelt and his Rough Riders might have been annihilated!

The U.S. military lost more than 5,000 lives. Ninety percent of the fatalities were due to disease and food poisoning. Blacks volunteered to aid the sick, to nurse the dying and to bury the dead. Their contributions were invaluable at the camps and hospitals in Cuba.

In less than twenty years later, America was again at war, WWI. And once again, Blacks served in an American segregated military. About 370,000 were soldiers and 1,400 were commissioned officers. A little more than half of these troops served in Europe while the others remained in American camps. Of the European troops, three black regiments were integrated into the French army and were trained by the French and fought with them. Praised by the French for their heroism and bravery, many were awarded medals and citations. However, at the war's end, when the black soldiers returned from Europe to America in 1918, they were met with the cruelties of Jim Crow once again, only worse than when they left. A resurrected Ku Klux Klan was leading the way in murder and mayhem in all parts of the country – North and South, East and West. Despite their having fought "Wilson's War," President Woodrow Wilson made no effort to honor them. Plus, he did nothing toward urging Congress to protect them, nor the rest of the black population.

NORTHERN MIGRATION

Once Reconstruction ended, southern Blacks sought redemption and hope. Their economic, social and political conditions were grave. Then two unrelated events occurred that facilitated opportunity for their exodus from the South to the North, in appreciable numbers. First the boll weevil, a small beetle, decimated the cotton crop in the South. And then later, WWI broke out in Europe. Subsequent to these events, the movement began, one of the largest population shifts in American History. It was called the Northern Migration.

Before their migration to the North, only a few Blacks lived there. Northern cities had a scattering of small pockets of them. This compared at this time with the South, where over eighty percent of all Blacks lived in the eleven Confederate states.[12] Around 1910, Blacks started edging out of the South, because economic conditions of deterioration were added to their already-woeful social and political situation. The South's agricultural economy, based on cotton, was threatened as the boll weevil gradually moved up from Mexico, destroying millions of acres of the crop. Northern lenders and merchants withdrew their support for cotton farmers. Unskilled agricultural workers, of whom larger numbers were Black, suffered from the disaster, along with their employers. The southern economy was in chaos: foreclosures, surplus labor, depressed wages and bankruptcies abounded. These conditions created gross unemployment for Blacks (and Whites, also), forcing many to turn their sights northward, where there was a worker-shortage – and plenty of jobs.

The immigrant labor force from Europe to the U.S. was quelled by WWI erupting in Europe in 1914. These immigrants had supplied the labor needs for the thriving northern industry. A dire need for workers arose without them. So by 1916 the black movement north accelerated. By summer it reached floodtide![13] Some sources estimated at the close of 1918 more than a million Blacks had fled the South. However, according to the 1920 U.S. Census report, the states of the North and West had netted gains of 330,000 Blacks. Whether one believes one or the other set of numbers, it is a fact that the Northern Migration of the early 20th century, not only caused a major demographic shift in the nation, but it also created a new social-political dynamic in the North between Blacks and Whites.

This epic change brought and spread more civil unrest in the North, simultaneous to the reemergence of the Ku Klux Klan, in both the South[14] and the North. Upon their arrival in the industrial North, many Blacks found themselves in furious competition with European immigrants and other Whites for menial jobs, and jobs in defense plants, shipyards, steelmills and meat-packing houses. The black newcomers in such cities as New York, Philadelphia, Detroit and Chicago, not readily absorbed, met with hostile and virulent challenges from Whites, often and constantly. With Klan agitation, oppression escalated into riots, floggings, lynchings, bombings and countless other acts of barbarity.

Black organizations such as the NAACP, the National Urban League, black churches and black newspapers waged a campaign, seeking intervention from the Presidents and Congress. Neither offered help nor support. Quite to the contrary: they enacted a proliferation of laws, bills, ordinances and a myriad of other forms of restrictions and prohibitions that segregated Blacks into ghettoes. These conditions made them more vulnerable to the brutal assaults and practices on them individually and collectively. They were besieged by the very cruelties that they thought they had left in the South. In some instances northern brutality perpetrated on the black newcomers exceeded some of the excesses of the South, as the bombings, burnings and murders rocked northern cities following WWI.[15]

Lynching Chart

	Number of Lynchings				Number of Lynchings		
State	*	**	**Totals**	**State**	*	**	**Totals**
Alabama	116	16	132	Nebraska	2	1	3
Arizona	1	3	4	Nevada	2	1	3
Arkansas	115	12	127	New Hampshire	-	-	-
California	10	2	12	New Jersey	-	-	-
Colorado	6	1	7	New Mexico	5	1	6
Connecticut	-	-	-	New York	-	-	-
Delaware	1	-	1	North Carolina	35	-	35
District of Columbia	-	-	-	North Dakota	2	3	5
Florida	141	29	170	Ohio	5	-	5
Georgia	240	62	302	Oklahoma	38	10	48
Idaho	2	-	2	Oregon	1	3	4
Illinois	12	1	13	Pennsylvania	1	-	1
Indiana	7	1	8	Rhode Island	-	-	-
Iowa	2	1	3	South Carolina	63	8	71
Kansas	8	-	8	South Dakota	1	1	2
Kentucky	58	10	68	Tennessee	73	3	76
Louisiana	145	27	172	Texas	181	21	201
Maine	-	-	-	Utah	1	-	1
Maryland	6	-	6	Vermont	-	-	-
Massachusetts	-	-	-	Virginia	25	1	26
Michigan	-	1	1	Washington	1	1	2
Minnesota	3	-	3	West Virginia	12	1	13
Mississippi	217	68	285	Wisconsin	1	-	1
Missouri	40	1	41	Wyoming	8	1	9
Montana	8	1	9	**Total**	**1595**	**291**	**1886**

* Exact location known. ** Exact location unknown.
Table of lynching by states during the period from 1900 to1931, according to data elaborated by Tuskegee Institute's Research Department.[16]

The Northern Migration exposed northern hypocrisy. Blacks quickly learned that Jim Crow did not live just in the South. But he symbolized what race meant throughout America . . .

PRESIDENTIAL ATTITUDES & ACTIONS TOWARDS BLACKS

American was a "new America" when William McKinley, Theodore Roosevelt, William Howard Taft and Woodrow Wilson held office, America moved increasingly toward political and economic poser on a world stage. Being engaged in two foreign wars, along with hemisphere skirmishes, different and more complex issues and problems, confronted them. However, each administration still wrestled with formidable domestic concerns. Economic strife persisted between the industrialists and the workers. And the old race problem surrounding Blacks continued to surface; but these issues received little or not favorable attention by these presidents. If black people received any response, it tended to be negative.

McKinley bridged the nineteenth and twentieth centuries to a newer and transformed America. Industrialism encouraged increased urbanization. Blacks made gradual moves northward to the cities. They were forced into ghettos by the North's Jim Crow practices; more social, political and economic problems plagued them throughout. And with the Indian Wars, virtually ended out West, Buffalo Soldiers were given new assignments; most prominent was their service in the Spanish American War. During McKinley's one term (his assassination occurred at the start of his second term), he did little to alter the plight of black people.

Upon McKinley's death, Roosevelt entered the White House. He brought a strong, dynamic personality. He pushed for reforms in Big Business. He injected progressivism in his political platform. He pressed for a greater U.S. presence in world affairs. He, in the beginning, even gave Blacks hope. He invited Booker T. Washington to dinner in the White House.[17] But, Roosevelt hastily backed off

157

– distancing himself from the occasion – when he realized his action offended the race-baiting South – so very much so, that white mobsters and supremacists made widespread attacks on Blacks. He did not intervene to curb the mayhem. In fact, Theodore Roosevelt abated the actions, as in the 1906 Brownville, Texas race riot, an ugly incident between white townspeople and black soldiers of the Twenty-fifth Regiment.[18] It was a frame-up. Again, an appeasing Roosevelt heavy handedly heaped dire reprisals on the entire Twenty-fifth Battalion. He dismissed them without honor, and disqualified each member from service in either military or U.S. civil service. Some called this "executive lynching." Ironically in 1898, the Ninth and Tenth Cavalry (Buffalo Soldiers) had made it largely possible for Roosevelt and his Rough Riders, to be victorious in the Spanish American War in Cuba.[19] In the end, Roosevelt's tenure yielded little good for black people.

Some Blacks began losing faith in the Republican Party on the heels of Roosevelt's unfavorable actions and policies concerning Blacks. This fading faith in the Republican Party's ability to improve their condition continued into William Howard Taft's administration. He too gave them very little consideration, and no favorable attention. As a result, an appreciable number of Blacks grew further away from the Republican Party during Taft's administration, and began to turn toward supporting the Democratic Party.

As the Democratic presidential candidate, Wilson contended that his wish was to see "Justice done to the colored people in every matter…." Disillusioned by previous administrations, many Blacks took Wilson's words at face value, and turned to the Democrats.[20] Their faith proved misplaced by his duplicitous words. Wilson betrayed them. Once in office, he pulled off one of his most egregious acts towards Blacks. By executive order instead of Congressional action, he mandated that "colored" federal employees be segregated in their use of public accommodations and facilities! At nearly every turn, Wilson seized the opportunity to demean, and to disenfranchise black people. His extolling of the virtues of D.W. Griffith's movie, *The Birth Of A Nation*, added the ultimate insult.[21]

Woodrow Wilson, a native Virginian, brought the worst of America to the White House. He exemplified racism. This whole period of Imperialism and Progressivism wrought more havoc upon black Americans. Through Wilson's actions during his presidency, it was clear that no constitutional support for Blacks was coming from either party.

IMPERIALISM & PROGRESSIVISM
Analytical Summary:
EFFECTS ON BLACKS

- **Buffalo Soldiers Saved Theodore Roosevelt and his Rough Riders in Cuba**
- **A Movement that Fostered Domestic Reforms, but Excluded Blacks**
- **Organizations that Worked to Regain Blacks' Civil Rights**
- **Black Media Established**
- **Blacks Fought in WWI in Segregated Units**
- **WWI and the Boll Weevil were Two Events that Colluded to Bring About the Exodus of Many Blacks from the South to the North**
- **Negative Responses**

Imperialism and progressivism shaped the political policies of this era. Presidents McKinley, Roosevelt, Taft and Wilson were charged with carrying out the tenets that in the political arena were fraught with dichotomies. This was a characteristic of politics where too much too often the action belies the rhetoric. There is a Native American expression which describes this as "speaking with forked-tongue." These presidents – particularly Roosevelt and Wilson – were notorious in this respect. Their endeavor to establish America as a world power, led them to commit imperialistic acts masked by moral veneer. This held true in their applying progressivism to curb laissez faire Big Business under the guise of guarding the nation's democratic principles.

Both imperialism and progressivism were based on power and money; two dynamics that are symbiotic. And the two tend to get in the way of morality.

160

America, from the days of the Founding Fathers had wrestled with this dilemma. Because black people were a pivotal part of America's beginning and ensuing dilemmas, they continued to play roles during this era of imperialism and progressivism, too.

The latter part of the 19th century European countries defined their nationalism through imperialistic plunder, brutalizing and exploiting the peoples of Asia, and Africa; competing to see which country could grow the biggest empire (England boasted that the sun never set on its empire). America wanted to join, too. The Europeans viewed the U.S. as not worthy. After all it was just the "new kid on the block" .... The government, pushed by Big Business, took this snipe to mean the dropping of the gauntlet – a challenge for America to prove it belonged and merited the right to compete on the world stage with the "big boys." True to its Yankee spirit, the U.S. dusted off its old manifest destiny mantra. Only this time, it used the rationale of the Europeans: Darwin's natural selection and survival of the fittest theories. America's show and tell was a strong new naval fleet, a robust economic system – and that indomitable, competetive Yankee spirit! Exhibiting these requisites, America plunged into the fray!

In 1898, the Spanish American War served as the nation's debut and launching. Vanquishing the hapless Spanish, the Yankee spirit took on an even more inflated hubris. U.S. duplicity was rife. Rather than calling newly appropriated lands colonies – Cuba, the Philippines, Hawaiian Islands and countless other Pacific and Caribbean island nations – the art of euphemism once again was applied. These conquered areas were referred to variously as annexations, territories, protectorates and even coaling stations despite the U.S. colonial treatment of the people. This was justified because it was America's duty to bring the white man's civilization to these dark and swarthy inhabitants. All this overseas imperialistic action was simultaneously juxtaposed against the domestic government policy calling for progressivism.

161

Roosevelt championed progressivism as well as imperialism. He agreed with the poet Vachel Lindsay that the magnificence of American wealth and its products contrasted with the American poor, whom the society had made "ox-like, limp and leaden-eyed." Industrialism put too much power in the custody of too few and it had left too many languishingly powerless. This was undemocratic. In theory how true, but in the real America only so much equality could be allowed. That is how capitalism works in a racist, class-based society. All the rhetoric in the world could not change matters. So being at the bottom of both social-political demographics, black people were overly-represented in Vachel Lindsay's ox-like, leaden-eyed segment in Jim Crow American society.

Shut out from the spoils of economic progressivism, but thrust into the fore-front in doing the nation's imperialist bidding, engaging in the skirmishes and the fighting in the wars, Blacks occupied their usual demeaning role. However, during this period, they amassed more and varied armaments to wage their own war against Jim Crow. The NAACP and the National Urban League organized using more and better focused strategies. The Black Press augmented their activi-ties buttressing the many phalanxes of black communities in the South and those that mushroomed into northern ghettos during the mid-nineteen hundred WWI period.

Once again Blacks had to draw from the well of self-determination and call upon the will of survival to overcome; to overcome another raft of American presidents dedicated to preserve and to maintain the status quo of a racist America. It is quite a paradox that this era was dubbed Progressive.

IMPERIALISM & PROGRESSIVISM END NOTES

1. In tracing the actions and policies of the U.S. Presidents, generally speaking, as far as Black people are concerned, the geography of these men's background played only a small part. The politics of the times dictated their presidential behavior and decision-making.

2. Beschloss, 305, 329.

3. _____, 315.

4. _____, 337.

5. DeGregorio, 411.

6. Franklin, "Negroes in the Spanish-American War," 418-425; "Enlistment of Negroes," 455-461; "Service Overseas," 461-470.

7. _____, "The Voice of Protest Rises," 486-493; Also see Lincoln, 84-91; Hodges, "Blacks Begin to Protest Anew," 283-286.

8. Lincoln, 85, 88.

9. Franklin, 418-425, 455-461.

10. Hodges, "Emergence of the NAACP," 290-291.

11. Franklin, 85, 88.

12. _____, Chapter 6 "Northern Migration," 84-106; Also Hodges, "Great Exodus from the South," 300-304.

13. Franklin, 472-473.

14. Hodges, "Upsurge of Violence," 279; "The Statesboro (Georgia) Riots of 1904," 279-280; "The Atlanta Riots of 1906," 280-281; "The Brownsville Disturbances of 1906," 281-282.

15. _____, "Hate in Postwar America," 304-305.

16. Lincoln, 81.

17. Hodges, "The Washington Furor," 277-279.

18. _____, "The Brownsville Disturbances of 1906," 281-282.
    Also see Franklin, 441-443.

19. Hodges, 276.

20. Adams, 245-247.

21. _____, 247. Also Hodges, "The Era of Woodrow Wilson," 292-293.

PANEL 10

Isolationism & Depression

1921~1941

President Profiles

Warren G. Harding
Term: 1921-1923

Calvin Coolidge
Term: 1923-1929

Herbert Hoover
Term: 1929-1933

Franklin Delano Roosevelt
Term: 1933-1945

President	Date	Birthplace	College	Profession	Party
29. Warren G. Harding	1865-1923	Ohio	Ohio Central	Editor	Republican
30. Calvin Coolidge	1872-1933	Vermont	Amherst	Lawyer	Republican
31. Herbert Hoover	1874-1964	Iowa	Stanford	Engineer	Republican
32. Franklin Delano Roosevelt	1882-1945	New York	Harvard	Lawyer	Democrat

Postwar America found the attempts to have the nation more involved in international affairs not to its liking. Wilson's failure of foreign policy left a bitter taste.[1] Hence his presidential successors – Warren Harding, Calvin Coolidge and Herbert Hoover – led the nation into isolation, turning their attention toward Big Business and promoting capitalism. They possessed little concern for other unrelated issues. Blacks happened to be a part of the unrelated, important issues. As Coolidge strongly made clear, "the business of government is business," the social-political needs went unattended.[2] The Republicans, whom they represented, held little interest in bettering the conditions of the common Whites. Their plight, an economic struggle, fostered the increased violence and persecution of Blacks and the resurrection of the Ku Klux Klan.[3]

All these Presidents – Warren G. Harding, Calvin Coolidge, Herbert Hoover and Franklin Delano Roosevelt – were northern-born and bred; two were

Northeasterners and two were Midwesterners. Their family backgrounds and communities dealt little with black people, politically or socially. Perhaps, in a superficial way, there may have been contact with some Blacks as domestic workers. They were products of the post Civil War, transitional years in America. At this time, there was a northern attitude of "benign neglect" toward Blacks.

An Ohioan, **Warren G. Harding** was born just months after the Civil War ended. Being the eldest of eight children from a rural family, he went to work at a young age to help out. His father held many jobs in supporting the family (farmer, homeopathic doctor, newspaperman, small businessman).[4] Harding learned to read at an early age. He did well in his studies in the local schools. At the age of 14, he entered Ohio Central College and graduated in 1882. For awhile, he taught grammar school. This was only the first of professions he tried – reading law, selling insurance – before settling on the newspaper business. Perhaps this was the residual influence of his days as an apprentice working on his father's newspaper.

Harding, early on, had a penchant for language and the printed word. With two friends, they bought a newspaper, "The Weekly Star." He became the editor and publisher. The editorials were overtly political, supporting strongly the Republican Party.[5] Besides his adeptness with the written word, his spoken word proved just as effective. In fact so much so, his oratory – and engaging personality – keyed his political successes. He served in many state offices, and they eventually led to the U.S. Senate in 1914. It was from this launching pad, that Harding was chosen in 1920 to carry the Republican banner for the presidency. He ran a "front-porch" campaign and adopted the slogan "Back to Normalcy." This appealed to the war-weary American electorate, and he and his running mate Calvin Coolidge won by a considerable margin. His normalcy and Big Business platform captured, overwhelmingly, the majority vote. Harding became the 29th president.

The Harding presidency was cut short when he suddenly died of a heart attack in 1923; **Calvin Coolidge,** as vice president, inherited the presidential reins. A stark change took place in the personality of the White House. Whereas Harding was affable and out-going, Coolidge was the opposite. He was so taciturn and reserved, his nickname was "silent Cal." From the beginning he was quite shy; however, his reputation of being witty and having a good sense of humor stood him in good stead, as he carved out a political career.[6]

Born John Calvin Coolidge, named after his father, he generally went by Calvin. This was to distinguish himself from the elder Coolidge.[7] His father ran the local post office and the general store in a small Vermont town. He also farmed. A community activist, Cal's father acted as a deputy sheriff, was a deacon of the church, and served as a state legislator. He encouraged young Cal to involve himself in community service and to be earnest about his education. After attending several preparatory academies, he entered Amherst College (Mass) in 1891. Four years later he graduated cum laude.[8] Coolidge distinguished himself in oratory and politics. He stayed in Massachusetts after completing college. Attracted to law, he took a position as a clerk in a law firm. He read his way to the law, and was admitted to the Massachusetts bar in 1897.

In 1898, Coolidge set up a law practice, and simultaneously plunged into Republican politics. He went from city councilman, mayor and on to governor of Massachusetts. His shrewd polemics engendered him to the National Republican Party, when the 1919 police strike captured national headlines. His pro-Big Business action, and anti-union rhetoric fit the party philosophy. So in 1920, he became the Republican pick, as Harding's running mate, during the presidential race. And then of course, he gained the vice presidency when the nation chose Harding for president. Coolidge served in this capacity from 1921 – 1923, ending when Harding suddenly died. He entered the White House, becoming the 30th president of the United States. Once he completed Harding's term, Coolidge ran on his own in 1924, and was successful continuing the patronization of Big Business. And he continued ignoring the deteriorating plight of Blacks.

In 1928, Calvin Coolidge opted not to run for re-election.[9] However, the American voters liked the Republicans' isolationist foreign policies, and their pro-business domestic actions, and put the party back in the White House. This time, **Herbert Hoover,** a millionaire businessman, carried the banner.

Herbert Hoover set a precedent. A native of Iowa, he was the first president born west of the Mississippi River.[10] However, he left Iowa at a young age. Both his blacksmith father and his Quaker-preaching mother, died by the time Hoover was 9 years old. Orphaned, he went to live with an uncle in Oregon.[11] This uncle was the principal at a Quaker academy. Here, young Herbert garnered his secondary education. With outstanding skills in math and science, his interests gravitated toward engineering. At 17, he enrolled in the newly-established Stanford University (California), and he graduated with a geological engineering degree in 1894. Using his expertise as a mining engineer, he established a prosperous business career. In many parts of the world he reorganized mines. By 1914 he was a millionaire. This same year WWI began. Belgium needed help. Hoover was hired as the food administrator. From 1914 – 1917 the superior management he did saved thousands of lives; he gathered and distributed food and raised relief funds for the Belgians.[12] When the U.S. entered the War (1917), President Woodrow Wilson appointed him to head the U.S. Food Administration. Following the Armistice, Hoover served in many appointed capacities. When Coolidge decided not to seek re-election, the Republicans nominated Hoover as their candidate. He was elected the 31st president in 1928.

Whereas Hoover's entrepreneurial skills brought him wealth, this was in stark contrast when compared to his successor. Born with the veritable "silver spoon" in his mouth, he grew up in an environment, oblivious to the trials of ordinary white Americans. **Franklin Delano Roosevelt** had wealth on both sides: his father was vice president of the Delaware and Hudson Railway; his mother's family gained riches from similar holdings. An only child, Roosevelt was pampered.[13] On his parents' Hyde Park Estate, in New York, his world was peopled with governesses, valets and tutors (and a doting mother, who followed him into the White House). His education was a typical elitist one. It stemmed from private tutoring, on to prepping at the school of the wealthy, Groton, through to Harvard University, and culminating with a law degree from Columbia Law School (N.Y.).

Coming from the influential world of money and power, Roosevelt easily parlayed his privilege into politics. This ascendancy was temporarily forestalled. In 1921 he was stricken with paralyzing polio.[14] Although a permanent cripple, this did not deter the future of the only four-term elected president. He continued to hold many appointed and elected positions prior to being tapped as the Democrats' 1932 presidential nominee, and to his subsequent election, the 32nd president.

ISOLATIONISM & DEPRESSION ISSUES & ACTIONS

- **Isolationism**
- **Resurgence of the Ku Klux Klan**
- **Black Response**
- **1929 Stock Market Crash**
- **The New Deal Programs**
- **Negro Renaissance**

By 1920, Americans turned inward. They were fed up with the fallout of fighting World War I: President Woodrow Wilson's postwar policies and actions, along with the staggering war debt. They wanted no more European entanglements. America turned to isolationism, hoping to be spared of foreign problems. So when Warren G. Harding's presidential platform hailed "returning to normalcy," the electorate embraced his isolationism and elected him president. He put the stamp of Big Business and capitalism on the government.[15] This also ushered in the nativist White Anglo-Saxon Protestant (WASP) foment.

This WASP foment led to the resurgence of the Klu Klux Klan. Their revival spawned all of the hate crimes targeting non WASPs – Blacks along with Catholics, Jews and foreign immigrants. Getting no support from the federal government, Blacks scrambled devising means and ways to fight, to cope. Civic and political groups sprouted throughout black communities.

In October 1929, the Stock Market crashed. Overheated, it literally exploded, collapsing the U.S. economy. The nation sank into an economic depression. Harboring fears of Socialism, President Herbert Hoover refrained from using governmental means in solving the people's economic problems.[16] After one term, his policies did not resonate with the voters and he was defeated in the 1932 presidential election by Franklin D. Roosevelt (FDR). He brought a different economic philosophy. He believed in governmental intervention.

FDR called this program that assisted Americans during this tumultuous period of economic, political and social strife, the New Deal. It proved to be relatively inclusive, inadvertently benefiting black Americans, too.

Many facets of the New Deal dealt with cultural enrichment – black artists, actors, writers, and musicians received a new impetus to the already arts and cultural pursuits known as the Negro Renaissance. This movement is also referred to as the Harlem Renaissance, because one of the most creative and flourishing art colonies was in Harlem, a section in New York City.

So it was during this 20-year span in American History of Isolationism and Depression, when the two major parties defined their divergent political, social and economic philosophies. The Republicans, advocates of Big Business, established a conservative philosophy, endorsing the status quo, referred to as *the right*. The Democrats' ombudsman of the people leaned to *the left*, because they evolved into a party of liberal causes and espousing change. The former stance was exemplified by the Harding, Coolidge and Hoover administrations; the latter was characterized by the Roosevelt administration. During this period when Blacks started to intrude upon the socio-political landscape again, the party demarcation was defined. Blacks began exercising their political voice, emanating from the Northern Migration cities.[17] And they began to martial their political capital with the Democratic Party, drifting away from the party of Abraham Lincoln.[18] Eleanor Roosevelt – FDR's wife – played a major role in aiding the black political switch.[19]

ISOLATIONISM

By 1920, Americans were disenchanted with President Woodrow Wilson's policies of WWI, which included the Versailles Treaty and his proposed League of Nations. They wanted no European entanglements. The war-weary nation struggled under the weight of farm problems stemming from high tariffs and surpluses. Added were labor set backs. Strikes and work unrest made more domestic upheaval, so when Warren Harding campaigned for president with his isolationist pitch, Americans readily embraced it.[20]

The inward-selfness created a counter-culture response. The Flapper Age with their short-skirted chemise and wild dancing were a part of the 1920's. This era in American History is also known as the Jazz Age, or the Roaring Twenties. Simultaneously, a temperance movement led to prohibition. Liquor was viewed as sinful. Congress passed the Volstead Act which prohibited the sale of alcohol. This Act turned into the 18th Amendment but was repealed later since the politicians determined this Amendment interfered with free-enterprise.

A revolt against this Puritanical attitude made for materialism and over-indulgence with the counter-culture segment of society. Night clubs called "Speakeasies" provided the venue with lots of drinking, dancing and entertainment provided by Blacks.[21] This rebellious attitude among Whites opened the doors for black bands, singers, dancers and other types of societal-defiant entertainment. Headliners included Louis Armstrong, Duke Ellington, Fletcher Henderson, Bessie Smith, the Cotton Club dancers and a myriad of other performers. Jazz and blues music swept the nation. New to Whites, in this anti-cultural mood, they grasped the black original American art form that grew out of the old slave and Negro Spirituals.[22] All of this served as a perfect vehicle to express defiance of Puritanism in the 1920's.

RESURGENCE OF THE KU KLUX KLAN

Bombings. Burnings. Lynchings. Unspeakable forms of hate crimes: harassment and intimidation became commonplace in the 1920's. These evil acts earmarked the resurgence of the Ku Klux Klan. No longer local only to the South, they spread north and west.[23] The Klan's destructive activities took many forms and involved many who hid behind their hooded attire, as they carried out their dastardly deeds. Throughout the 20's, they controlled governments with Oregon, Indiana and Colorado being chief among them. Mayors, governors, legislators, police chiefs and the police departments held Klan memberships and followed and carried out insidious operations.

The murdering, maiming, destroying property, depriving justice and the miscarriage of it scoured the nation. The Presidents and Congress made little effort to protect or intervene on behalf of the Klan victims. Blacks were their main target; however, they also attacked other racial and ethnic groups,[24] any group not White Anglo-Saxon Protestant (WASP).

BLACK RESPONSE

Jim Crow evils grew and intensified. The federal government under Presidents Harding, Coolidge and Hoover, failed to address the problems. As Ralph Ellison, the famous black author pointed out in his book, "Blacks were the invisible men." [25] Another black voice was Ida B. Wells, the journalist and relentless crusader. She tried in vain to get the presidents' and Congress' attention to enact legislation to stop the lynching. She, as well as others, went unheeded.[26]

Many approaches were taken to lessen the abuse. On the legal end, the NAACP fought through the courts. On the economic front, the National Urban League struggled. A. Phillip Randolph organized a black union that affiliated with the Congress of Industrial Organizations (CIO).[27] Black churches were forever waging an uphill battle. The deaf ear and denial of constitutional rights pervaded the country, seemingly wherever Blacks were or went.

Some Blacks chose to separate from white America. They established black communities and towns.[28] Various states were home to these all-black towns. Some Blacks went so far as to seek refuge in the Marcus Garvey Back-to-Africa Movement, the Universal Improvement Association.[29]

Despite the oppressive political-social conditions, most Blacks continued the fight for their rights as full-fledged Americans, as they gained more voting power.

THE STOCK MARKET CRASH OF 1929

On October 29, 1929, the Stock Market crashed.[30] Banks failed, factories shut down, stores closed, unemployment sky-rocketed. America plummeted into a deep, economic depression! Poverty extended throughout, affecting all Americans – black and white. President Hoover felt it unfitting that the Federal Government bail out citizens; its role was to help business. This was the Republican philosophy of government. So conditions deteriorated steadily until the election of Franklin Delano Roosevelt in 1932.

THE NEW DEAL PROGRAMS

After the Stock Market Crash in 1929, Franklin Roosevelt and the Democrats took over the federal government. Economic depression engulfed the nation. The New Deal did not end discrimination, but some of the programs, by default, brought improvements. Through first lady Eleanor Roosevelt's advocacy, Blacks got some recognition and consideration.[31]

Programs such as the CCC (Civil Conservation Corps), the PWA and the WPA (Public Works and Works Progress Administrations) hired Blacks and helped them benefit from relief and recovery because so many were poverty-stricken. The Federal Theatre Project and Writers' Project further advanced black creative arts. Roosevelt's Executive Order 8802, issued in June 1941, mandated fair employment. It prohibited discrimination where businesses held federal defense contracts.[32]

Many Blacks hailed this as significant as the issuance of the Emancipation Proclamation. The New Deal did not end depression or discrimination, but it advanced confidence in the government. Many Blacks began to switch from the Republican to the Democratic Party. Roosevelt was returned to office three more times, receiving the overwhelming support and the vote of Blacks.[33]

THE NEGRO RENAISSANCE

This postwar period spawned the coming of age of black cultural expression. Cultural colonies sprang up in the large northern cities following the Northern Migration. New York and Chicago were chief among them. Artists, musicians, writers and actors added an untapped and fresh dimension to the cultural world. They performed during the Roaring Twenties in the underworld speakeasies. Jazz greats Louis Armstrong, Duke Ellington and others gained fame. Singers of many stripes performed songs from the classical to the blues-belters among whom were Marian Anderson, Paul Robeson, Roland Hayes, Bessie Smith and Ma Rainey. The literary contributions loomed large. Works by Langston Hughes, Zora Neal Hurston, Richard Wright and Gwendolyn Brooks stood out. The fine arts works of Jacob Lawrence, Horace Pippin, Hale Woodruff and Augusta Savage brought another perspective. With the advent of Roosevelt's New Deal, the arts received even greater impetus.[34]

It is during this period that Blacks used the arts as therapy, and a catharsis. They released their pent-up feelings and frustrations; they found solace from the inflicted hurts continuously heaped upon them. The visual arts, the literature, the dance and theatre along with music, offered modalities of cultural expression. These varied forms of the Negro Renaissance served strategically in enabling Blacks' adjustment to the urban ghettos. This was comparable to the role the Negro Spirituals played in helping the bondsmen cope with slavery.

ISOLATION/DEPRESSION
Analytical Summary:
EFFECTS ON BLACKS

- **WWI Fallout Led to American Move to Rid Itself of European Entaglements**
- **Political Unrest Spawn Increased Hate Crimes Against Non-WASPS**
- **Civic and Political Groups Organize to Fight, to Cope**
- **U.S. Economic System Collapsed**
- **Franklin Roosevelt's Economic Recovery Program**
- **Black Cultural Arts Flourished**

President Woodrow Wilson's political policies and actions left in their wake a disconsolate nation. America's fighting in WWI proved to be a disillusionment. None of the expected glory and nor the expected wealth materialized. Rather bitter disappointment enveloped the bulk of America. The staggering-incurred debt, the needless blood-shed, the foreign entanglements and the spiraling domestic problems manifest into a call for political change: Isolationism. So for the next three terms the Republicans wrested the helm from the Democrats and practiced insular politics. However one practice they did not change was abetting Jim Crow and racism.

Warren G. Harding, Calvin Coolidge and Herbert Hoover presided over the nation's ills with such insensitivity and dispassion that most ethnic-racial discord and violence barely received federal intervention. The resurgence of the Ku Klux Klan reeked havoc throughout the country. As per usual, black people topped their list of victims. Lynchings, shootings, fire bombings, tarring and featherings were but a few of the heinous crimes perpetrated upon them. Blacks, despite

177

their getting no help from the presidents or the congress, most continued to struggle for their constitutional rights. However, some lost faith and sought solace with Marcus Garvey's Back-to-Africa Movement. America raged with hatred and immorality. It is not until Franklin Roosevelt took office that Blacks got some redress.

The stock market collapsed in 1929 and sent America plummeting into a virtual economic abyss, a depression. Hoover was president. And as he was wont, his actions were not people-friendly. Blacks, and nearly every other American suffered. Fortunately, Roosevelt succeeded Hoover – just in the nick of time. He implemented a national recovery plan called the New Deal. Although it did not affect total recovery – it provided enough federal assistance to rescue the nation – and black people.

There were a myriad of agencies under the New Deal. Various facets of the economy and other parts of the infrastructure were addressed. Jobs resulted. Although not an affirmative action set aside program, black people benefited from it in many ways. The arts and related cultural pursuits received a savings-boost. The Negro Renaissance owed much of its continuing life to President Roosevelt's New Deal.

Once again in American history, when circumstances for black people are so dire and the outlook appears heading toward futility, a combination of serendipity and the indomitable spirit enables them to overcome – depression, oppression, Jim Crow and racism.

ISOLATIONISM & DEPRESSION END NOTES

1. Johnson, Wilson's failure with Congress over the League of Nations. 654-655.

2. Taranto, 148.

3. Hodges, "Hate in Postwar America," 304-305.

4. Beschloss, 351.

5. DeGregorio, 436.

6. McPherson, 214.

7. DeGregorio, 447.

8. _____, 449.

9. McPherson, 216.

10. _____, 218.

11. DeGregorio, 464, 465.

12. Beschloss, 368.

13. _____, 377.

14. _____, 378.

15. Paul M. Roberts and Paula A. Franklin, *Comprehensive United States History* (New York: AMSCO School Publications 1986), 412.

16. Hodges, *Hoover Alienates Blacks*, 338-339.

17. In the northern large city ghettos, Blacks began to assemble some voting power, particularly by the 1930s.

18. Hodges, *The New Deal for Blacks*, 336-338; *Blacks Leave the Republican Party*, 339.

19. _____, *The Roosevelts Befriend Blacks*, 341-342.

20. Isolationism is a doctrine that calls for a nation not to engage politically, or in other ways, with other nations, no entanglements.

21. Lincoln, 122.

22. _____, 122.

23. See #3.

24. The Ku Klux Klan attacked other ethnic and racial groups besides Blacks. They targeted anyone or ones, who did not fit into the White Anglo Saxon Protestant culture (WASP). Also see Lincoln, 85. 29. Hodges, "Marcus Garvey: The Black Messiah," 309-318.

25. Ralph Ellison, *Invisible Man.* (New York: Signet Books, 1952).

26. Dorothy Sterling, *Black Foremothers: Three Lives* (New York: Feminist Press at the City University of New York) "Two: Ida B. Wells," 61-103.

27. Hodges, 325, 344.

28. Black Towns: following the unfulfilled promise and the betrayal of Reconstruction, a movement spread to establish Black Towns. These were not enclaves within cities, but separate municipal entities, peopled and governed by Blacks. They sprang up throughout various parts of the U.S. Some of these Black Towns were: Mount Bayou, Mississippi; Nicodemus, Kansas; Dearfield, Colorado; Boley and Taft, Oklahoma.

29. Hodges, Marcus Garvey: *The Black Messiah*, 309-318.

30. _____, 310.

31. In spite of her husband, President Franklin Roosevelt's less than intense interest in the plight of black Americans, Eleanor made it her business. She constantly nagged, cajoled and demanded, in some instances, that FDR not ignore Blacks. The Tuskegee Airmen, the all-Black fighter wing of the U.S. military, during WWII, is one the most stirring results of her efforts and influence. Another of her interventions that stands out was her stalwart steadfastness, on behalf of Marian Anderson. Mrs. Anderson, a marvelous world-famous concert singer, who was black, was barred by the Daughters of the American Revolution (DAR) from singing in Constitution Hall, in 1939. Mrs. Roosevelt was a DAR member. In response to the indignity perpetrated upon Mrs. Anderson, Eleanor Roosevelt withdrew her membership! And she then arranged it so that Marian Anderson could, on Easter Sunday, 1939, sing from the steps of the Lincoln Memorial in Washington, D.C. Also see Adams, 258-59; 260, 268.

32. Adams, 256-266. Also see Hodges, 344.

33. FDR set up a new federal agency to deal with black Americans during the Depression. The agency was composed of prominent black officers and advisers. They often were referred to as the "Black Cabinet." This kind of recognition swayed large numbers of black voters to switch from the Republican Party to the Democratic Party. Also see Hodges, 340-344.

34. Hodges, 318-325. Also see Lincoln, 120-123. 18. Paul M. Roberts and Paula A. Franklin, *Comprehensive United States History* (New York: AMSCO School Publications 1986), 412.

PANEL 11

World War II
& Postwar Prosperity

1941 ~1955

President Profiles

Franklin Delano Roosevelt
Term: 1933-1945

Harry S. Truman
Term: 1945-1953

Dwight David Eisenhower
Term: 1953-1961

President	Date	Birthplace	College	Profession	Party
32. Franklin Delano Roosevelt	1882-1945	New York	Harvard	Lawyer	Democratic
33. Harry S. Truman	1884-1972	Missouri	None	Business	Democratic
34. Dwight David Eisenhower	1890-1969	Texas	West Point	Soldier	Republican

Franklin Roosevelt's background contrasts considerably from those of presidents Eisenhower and Truman. The comparisons can be made by review of the President Profile in Panel 10.

Harry Truman's background, unlike Roosevelt's northeastern aristocracy, was a humble one, stemming from rural Missouri. His Kentucky-bred grandparents owned slaves. They brought them into Missouri, a slave state, when they immigrated there in the 1840's.[1] While Truman was growing up, his environment was segregated. Although his family was not wealthy, he and his two siblings enjoyed a comfortable life. Having an educated and cultured mother, who instilled in him the love of books, and the joy of music, Truman was a life-long learner. But oddly, he never went to college. He aspired to attend West Point; poor eyesight negated that, rendering him physically unqualified.[2] Instead, Truman entered business (although he served a short stint in the U.S. Army during WWI).

As a businessman, Truman was a community activist. His connections led him into politics. Moving from the state level, he eventually represented Missouri in the U.S. Senate. Here he became very powerful and highly respected in the Democratic Party.[3] So when Franklin Roosevelt ran for his fourth presidential term, he picked Truman for his vice president. Besides completing FDR's un-expired term, Harry Truman was elected to a term in 1948, serving until **Dwight David Eisenhower**'s election in 1952.

Whereas Truman aspired to West Point, Eisenhower qualified, entered and graduated from there.[4] It was this background and training that led him to a distinguished military career with service in both WWI and WWII. In the latter war, he was named and served as Supreme Commander of the Allied Expeditionary Force in Europe, from 1943 until victory in 1945. After retiring from active duty in 1948, he became president of Columbia University (N.Y.).[5] Then two years later, prior to his election as U.S. President, he was made NATO Commander (North Atlantic Treaty Organization). Once again, his organizational skills and adeptness to martial men, gained him plaudits and admiration. This hero stature led the Republican Party to select him as their presidential nominee in 1952.[6]

Eisenhower's life exemplified that of the mythical Horatio Alger heroes.[7] He came from lowly beginnings, and rose to great heights. His German-Swiss ancestors were pacifists. They came to America for religious freedom; they did not believe in war or any kind of violence. The family first settled in the slave-holding state of Texas, where Ike (his nickname) was born. When Ike was two years old, he, his father, mother and two brothers moved to Kansas. Four more boys were born to the family in Kansas, a Jim Crow state.

The Eisenhowers were very poor. Ike's parents raked and scraped, using every means possible, to eke-out a living for him and his six brothers. Being the third oldest he went to work, supplementing the family income. His father worked as a mechanic in a dairy; his mother farmed, growing fruit and vegetables. Ike worked at a part-time job at the creamery, and also peddled produce. However, he did not neglect his education, despite his working. He did well in school. The 1909 high school yearbook predicted that some day he would be President of the United States! [8]

WWII & POSTWAR PROSPERITY ISSUES & ACTIONS

- **Pearl Harbor Attack 1941**
- **War Industries /Black Fighters in WWII**
- **President Roosevelt's Death /Atomic Bomb**
- **GI Bill (Servicemen's Readjustment Act 1944)**
- **Korean War**
- **Roosevelt, Truman and Eisenhower Administrations**

Franklin Roosevelt's success, that he experienced overseeing the Great Depression, continued as he led the nation into World War II (WWII) after the Japanese attack on Pearl Harbor.[9] He played a pivotal role in helping America and the allies defeat the Germans, the Japanese and the Italians.

With the Japanese attack on Pearl Harbor, Hawaii, in 1941, the New Deal ended. World War II began for America. Drafted Blacks, in segregated units, fought in both Theatres of War: Pacific and Europe. War plants and related industries opened nationwide. Many work opportunities became available to black civilians. They migrated from the South to various areas of the country, north and west.

Months before the Japanese surrendered, upon the dropping of the atomic bomb in 1945, Franklin Roosevelt died suddenly. Harry Truman assumed the presidency, providing the leadership between wartime and the return to peace. After this, the nation vaulted into prosperity; a goodly part of it was due to the transforming GI Bill; a black middle class was established.

In an effort to stem the spread of Communism in Asia, U.S. intervention brought on the Korean War. Once again, Blacks fought, but this time in an integrated military, in 1950 thanks to President Truman's executive orders. The War ended in 1953 during Eisenhower's administration.

This period of dramatic national and international changes, caused largely by the fighting of WWII and its postwar consequences, impacted heavily the lives of black Americans. The administrations of Presidents Franklin Roosevelt, Harry Truman and Dwight Eisenhower figured significantly in most of the marked changes. However, oft-times their actions that resulted in black advancement came due to intense pressure. Some of it was applied by black leadership and civic/fraternal organizations which continuously battled Jim Crow.

PEARL HARBOR ATTACK

The U.S. took over Hawaii as an American territory in 1893. Pearl Harbor, one of its principal ports, became an American naval base. When WWII broke out in Europe in 1939, the United States helped allies England and France with aid, but it was not an official part of the combatants who fought Hitler and his henchmen.[10] Simultaneously, the Japanese waged war in Asia and the Pacific, where Hawaii is located. Their efforts to control that part of the world, led to the bomb attack on U.S. installations on December 7, 1941. This provocation led to the U.S. declaration of war, and it began America's fight on two fronts, Europe and Asia in WWII. Black men and women joined other Americans participating in the War on the home front and the war front; working in war industries and serving in branches of the military.

WAR INDUSTRIES/ BLACK FIGHTERS IN WWII

Thanks to many of the skills and jobs Blacks acquired during the New Deal, they were able to transfer them into war work. Jobs in the aircraft industries, ship building, welding, automotive mechanics, electricity and radio, black workers plied their trades. They migrated to the various sites of employment in large numbers to the North and the West. This migration led to a considerable population shift of Blacks from the South to these various areas. This wartime employment became a turning point in economic advancement for Blacks.[11]

Drafted Blacks served largely in the U.S. Army. They also made up ranks in the Navy, the Coast Guard, the Marine Corps and in the Women's Auxiliary units. Thanks to Eleanor Roosevelt, Blacks trained and flew in the Army Air Corps under the banner of the Tuskegee Airmen. They distinguished themselves as one of the most prestigious fighting units of the American military. Though segregated in separate troops throughout the War, Blacks participated in all the Theatres of Operation. Both black men and black women numbered approximately one million or more, from a total black population of 12 million![12]

ROOSEVELT'S DEATH/ATOMIC BOMB

Roosevelt was a very sick man when he was elected to a fourth term in 1944. Less than three months later, he died of a stroke, on April 12, 1945. Harry Truman took the reins, making the decision to drop the new lethal weapon, the atomic bomb, on Japan.[13] In early August, two bombs struck Japan. World War II ended. At last, peace. But the Blacks, like the rest of the Americans, confronted new political-social issues and problems.

GI BILL (SERVICEMEN'S READJUSTMENT ACT)

The Servicemen's Readjustment Act passed in 1944. It is also known as the GI Bill. It provided cash payments, education at government expense, unemployment benefits and loans to buy homes, farms and businesses. This bill was designed to ease the millions of newly-released service people's return to civilian life. Blacks took advantage of these benefits. They went to college; they obtained degrees and training. Better education yielded better jobs. Some bought homes, some started small businesses. These gains helped to establish a black middle class.[14]

Despite all this prosperity and gains, Blacks still confronted Jim Crow. Segregation persisted throughout America in all walks of life. Despite blood-shed and sacrifice made by Blacks during the War, they were still kept at bay, denied the rights whites continued to enjoy.[15] However, the boost from the GI Bill helped to initiate political action, eventually giving impetus to the Civil Rights Movement of the 50's and 60's.

THE KOREAN WAR

Peace did not last too long. Five years later in June 1950, American troops were sent to Korea. Not a declared war, this was called "police action" to prevent the spread of Communism. This represented part of Truman's containment policy. Once more, Blacks answered the call to do their patriotic duty. But this time, as a part of Truman's Fair Deal policy, they fought in an integrated military. The first time in American history! They served as officers as well. Major General Benjamin O. Davis, Jr., was the most famous.[16]

The Korean War extended into the first term of Dwight Eisenhower. An armistice ended the fighting in 1953.

ROOSEVELT, TRUMAN, EISENHOWER ADMINISTRATIONS

During the war years, 1941-1945, under FDR, Blacks participated on the battle-front and the home-front. Due to the influence of his wife Eleanor, Roosevelt authorized the organizing and training of the Tuskegee Airmen.[17] This all-black fighter wing of the military distinguished itself in the European Theater of Operations. And as war industries proliferated, Blacks flocked to the many sites, nationwide. In assuring black workers their right to employment, Roosevelt issued the Executive Order #8802. It mandated no racial or religious discrimination on federal-contract jobs. His action, however, did not come voluntarily. A. Phillip Randolph, a black union and labor leader, brought pressure: he threatened to lead a protest march on Washington in 1943![18] This action would surely have affected adversely in fighting the war, because the United States presented itself to the world as the "arsenal of democracy." Harry S. Truman carried on the same action when he became president. As Roosevelt's vice president, he assumed the presidency following FDR's demise. In April 1945, Roosevelt was suddenly stricken with a fatal stroke.[19] Truman saw America through the end of WWII when it and the Allies defeated Japan. It surrendered after the atom bomb was dropped on two Japanese cities in August, 1945. The new secret weapon was ordered to be dropped by Truman to save lives.[20]

As successors to Franklin D. Roosevelt, Harry Truman and Dwight D. Eisenhower, though each grew up in a segregated environment, they viewed Blacks differently. Truman was pro-active; Eisenhower was reactive. Truman made concerted efforts to get civil rights legislation enacted. He appealed to Congress to pass laws against lynching and poll taxes. It went for naught. A southern Democrat-controlled Congress stifled these many endeavors. However, Truman persisted. In 1948, knowing he could not get it done through the Congress, Truman issued an executive order decreeing the end to a segregated military![21] So when the U.S. engaged in the Korean War in 1950, Blacks fought for the first time in American History, in integrated units. He also appointed the first black federal circuit judge, and chose Blacks for other federal offices. President Harry S. Truman turned out to be a surprising ally of black people.

On the other hand, Eisenhower entered the presidency viewing Blacks with a "benign neglect" attitude.[22] And he did only what he was coerced into doing. That proved to be plenty, for unforeseen and unexpected issues and events forced his hand. Things started with his appointment of Earl Warren as Chief Justice of the U.S. Supreme Court. It is this precedent-setting court that nullified the Plessy v Ferguson Decision of 1896. The decree kept America in the stranglehold of segregation until the Warren Court unleashed it with the 1954 Brown Decision, outlawing segregation. And subsequently, the Civil Rights Movement rushed over the dam, in full force. The Montgomery Bus Boycott of 1955 ushered in by Dr. Martin Luther King, Jr., was only the beginning for President Dwight D. Eisenhower to get involved on Blacks' behalf. [23]

Paradoxically, while this period is labeled one of prosperity and peace, it really translates, for Blacks, another kind of prosperity and peace. It harkened the Second Reconstruction.

WWII & POSTWAR PROSPERITY
Analytical Summary:
EFFECTS ON BLACKS

- **U.S. Enters WWII**
- **New Work Opportunities; Drafted in Segregated Units**
- **Harry Truman Became President**
- **WWII Ended**
- **Law Helped Establish Black Middle Class**
- **First War Fought With Integrated Military**
- **Set the Stage for a Second Reconstruction**

The Japanese bombing of Pearl Harbor, Hawaii on December 7, 1941 marked the U.S. official entry into WWII. It also ended the Depression. The New Deal generated-jobs did not fully create a free market economy; but industries established by war-needs, infused energy, capitol and productivity into the recovery market. Jobs proliferated. Employment work opportunities spread throughout the nation, all but eliminating the unemployment scourge. And of course, the drafting of men mainly, to people the military and to fight the war, reduced civilian-labor surplus rendering a wide open labor market.

Like the rest of America, Blacks partook and participated. They became a large part of a major demographic shift. Before the War, eighty percent of black people lived in the South. Their numbers dissipated exponentially. Whether their leaving stemmed from civilian causes or from military commitments, the black population underwent a dramatic transformation, along with the rest of America.

Another dramatic stroke occurred. WWII was just months away from America and the Allies' declaring victory over Germany and Japan. After being subjugated to man-killing, physical, mental and emotional stresses in seeking ways to solve virtually insurmountable problems, over his three plus terms – got to be too much – President Franklin D. Roosevelt died. Harry S. Truman acceded to the presidency.

Truman shepherded the nation to a successful ending of WWII. He also oversaw significant issues and acted decisively in a manner that proved favorable for black Americans. Uppermost among the actions was his issuance of the Executive Order #9981 in 1948. With the stroke of his pen, he expunged a Jim Crow U.S. military! A racist policy so engendered from the days of the Founding Fathers, it endured until the Korean War in 1950. It became the first war fought with an integrated military.

One of the rewards for military service that Blacks found beneficial was the GI Bill. Its implementation furthered the emergence of a black middle class. And a significant coterie of black political and civic organizations sprouted and mounted a leadership with clout. This societal strength gave impetus to the ensuing Civil Rights Movement.

During this era of WWII and Postwar Prosperity, Blacks made considerable social-political gains. Presidents Roosevelt and Harry Truman contributed significantly. They showed moral authority, a virtue absent in governance since Reconstruction. Even though some actions resulted from pressure, they still furthered the cause of black people. This became more evident in exacting any forward action from President Dwight Eisenhower as the Civil Rights Movement loomed, a Second Reconstruction.

WWII & POST WAR PROSPERITY END NOTES

1. *The World Book Encyclopedia*, Volume 19 (Chicago: Marshall Fields) 380-382.

2. _____, 381.

3. _____, 382-384.

4. William A. De Gregorio, *The Complete Book of U.S. Presidents.* (New York: Random House, 1997).

5. Elizabeth Jewel, *U.S. Presidents Factbook.* (New York: Random House, 2005).

6. *The World Book Encyclopedia*, Volume 6, 104-107.

7. Horatio Alger was a 19th century American author, who wrote books for boys. His heroes rose from poverty to wealth and respectability. This "rags-to-riches" theme symbolized the American Dream.

8. *The World Book*, 106.

9. McPherson, 224.

10. Lincoln, 110.

11. _____, 112. Also see Franklin, "The Home Fires," 592-607.

12. _____, 110-114.

13. McPherson, 236.

14. Adams, 264.

15. _____, 265.

16. Bernard C. Nalty, *Strength for the Fight: History of Black Americans in the Military.* (New York: MacMillan Free Press, 1986) 137-142.

17. _____, 136, 147, 151-152, 160, 231-232, 245, 313.

18. Franklin, 578-580.

19. McPherson, 234.

20. _____, 236.

21. Nalty, "Postwar Transition," 204-217.

22. Adams, 273-279.

23. McPherson, 247.

Great Society
& Civil Rights
1955 ~ 1969

President Profiles

Dwight D. Eisenhower
Term: 1953-1961

John F. Kennedy
Term: 1961-1963

Lyndon B. Johnson
Term: 1963-1969

President	Date	Birthplace	College	Profession	Party
34. Dwight D. Eisenhower	1890-1969	Texas	West Point	Soldier	Republican
35. John F. Kennedy	1917-1963	Massachusetts	Harvard	Author	Democrat
36. Lyndon B. Johnson	1908-1973	Texas	SW Texas State	Teacher	Democrat

The fifties and sixties symbolized America's struggle with Communism on the world front, and Civil Rights on the home front. Dwight D. Eisenhower, John F. Kennedy and Lyndon B. Johnson, during their White House stints, found commonality in confronting issues and problems stemming from these struggles, although each came from quite diverse backgrounds. Kansas-reared Eisenhower spent his early years in poverty;[1] Kennedy enjoyed privilege and wealth during his formidable years spent between Massachusetts and New York; coming from one of the more economic-stressed areas of West Texas, Johnson learned the resourcefulness of hard work.

Born in a Boston suburb, **John Kennedy** was one of eight children of an Irish Catholic family.[2] Both of his grandfathers were powerful political bosses in Boston and the state of Massachusetts. His father was a self-made millionaire. As Kennedy's family grew wealthier, it moved to richer suburbs of New York City. Enjoying the best life that money could buy, he attended the most prestigious prep schools; among them was Choate. In 1935, he entered Princeton University; however, an illness forced him to drop out for a year. But within a year, he enrolled in Harvard. From here he graduated cum laude, in 1940. He majored in government and international relations.

After a short stint in grad school at Stanford University, student-Kennedy left to travel South America. Upon his return to the U.S.A., he enlisted in the U.S. Navy as a seaman. Then, when the Japanese attacked Pearl Harbor in 1941, and America entered WWII, Kennedy applied for sea duty. Assigned to a PT boat squadron he became an ensign commanding a small craft.

Off the Solomon Islands in the South Pacific, on midnight August 2nd, 1943, a Japanese destroyer cut his boat in two! Some of his crew died. All through the night he and the rest of the crew clung to the wreckage. Despite a badly injured back, Kennedy spent four days in the water searching for help for his men. On the fifth day, he found friendly natives. They aided him, and rescued his crew, who had swum to a nearby island. For his heroism and leadership, Kennedy was awarded the Navy and Marine Corps Medal. In addition, for being wounded, he received the Purple Heart. Besides his back injuries, he suffered from malaria. For the rest of his naval service, he spent considerable time in various military hospitals in recovery. At war's end he became a lieutenant and an instructor.

Kennedy had planned to be a writer or a teacher. His oldest brother Joe was expected to be groomed for politics. But he was killed in a plane crash; John's future changed. At his family's urging, he entered politics. As a Democrat, he became very successful, first as a U.S. Representative and later as U.S. Senator from Massachusetts. In 1960, the Democrats picked him to be their presidential nominee. Many thought his chances of being elected were not good, because he was Catholic – only Protestants had been elected to the presidency. He defied history. John F. Kennedy became the first U.S. President of the Catholic faith, the only one thus far.

Like Kennedy, **Lyndon Johnson** served in WWII as a naval officer. However, compared to Kennedy, his prior years were very different. Born in a farmhouse in Central Texas, Johnson was the oldest of five children.[3] His father was a farmer and a school teacher. He was also a politician who served four terms in the Texas legislature as a representative. Johnson's mother was a teacher, too. Education was very important in Johnson's growing years. And he did well in school. He stood out as a very skillful debater. At 15 years old, he graduated from high school.

Afterward, Johnson grew restless, and a bit burnt out on education. Much to his parents' dismay, he deferred going to college. He took off, with some buddies, and went to California. The stay was not too pleasant. He returned home in seven months. College was still not in his plans, despite parental urging. But after working odd-jobs for four years, he decided to go to college. In 1927, he enrolled in Southwest Texas State Teachers' College (SWTC). Paying his own way, he incurred an interruption on his way to his teaching degree, when his money ran out. Upon his return to college, he became an outstanding student leader; he was involved in campus politics, served as the editor of the college newspaper, and earned excellent grades. He graduated from SWTC in 1930. Following his graduation, he took a teaching job in a Houston high school. He taught public speaking and debate.

Johnson's teaching career was brief. After a year, he left it to go into politics – for the Democratic Party. In 1931, he campaigned and made speeches for a Democratic candidate for the U.S. House of Representatives. The successfully elected new congressman went to Washington and took Johnson along with him as his secretary. Rapidly gaining the reputation as "an operator," at age 26, he received an administrative appointment from President Franklin Roosevelt to carry out the National Youth Administration, New Deal Program, in Texas. Using these political stepping stones, Johnson carved out a long and distinguished career in

Congress. He served from 1937 until 1960, save for a short stint in the U.S. Navy during WWII. It was Johnson's stellar political record and performance that led to his being tapped as John F. Kennedy's running mate in the 1960 presidential election. And when Kennedy got the nod from the voters to be the nation's 35th president, Johnson automatically assumed the office of vice president.

GREAT SOCIETY & CIVIL RIGHTS ISSUES & ACTIONS

- Brown Decision
- Black Social-Political Action
- Presidents Eisenhower, Kennedy, Johnson Responses to Black Social-Political Actions
- President Kennedy's Assassination
- Civil Rights Laws
- Entitlement Programs
- Vietnam War

Monday, May 17, 1954, was a day that marked a turning point for blacks in American History. The U.S. Supreme Court, headed by Chief Justice Earl Warren, unanimously handed down the Brown Decision. It struck down the decisive doctrine of "separate but equal." This ruling also provided blacks with constitutional leverage in their fight and struggle for civil rights.

Blacks seized upon this impetus. They initiated stirring social-political action. The courts and streets served effectively as venues in their pursuit for first-class citizenship. Dr. Martin Luther King, Jr. was in the vanguard, forging to the fore-front with his direct-action, non-violent philosophy and approach, in leading the Montgomery Bus Boycott in 1955.

Presidents Eisenhower, Kennedy and Johnson were confronted throughout their administrations with black social-political issues and problems, amid their wrestling with the ever-nagging throes of Communism. These two-pronged dilemmas created political havoc for each of them in figuring sound government politics.

President Kennedy was assassinated in 1963; Johnson became president high-lighting further the period of the Great Society and Civil Rights which produced a myriad of civil rights laws. Entitlement programs proliferated, also. This was a particularly pronounced signature of the Johnson presidency. A great admirer of Franklin Roosevelt (FDR) and the New Deal, Johnson's domestic actions and policies reflected the FDR influence.

Tangents from WWII persisted in dealing with foreign policies. The Communist v Freeworld tussle over world supremacy continued to break out with Asia as the prime "hot-bed." Police-actions, skirmishes and full-blown wars plagued the postwar occupants of the White House. But Johnson suffered the most: Vietnam. His unprecedented achievements in civil rights were all but obliterated by it because he inherited the Vietnam morass. It was a problem that plagued the Eisenhower and Kennedy administrations, growing steadily worse with each. But once Johnson took the helm, his imprudent and inept decision-making made a grave situation irreconcilable.

Some historians view this era in American History as the Second Reconstruction. For it is during this period, that some of the early civil rights promised to blacks in the First Reconstruction finally reached fruition.

THE BROWN DECISION

On May 17, 1954, the U.S. Supreme Court handed down the landmark, unanimous ruling: the first Brown Decision (Brown v Board of Education of Topeka, Kansas).[4] It outlawed segregation in public schools, and overturned Plessy v Ferguson (1896) that legalized segregation under the "separate but equal" clause. This decision was made by the liberal court led by Chief Justice Earl Warren. In his opinion he declared, "To separate (black children) from others of similar age and qualifications solely because of their race, generates a feeling of inferiority as to their status in the community, that may affect their hearts and minds in a way unlikely ever to be undone." He further wrote, "We conclude that in the field of education, the doctrine of 'separate but equal' has no place." And, he added, "Separate education facilities are [thus] inherently unequal."

The Brown case actually consisted of five different cases that were consolidated under the umbrella of Brown v Board of Education of Topeka, Kansas.[5] The persuasive and legally strategic argument was presented before the court by a team of outstanding NAACP lawyers. Thurgood Marshall led the team. He later became the first Black to be a justice of the U.S. Supreme Court. President Lyndon Johnson appointed him in 1967; he served until 1991.

The Brown Decision has proven to be one of the most significant rulings ever handed down by the U.S. Supreme Court. It changed America. Its social and political impact has been unfathomable, not only for black Americans, but for all Americans.

BLACK SOCIAL-POLITICAL ACTION

The Brown Decision provided Blacks constitutional leverage to wage war against segregation and discrimination. Various forces of black leadership united their strengths and resources in fighting the Civil Rights battle. Black churches, the NAACP, the National Urban League, college student groups, and countless other civic and fraternal groups formed a determined coalition. They utilized a creative arsenal of non-violent protest strategies: boycotts, sit-ins, marches, voter registration campaigns, school desegregation drives and many other formidable approaches. Perhaps the most epic event that buoyed the nation, and captured worldwide attention came during the Kennedy administration. It was on August 28, 1963 – the March on Washington!

Here Dr. Martin Luther King, Jr. – who had earlier gained fame from leading the historic Montgomery Bus Boycott – delivered the galvanizing and electrifying "I Have a Dream Speech."

Black social-political action of the fifties and sixties stood as a beacon of hope against oppression. Throughout the South – Montgomery, Birmingham and Selma, Alabama; Little Rock, Arkansas; New Orleans, Louisiana; Oxford, Mississippi; Albany and Atlanta, Georgia; Greensboro, North Carolina – this light of determination shone brightly.[6] Blacks began overcoming some of the social-political injustices stemming from the legacy of American slavery. Now, Blacks could exercise their constitutional rights under the First Amendment!

PRESIDENTS EISENHOWER, KENNEDY, JOHNSON RESPONSES TO: BLACK SOCIAL-POLITICAL ACTION

The Brown Decision unleashed the pent-up yearnings of Blacks for the justice Reconstruction had promised. It took nearly a hundred years! To this social-political fervor, the Eisenhower, Kennedy and Johnson administrations had to respond. Although it was applied in varied degrees, the attention and action on civil rights could no longer be ignored by the occupants of the White House at this time.

It was during Eisenhower's second term that he was forced into action. Ironically, this resulted from the Earl Warren appointment he made during his first term. (Warren became Chief Justice of the U.S. Supreme Court in 1953.) This appointment led to a liberal court. Under Warren, it handed down favorable civil rights rulings, of which the most precedent-setting was the Brown Decision. Because it established the law that discrimination and segregation were unlawful in public schools, when it was tested in Little Rock in 1957, the federal government was drawn in. Nine black students tried to enroll and desegregate Central High School. The governor of Arkansas defied the new law. He called out the State National Guard to prevent the students from carrying out their mission. The scene was ugly. A hostile gathering of Whites did unspeakable things – all the while protected by the Guard. National media, particularly television, flashed the despicable display throughout the nation – and to some parts of the world. A cry of outrage was pervasive. Strident voices demanded action: action to protect the students and to uphold the law!

At the onset, Eisenhower was reluctant and hesitant.[7] He did not want to bring in the federal government. It was clear to many civil rights advocates that as far as Blacks and civil rights were concerned, Eisenhower's actions tended never to be proactive. Martin Luther King, Jr., remarked, "That men like Eisenhower are more devoted to order than to justice … they prefer a negative peace, which is the absence of tension to a positive peace which is the presence of justice."[8] Alas, Eisenhower intervened. He dispatched federal troops to Little Rock to enforce the law. The following week, Congress passed the 1957 Civil Rights Bill, and it was signed by Eisenhower. This was the first civil rights legislation passed by Congress since 1875! And, this 1957 bill signaled the message that the federal government could not any longer ignore the plight of Blacks in America.

Civil rights became even more indelible for John F. Kennedy, even before his election to the presidency. During Kennedy's campaign as the Democratic nominee for president, Martin Luther King, Jr., was jailed. Although the charges as a parole violator camouflaged the real reason for his incarceration – he had led a protest civil rights activity in Atlanta – King faced four months in prison, at hard labor! King's supporters appealed to Kennedy for help. Using his personal influence, Kennedy called the Governor of Georgia. His intervention led to King's release. Black newspapers throughout the nation heralded the story; Kennedy was perceived as a champion of civil rights, and a friend of Blacks. His actions translated into votes. Kennedy's 1960 narrow victory over Richard Nixon for the presidency came largely from the votes of southern Democrats and urban Blacks. However, once in office, Kennedy took a cautious approach toward civil rights, despite his debt to Blacks. He feared offending the South. But, like Eisenhower before him, political circumstances forced his hand. The media made civil rights "the news."

In 1962, James Merideth enrolled in Mississippi University, which was still segregated and all white. Merideth was black. The next year, there was a battle to desegregate the University of Alabama. At the same time, civil rights protests erupted in various other forms and means throughout the South.[9] Kennedy began to realize – with considerable urging from his Attorney General brother, Robert Kennedy – civil rights no longer were just legal or legislative, but they were a moral issue. He authorized increased federal involvement. Yet, to just how much this action would have impacted civil rights and the overcoming of discrimination and oppression of Blacks was mooted by Kennedy's assassination on November 22, 1963 in Dallas, Texas. Lyndon Johnson was left to pick up the torch.

Johnson approached civil rights with relentless zeal. In addressing Congress to support the Voters' Rights Act in March 1965,[10] he proclaimed its importance because, "This is no issue of states' rights... it's human rights!" Johnson proved preeminent among all U.S. Presidents, to date, in dealing with and acting on issues and events specifically related to Blacks. He took the initiative and led the crusade. His Great Society and War on Poverty programs have yet to be exceeded in their excellence in domestic reform—socially, politically and economically. Blacks and the nation owe Johnson a debt of gratitude in this respect.

PRESIDENT KENNEDY'S ASSASSINATION

In Dallas, Texas, on November 22, 1963, the Friday before Thanksgiving, John F. Kennedy was shot. He died shortly after. His assassination was the fourth of a president in American History. The nation fell into mourning. As it was when Lincoln was killed, Blacks were heavily struck and overcome with grief. They held unsettling concerns and grave trepidations. They nervously wondered what would happen to them and to the Civil Rights Movement? All in all, they knew little about his successor, Lyndon Johnson – a southerner from Texas... history, however, has shown that Blacks needed not to have been distressed: Johnson proved to be a most unexpected and an unlikely ombudsman for black people.

CIVIL RIGHTS LAWS

During the Lyndon Johnson administration, civil rights laws proliferated.[11] Below is a synopsis of some of the major ones that have had a significant impact on Blacks' strides toward justice and equality.

- **Civil Rights Act of 1964**

This law barred discrimination in employment as well as in hotels, restaurants and other public facilities. It also authorized the attorney general to initiate desegregation suits. The Women's Liberation Movement and the Gay Rights Movement stemmed from this law.

- **The Civil Rights Voting Act of 1965**

This law outlawed discrimination to prevent voting by using literacy tests. The federal government was authorized to promote voter registration; it resulted in marked increases in minority voting.

- **The Civil Rights Act of 1968**

This law barred discrimination in sale and rental of housing and stiffened federal criminal penalties for civil rights violations.

These laws made the greatest strides in civil rights since Reconstruction. They were considered affirmative action, a means to remedying the years of unfairness and injustice.[12]

President Lyndon Baines Johnson signing the Civil Rights Act of 1968
Photo courtesy of Library of Congress

ENTITLEMENT PROGRAMS

Lyndon Johnson's Great Society, besides targeting civil rights, encompassed the War on Poverty. Johnson, in his 1964 State of the Union address, bemoaned the plight of the poor, a group social subset that included a large percentage of Blacks. He stated, "… Many Americans live on the outskirts of hope, some because of their poverty and some because of their color, and all too many because of both." Then he summed up the goal of the War on Poverty. "Our task is to help replace this despair with war, unconditionally."[13] To accomplish this, he proposed and shepherded the implementation of many entitlement programs. Listed are some of these, all of which were incorporated under The Economic Opportunity Act of 1964.

- **The Job Corps** – It provided vocational training in residence to disadvantaged youth aged 16 to 21.
- **Volunteers in Service to America (VISTA)** – This was a domestic Peace Corps. It entitled volunteers to work and teach in ghettos.
- **Work-Study Program** – This program provided jobs to enable students of low-income families to work their way through college.
- **The Work Experience Program** – It provided child day care and other support services to poor heads of households.
- **The Community Action Program** – This contained many segments:
  Head Start that instructed disadvantaged preschoolers;
  Upward Bound tutored disadvantaged high school students;
  Foster Grandparents used elderly volunteers to befriend institutionalized children, and it also provided legal aid services to the poor.

In addition, there was Medicare and Medicaid (1965). Medicare was funded through the Social Security System. It provided hospital insurance and, for a low monthly premium, there was medical insurance for persons 65 years or older. Medicaid provided hospital and medical benefits for the poor and needy of any age.

Johnson's War on Poverty Program was reminiscent of Franklin Roosevelt's efforts to rescue the Nation from the ravages of the Great Depression of the 1930's. As a young man, Johnson administered some of those New Deal Programs. He no doubt was greatly influenced by the New Deal, as a template on which to hinge his War on Poverty Program.

VIETNAM WAR

At the close of World War II in 1945, a struggle for world supremacy ensued between the U.S. and U.S.S.R. (Russia). Despite their being allies during the War to eradicate Hitler, Mussolini and Tojo, at the close of all the warfare, it became abundantly clear the two were at loggerheads over ideology: Will the world be democratic and free; or will it be communist and not free? Winning over Asia topped both powers' lists, as the prime area to settle the supremacy contest. Promulgating a policy of containment, Harry Truman employed this strategy for military policing the "hot spots." This was called the Truman Doctrine.[14] It held sway as the anchor of U.S. foreign policy throughout the Eisenhower, the Kennedy and the Johnson administrations. Although officially not declared-wars, the Korean War and the Vietnam War emerged as a result of this policy. The latter was devastating, as it nearly tore the country – America – apart. And it escalated at its zenith, when the nation was most domestically vulnerable: enmeshed in the battle over civil rights.

Blacks made up a large part of the U.S. military personnel. Many made it their career. Comparable to the occupational climate at the end of the Civil War, the military again offered Blacks a more feasible way of making a living and pursuing a less threatened life-style found in the civilian world rife with discrimination and prejudice. Truman's desegregation of the military helped to mitigate these menaces, somewhat.

In the Vietnam War, black representation far exceeded their proportional number in the general U.S. population. This reflected glaringly in the casualties of dead and wounded. The War also made Lyndon Johnson a casualty, too. His efforts to wage a domestic war and a military war simultaneously, proved his undoing. The national debt mounted. The non-violent civil rights movement turned violent. Whites became disenchanted with Johnson's "catering" to the needs of Blacks, and the nation, in general, grew increasingly hostile with his imprudent and dishonest handling of the Vietnam War. What once had so much promise toward a brilliant presidential legacy for Lyndon Johnson, in the end, turned terribly sour. Nevertheless, regardless of how many Whites have viewed him, Blacks found his fearlessness on their behalf to be a god-send;[15] this was soundly affirmed by Dr. Martin Luther King, Jr.

GREAT SOCIETY & CIVIL RIGHTS
Analytical Summary:
EFFECTS ON BLACKS

- **U.S. Supreme Court Outlawed Segregation**
- **Using Constitution, Blacks Launched Civil Rights Campaign**
- **Presidents Eisenhower and Kennedy Forced to Act**
- **President Johnson Provided Strong Leadership and Support After Kennedy's Death**
- **Legislation and Domestic Programs Improved Blacks' Status**
- **Disproportion Number of Casualties**

The impetus for the Great Society/Civil Rights Era came from the Warren Court. The Brown Decision of 1954 gave black people social-political leverage. It became the link necessary to hook up where Reconstruction left off, in righting some of the wrongs that were perpetrated against black people. The over-turning of legalized segregation paved the way for utilization of the Constitution in buttressing their civil rights battle. Many heart breaking years elapsed, many black lives were sacrificed, and many presidents came and went before any appreciable dent could be made in the Jim Crow wall.

During this long gruesome period between Reconstruction and Brown, Jim Crow built an American apartheid wall. It started in the waning years of President Ulysses S. Grant's last term, fostered forward from the Rutherford B. Hayes election until the Warren Court – over more than seven decades! And in these intervening years, the barriers against Black people seemed to have no parallel nor seemed to have no end. The Klan ran amok; the president and congress paid little attention to their plight. Then came World War II.

Its global engulfing and aftermath spawned the United Nations. Its mission: human rights. American apartheid could no longer go unabated – the hypocrisy was exposed! However, all along, during the Jim Crow years of oppression, Black people never succumbed. They persevered. And with the issuance of Brown, Black activists amped-up their arsenal. Many creative steps were employed. Just as their slave ancestors used spirituals and other slave songs, the Civil Rights Movement resurrected them, and added more ways. The dynamic leadership of Dr. Martin Luther King, Jr. galvanized the struggle around a non-violent philosophy (an adaptation of Mahatma Gandhi's strategy used to free India from British control). This form of civil disobedience, so inflamed the South that it resorted to brutal retaliatory tactics to thwart the movement.

Unfortunately – for the southern sheriffs and police chiefs – they could no longer get away with this behavior. Television exposed them! Just coming into its own as a communication source, its pictures spoke louder than words. T.V. was piped into homes all over the nation – and to many parts of the world – people became incensed over what they saw. Instead of quashing the demonstrations, the southern lawmen inadvertently abetted the cause. Thousands joined the movement.

The southern behavior became an embarrassment to the U.S. government, too. And the time had come when American presidents could no longer skirt the issue of Jim Crow. Presidents Eisenhower and Kennedy found no escape, they were forced to confront the issue: Eisenhower and the integration of Little Rock, Arkansas' Central High School and Kennedy's handling of the 1963 March on Washington. Neither exerted strong moral leadership. Not until Kennedy's assassination, and Lyndon Johnson assumed the presidency, did black people witness resolve and benefit directly from a president's actions.

Johnson ramroded legislation through Congress so swiftly and decisively, it left most Blacks disbelieving, euphoric. Never had a U.S. President centered his governmental agenda around Black – in a positive way. Johnson, true to his word, did. Many of the social/political promises made during Reconstruction were finally realized under Lyndon Baines Johnson, via the passage of empowering Civil Right Laws and strengthening Entitlement Programs.

Although Johnson was eligible to seek a second term on his own, he chose not to run. The Viet Nam war – that he inherited – sabotaged his chances. It divided an already aroused nation so irreparably, Johnson realized his chances were futile, he made too many unwise decisions in regard to the Viet Nam War.

The era of the Great Society/Civil Rights proved – to many Blacks – that hope still exited – they possibly, finally cash in on their "We the People" membership.

GREAT SOCIETY & CIVIL RIGHTS END NOTES

1. McPherson, 247. Also see Adams, 273.

2. Beschloss, 417-419.

3. _____, 431-433.

4. Charles J. Ogletree, Jr., *All Deliberate Speed: Reflections on the First Half Century of Brown v Board of Education.* (New York: W.H. Horton, 2004) Chapter 1, 1-17. An excellent capsule summary of the Brown Decision.

5. _____, 4-6.

6. Franklin, "The Negro Revolution," 623-639. Also see Adams, 281-283.

7. McPherson, 247. Also see summary of Eisenhower's philosophy re: federal intervention. Adams, 273-279.

8. Adams, 279.

9. Franklin, 623-639.

10. Beschloss, 438-439.

11. De Gregorio, 574-575.

12. Adams, 302-303.

13. De Gregorio, 547.

14. McPherson, 237-238.

15. Adams, 293. Also see De Gregorio, 441.

PANEL 13

Conservatism v Liberalism

1969 ~1993

President Profiles

Richard M. Nixon
Term: 1969-1974

Gerald R. Ford
Term: 1974-1977

James (Jimmy) Carter
Term: 1977-1981

Ronald Reagan
Term: 1981-1989

George H.W. Bush
Term: 1989-1993

President	Date	Birthplace	College	Profession	Party
37. Richard M. Nixon	1913 - 1994	California	Whittier	Lawyer	Republican
38. Gerald R. Ford	1913 - 2006	Nebraska	Michigan	Lawyer	Republican
39. James Carter	1924 -	Georgia	US Naval Academy	Business	Democrat
40. Ronald Reagan	1911-2004	Illinois	Eureka	Actor	Republican
41. George H.W. Bush	1924 -	Massachusetts	Yale	Business	Republican

During this period following President Lyndon Johnson's liberal actions and policies, many white Americans wanted, and called for change. Nixon called them "Middle America." They were disenchanted with Johnson's courting of Blacks and the ramrodding of his civil rights agenda. Plus, his disingenuous handling of the Vietnam War, further turned them off. The political pendulum swung from liberalism to conservatism. This change caused the Democrats to relinquish the White House control to the Republicans.[1] Four out of the next five presidents were conservative Republicans. Richard Nixon, Gerald Ford, Ronald Reagan and George H. W. Bush indelibly answered the national clamor for less government intervention and regulation. Jimmy Carter, though a Democrat, was squeezed into the conservative vice, too.

Richard M. Nixon, who led the vanguard, was born and grew up in California. He came from a devout Quaker family, one of limited means. His father, originally from Ohio, did not finish high school. When he moved to California, after working odd jobs for a time, the elder Nixon improved the family income, somewhat. By operating a gas station and a small market, his father made a steady living. As a boy, Richard worked long hours at the store before and after school.[2]

Richard Nixon was a diligent student. According to his memoirs, he studied into the wee hours of the night after his work at the store ended. In 1930, he graduated first in his high school class. This was at the time when America was sinking into an economic depression. So when Nixon won a partial scholarship to Harvard, he could not accept. His family's finances made it prohibitive. He instead attended Whittier College (California). His classroom excellence and campus activities led to a ranking of second in his 1934 class. Upon his graduation, he received a scholarship to Duke University Law School. This time he was able to accept the scholarship. Nixon did well and graduated in 1937. The same year, he was admitted to the California bar.

Following Nixon's admission to the bar, he successfully practiced law until the U.S. entered WWII. In 1942, he took a job with the federal government working in the Office of Price Administration in Washington, D.C.[3] The job lasted for only a short duration. He grew unhappy with the bureaucracy. Resigning, he joined the U.S. Navy. So from June 1942 to March 1946, he was an officer, rising from lieutenant junior grade to lieutenant commander. His outstanding service in the South Pacific earned him a citation for meritorious and efficient performance. Nixon was released from active duty in 1946, but remained in the Naval Reserves until June 1, 1966. However, he had begun his political career in California, in 1946.

Nixon made a name for himself when he went to Washington in 1947. He was elected for two terms as a U.S. Representative from California. His reputation as a fearless fighter against Communism led to his election to the U.S. Senate in 1950.[4] He continued his crusade until the Republicans picked him to be Dwight Eisenhower's running mate in the 1952 presidential election.[5] Eisenhower was elected and Nixon served two terms as vice president. Then in 1960, he tried for the presidency, but was defeated by John F. Kennedy, the Democratic nominee. Nixon's political career took a further setback when he lost his bid for governor of California. He went back to practicing law, but this time in New York. However, he still kept involved in the Republican Party. In 1968, he garnered the party nomination for president. With his election, he became the 37th U.S. President.[6]

Nixon was elected president twice. The first term he began to appeal to the southern Democrats as they gradually changed their affiliation to the Republican Party. By the second term, he won by a landslide. Only Massachusetts and Washington, D.C. did not vote for him. Yet, by the middle of the term, his scandalous behavior in an attempt to amass more political power, led to his downfall. Even before entering the White House, Nixon was known to be devious. He was called "Tricky Dick." In June of 1972, five agents of the Committee to re-elect the President (CREEP) were caught burglarizing the Democratic National Headquarters in a Washington, D.C. complex named Watergate. The scandal became known as Watergate.[7] Nixon's denial and attempts to cover-up his involvement led to his forced resignation. (Thus far, he is the only president to resign.) Gerald R. Ford was his vice president; he assumed the presidency.

Gerald Ford was born Leslie Lynch King, Jr. in 1913 in Nebraska. His parents separated and subsequently divorced. At a young age, he and his mother moved to Michigan. In 1916, she remarried to Gerald Rudolph Ford. When young Leslie was four, his stepfather adopted him and changed his name to Gerald Rudolph Ford, Jr. The family grew to four children. Ford had three half brothers. Despite difficult economic conditions, his father managed to make a modest living for the family.[8]

Ford received a public school education. He did well. In high school, he excelled in history and government. At the end of his junior year, he became a member of the National Honor Society. He was popular and active in school.

As the center for the football team he made All-City. Following his graduation in 1931, he entered the University of Michigan on a partial scholarship. As a pre-law student, he majored in economics and political science. He helped work his way through college busing tables and washing dishes. As he had in high school, he played football for Michigan. His athletic skills were so outstanding, that he received two offers of lucrative professional football contracts. He rejected them. Instead, Ford pursued law at Yale, and graduated in 1941.[9]

Shortly after Ford passed the Michigan bar in 1941, the U.S. entered WWII, following the Japanese attack on Pearl Harbor. He enlisted in the U.S. Naval Reserves. His stint lasted forty-seven months. In February 1946, he was discharged with the rank of lieutenant commander. Returning to Michigan, he resumed practicing law. However, after a while, law began to bore him and he turned to politics. At the urging of his family and friends, he plunged head-long and was elected U.S. Representative from Michigan in 1948. His political career blossomed. As a Republican, his influence was so great he was named House Minority Leader. He was an ardent Nixon supporter. So when the Nixon administration began unraveling, Ford inherited two offices: first Nixon appointed him vice president when Spiro Agnew resigned the office in 1973; then with Nixon's exit – having to resign the presidency over the Watergate scandal – Gerald Ford became the thirty-eighth U.S. President.[10] He is the only vice president and president who was not elected for either office.

With Ford's assumption of the presidency, he took on the vitriol hurled at the Republican Party. Thus, when he ran to reclaim the office, he lost to an unknown, dark horse Democrat, Jimmy Carter.[11]

He was born **James Earl Carter, Jr.** But, he took on the name Jimmy and has basically used the name throughout most of his life; he signs himself as Jimmy. Perhaps this was to distinguish himself from his father. The elder Carter was a prosperous peanut farmer who owned over 4,000 acres of rich Georgia farmland. Over 200 black tenant farmers worked the acreage. The farm was located near a largely black community. Jimmy grew up playing and interacting with Blacks at the displeasure of his segregationist father.

This was not the view held by his mother, who engaged Blacks, which was an exceptionally enlightened attitude for a white southerner during this time in American history.[12]

By his first grade teacher, Carter was remembered as a model student, well-behaved and eager to learn. He displayed this behavior throughout his public school education. He did well academically; so well that in 1943 he was admitted to the U.S. Naval Academy at Annapolis, Maryland. During his cadet days, he endured unrelenting ridicule of his southern drawl. Nevertheless, this did not deter him from his studies or his focus toward a naval career. He graduated in the upper ten percent of his class in 1946. Accepting a commission as ensign junior grade that same year, Carter embarked on a military career. It lasted until 1953. His father died that year also, so he returned to Georgia to run the family peanut business.[13]

Once back home in Georgia, he became active in the local civic affairs. Amid all the acrimony over the desegregation decision by the U.S. Supreme Court in 1954, Carter raised his voice, pleading for reason. This almost cost him the election when he ran for Georgia state senator in 1962. But his honesty and leadership shone through and it was proven that his opponent had won by fraudulent means. Hence the election was overturned in his favor. Carter was seated. He followed up by being elected two years later for another term. He tried for the governorship in 1966, but failed. However, four years later he was elected. The governorship brought him visibility and recognition in the National Democratic Party. He was soon heralded as a leader of the "New South."[14] His policies and actions made Blacks a big part of his political legacy. As head of the National Democratic Campaign committee in 1974, Carter led Democrats in overcoming some of the Republicans' political superiority; superiority they built up from the party switching that took place after the nation's disenchantment with President Lyndon Johnson. By virtue of his surge to national prominence, Carter got the Democratic presidential nomination in 1976. Surprisingly, as a dark horse, he defeated incumbent Gerald Ford. James Earl Carter became the first U.S. president, since Reconstruction, to come from the Deep South.

Jimmy Carter served only one term as U.S. president. As something of a Washington outsider, his presidency proved less than successful. Both his domestic and foreign policies met with reoccurring opposition. He was succeeded by Ronald Reagan, an actor turned politician.

Ronald Reagan's exposure to politics, growing up in Illinois, was an immersion in Franklin Roosevelt's New Deal. His father was a staunch liberal Democrat. As an Irish Catholic – a faith young Reagan did not follow – he abhorred bigotry and the Ku Klux Klan. However, he had a pronounced weakness for alcohol. His alcoholism made for a very unsettled family life for "Dutch," as his father nicknamed him, and also for his older brother. But fortunately he had a strong, dedicated mother who stabilized the family somewhat.[15] Yet, despite the poverty and dysfunction, Reagan's memoirs called his childhood the happiest time of his life.

Educated in the public schools, Reagan received a good education. And he was a good student, as well as a student athlete. He played football, basketball, and ran track. Besides the athletics, Dutch appeared in school plays, wrote for the school yearbook, and was student body president. Receiving a partial scholarship, he continued his education in the small Illinois college, Eureka. The rest of his tuition was supplemented by washing and busing dishes at fraternity houses. However, he continued to participate in athletics, student government, the yearbook and school plays. Reagan later admitted that extracurricular activities so ate up his time that his average grade was closer to the "C" level, required to maintain eligibility, than it was to straight "A's."[16] However, he received honors for his acting, a portent of his future and fame as a Hollywood actor.

Before parlaying his acting stakes in Hollywood, Ronald Reagan spent the early Depression years (1932 -1937) as a popular sports announcer in the Midwest. He used his regional celebrity success as stepping-stones to an acting career. Reagan possessed good looks and a good voice. His moves from the Midwest to California, and from radio to the Hollywood screen paid off handsomely for him. During WWII, he made many movies glorifying American war ingenuity and heroics. Reagan suffered all his life from poor eyesight. This negated his acceptance into the military. His contribution to the war effort came through his acting. Although at the war's end, his career languished, he was elected president of the Screen Actors Guild (1947-1952 and 1959-1960). During this time, the witch-hunt for Communists set off a political craze. The entertainment industry was heavily targeted by various federal and congressional investigative bodies. As spokesperson for the actors, Reagan testified at many hearings. He blew the whistle on many of his colleagues, causing irreparable damage to careers and in many cases unjustifiably. It was later revealed that Reagan was an FBI informant.[17] It is also at this time when he switched his liberal-leanings as a New Deal Democrat to the staunch Republican conservatism.

He plunged deeply into California politics, and headed the Democrats-for-Eisenhower group in 1952 and in 1956. In 1960, he delivered over 200 endorsement speeches for Richard Nixon when he ran for president. By 1962, Reagan officially changed his voter registration from Democrat to Republican. In 1967, he was elected governor of California on the Republican Party ticket. His record of conservatism drew national attention and high party praise. In 1980, he defeated the incumbent President Jimmy Carter as the standard bearer for Republican conservatism. His tenure in Washington became the signature period of turning-back the political and social clock for black people. He made efforts to eliminate the entitlement policies such as affirmative action, and he wanted to eliminate the Department of Education because it symbolized the Brown Decision. He wanted to dismantle the Democrats' liberalism that aided Black and poor people. Wealthy and big business people were his main focus.

George Herbert Walker Bush was Reagan's vice president. He was steeped in "Reaganese." So when Reagan's administrations ended, Bush became the heir-apparent. As the Republican nominee for president in 1988, he was elected over the Democratic Michael Dukakis, governor of Massachusetts.

George H.W. Bush's background – far different from Ronald Reagan's – stemmed from New England aristocracy whose ancestry stretched as far back as mid-17th century.[18] His English ancestors settled on Cape Cod, Massachusetts. These forefathers established an inheritance of business and political success. From both his father's and his mother's families, George acceded to wealth and social position. Prescott Bush, his father, was a prominent businessman and U.S. Senator. His mother came from a Maine banking investment family. George never experienced a need for anything material. As an infant, his family moved from his Connecticut birthplace to an exclusive New York suburb. Amid this wealth and comfort, his environment provided him with chauffeurs/handymen, nannies and housekeepers to cater to his needs. Boating, yachting, deep-sea fishing, tennis and golfing filled his off-hours and vacations which were often spent at his maternal grandfather's sprawling estate at Walker's Point in Kenneb-unkport, Maine. Prestigious schooling was commensurate with his privileged life. He attended prep schools for the offspring of the wealthy, and he entered Yale in 1942. However, WWII interrupted his studies, but he resumed them after the war. Bush graduated with honors – achieved Phi Beta Kappa his junior year – from Yale in 1948.

George Bush's military service lasted from June 1942 until September 1945. He enlisted as a seaman second class in the U.S. Navy. He rose to lieutenant. Earning his wings in 1943, he became the youngest pilot, then, in the navy. Bush's exploits in the Pacific are legendary. He flew 58 combat missions against the Japanese. For his many near-death heroics, he was awarded the Distinguished Flying Cross, returning as a true "American Hero."[19]

Upon graduation from Yale, Bush opted not to follow his father and grandfather in the New York banking business. Instead, he went to Texas, where he learned the oil business.

With money secured from an uncle, he co-partnered in establishing an oil development company. Its merger with a larger petroleum company paid dividends. It thrived, and so did Bush. He bought out his partners and became a millionaire in his own right. His move to Texas, and his oil business success cultivated for him political contacts. This led to his leading role in the National Republican Party. Selling his oil interests, he directed his full attention to politics.[20] At various times from 1966, until he became U.S. President in 1988, George H.W. Bush held congressional office, ambassadorial positions, head of the CIA and National Chairman of the Republican Party, besides being Reagan's vice president.

CONSERVATISM v LIBERALISM
ISSUES & ACTIONS

- **Middle America**
- **Party-Switch**
- **Black Power/Urban Riots**
- **Court Appointments**
- **Entitlement Reforms**
- **Watergate**
- **Review of Reinstituting Republican Conservatism**

The liberal politics of the Democrats and President Lyndon Johnson during the Civil Rights Era took a back seat when the Republicans controlled the White House. Starting with President Richard Nixon, the nation's politics took an abrupt turn to the right, ushering in conservatism. He signaled a change in government policy. Using the term "Middle America" as a euphemism for white people, Nixon let it be known that government attention would be directed toward them, and that civil rights and black people would no longer be the focus. This message so enthralled and energized southern Democrats that they made a wholesale defection to the GOP.

Around the same time, some Blacks changed their minds about Dr. Martin Luther King, Jr.'s non-violent approach to civil rights. They embraced "Black Power," denouncing integration and "turn-the –other-cheek" posture. Republicans added this to their political arsenal in calling for change from liberalism to conservatism.

Also during this period, eight U.S. Supreme Court Justices were appointed shifting the Court from left to right. Republican-led legislation passed, reforming numerous entitlement programs. Even after Nixon's resignation over the Watergate scandal, the liberal shift to the conservative trend continued. All the Republican presidents who followed vigorously pushed the same ideology; one that paid little positive attention toward black people.

MIDDLE AMERICA

More and more, Whites grew disgruntled over civil rights, feeling too much attention went to Blacks. The political changes of the fifties and the sixties created fear and anger. Busing in the schools, affirmative action in employment and the courts, and fair housing laws that spurred "white flight" – the Republicans seized upon these emotions. White middle-working class, the most impacted by the changes, were targeted and euphemistically dubbed by President Nixon as "Middle America"– the "Moral Majority." Political mileage became increasingly accelerated as more northern Whites felt the changes.[21]

PARTY-SWITCH

Since the Civil War, the Democratic Party had always been the political party of the South. The Republican Party was associated with Abraham Lincoln and the freeing of slaves. But during the Civil Rights Era, when the Democrats under Lyndon Johnson embraced the movement, wholesale defection took place by southern Democrats. Republican conservatism addressed their hopes of reversing the social-political changes. This represented a big part of the southern strategy. The "Solid South" became GOP.

BLACK POWER/URBAN RIOTS

In the black community, another voice emerged. Black Power was its mantra. It discounted Martin Luther King's non-violent, integration philosophy. Organizations such as the Black Panthers and the Black Muslims called for separation, and an any-means-possible approach to get Blacks civil rights. Many urban ghettos erupted in rioting conflagrations. The older coalitions under King such as the NAACP, the Urban League and the Southern Christian Leadership conference lost followers and converts to these militant groups. King's assassination in 1968 added more "fuel" to the fire. The split in the black community divested itself in many ways: separation of the black middle class from poor Blacks, and the gradual moving of some former Democrat Blacks to becoming Republicans.[22]

In all, by the end of the Sixties, King's assassination proved to be a big blow to Johnson's goal to carry out civil rights changes in a non-violent way. This legitimized the Nixon need and demand for "law and order."

COURT APPOINTMENTS

During this period more U.S. Supreme Court appointments occurred than any other time in U.S. History. A total of eight – Nixon and Reagan made the most appointments, five between them. This completed the transformation from a liberal court to a conservative one, a turn around from the Warren Court.[23]

Supreme Court appointments by Nixon, Ford, Reagan and Bush made an indelible impact on the highest court of the land. As the liberal justices of the Warren Court aged and retired, these Republican presidents replaced them with conservative judges. Among the eight replacements was a second black judge, Clarence Thomas. Unfortunately for Blacks, his judicial rulings and actions, thus far, conform to the conservative-bent.[24] Jimmy Carter had no opportunity to make a U.S. Supreme Court appointment.

ENTITLEMENT REFORMS

These conservative presidents made it their mission to reform, dismantle, change or completely eliminate many of the entitlement programs of Johnson's Great Society. Many blows were struck against black social-political progress. Affirmative Action was key among them.

WATERGATE

President Nixon won his 1972 reelection by a landslide. But, on the way, his committee to reelect the president employed illegal tactics. In their zeal to assure his reelection, they resorted to breaking into the offices of the Democratic National Committee. The offices were located in the Watergate building in Washington, D.C. The group, led by G. Gordon Liddy, got caught. They tried to gather intelligence for use against the Democrats. Supposedly this was done without Nixon's knowledge; however, when he learned of the break-in, he tried to cover it up. Items found in the groups' possession suggested a White House link.

Nixon stonewalled. He fabricated stories, using all means in obstructing justice. But, his secret taping system trapped him: the "smoking gun." Left with the choices of resignation or impeachment, he opted for the former. So, on August 9, 1974, he left office, being the first, and only, president to find himself forced to resign. Vice President Ford became president and completed Nixon's term.

- It is interesting to note that despite Nixon's resignation and Watergate, the trend from liberalism to conservatism continued.

REVIEWING OF REINSTITUTING REPUBLICAN CONSERVATISM

In reviewing the method in which Richard Nixon, Gerald Ford, Ronald Reagan and George H.W. Bush reinstituted and reconstituted the Republicans' conservative agenda, it is clear, once again in American history, Blacks were the scapegoats. When the political, economic and social conditions began edging toward equality and justice for Blacks, the government jerked the first class citizenship rug from under them. Roosevelt's New Deal and Johnson's Great Society were too liberal and too threatening in their attempt toward equalizing opportunity and achievement between Blacks and Whites. It was checkmate time once more:

- Appointments to the federal courts and U.S. Supreme Court were packed with conservative judges to recover and maintain the status quo

- Entitlement programs were reduced or eliminated altogether
- Racism was courted and encouraged through divisive institutional actions and means; and duplicitous, inflammatory language deepened the wedge. This Post Civil Rights Period fell just short of reprising Post Reconstruction.[25]

Initially, Nixon's recommended reforms on school desegregation and welfare were moderate. But, as his first term moved closer toward reelection, he stepped up actions calling for stronger measures to curtail black progress. Successfully gaining a second term, pressures from his newly-acquired southern constituents caused the southern strategy to kick in. It turned further right and farther away from favorable actions toward issues important to Blacks.[26] Before he could intensify his added efforts, Nixon's Watergate scandal ended them. He resigned in the middle of his second term in 1974. His vice president, Gerald Ford, took the reins.

Ford spent his short time dealing with a failing economy, and a collapsed Vietnam campaign. Nixon's Watergate scandal derailed the Republican quest temporarily. As a result, Gerald Ford failed in his presidential try. The Democrats returned to the White House under a Washington "outsider," Jimmy Carter. His victory was narrow, although he received 90% of the black vote. He had gained their favor and that of the black leadership based on his governorship in Georgia.[27]

"Moderate to ambivalent" characterized Carter's stint. He found himself constantly juggling and weighing his actions between the working-class Whites and pressuring Blacks. The Bakke Case elicited such decision. He called for "flexible" affirmative action. However, Carter made significant accomplishments in the area of civil rights by some of the appointing of Blacks: Andrew Young to the United Nations, Patricia Harris as Secretary of Housing and Urban Development, Eleanor Holmes Norton to chair the Equal Employment Opportunity Commission and innumerable Blacks placed in the federal judiciary.

Carter's bid for a second term failed. He received a sound defeat by Ronald Reagan, who as governor of California, proved his less-than-charitable attitude toward Blacks. When he restored the power of the Republicans in controlling the nation by revitalizing the coalition between traditional conservatives and disgruntled working-class Whites, he picked up where Nixon left off. His movie-actor charisma enabled him to easily carry out the conservative agenda. And he made it very clear to the angered Whites as to which side he was on when he launched his candidacy for president in Philadelphia, Mississippi – the place where the Klan killed three civil rights workers in 1965. This action made it clear to Blacks, also.

As Nixon did before him, Reagan's focus on law and order, strict constructionist judges, welfare reform and affirmative action allayed the fears of Whites over the issues of loss of jobs, choice of schools, busing and their children's bus ride, plus the fright over their neighborhoods. He was immensely popular – with Whites. Reagan justified his actions stating he was making America a "color-blind society."[28] This gave aid and comfort to racism, and to those he called the "Moral Majority."

"A kinder, gentler society," was promised by his successor, George Herbert Walker Bush. It did not apply to Blacks. His attacks on affirmative action – reducing funding of entitlement programs and steadily whittling away at liberal courts and judges – marked his tenure as one that further eroded the progress black people accomplished under Johnson's War on Poverty and the Great Society.

CONSERVATISM v LIBERALISM
Analytical Summary:
EFFECTS ON BLACKS

- Euphemism Placing Emphasis on Whites
- Southern Democrats Change Political Party to GOP
- Separation/Segregation v Integration
- Shifts from Liberal to Conservative
- Many Programs Modified or Eliminated
- Watergate Scandal did not Stop Change of Liberal to Conservative Trend
- Blacks were Scapegoats

Is there such a thing as the status quo in politics? Or at least, is it possible to return to yesteryear? Of course it is impossible to replicate or duplicate anything of the political past exactly. However, by extracting key elements from the "good ole days" that gives a modicum of satisfaction and the desired comfort to the disgruntled, a political 180 degree can be achieved. This is what the Republicans did during the 1969 – 1993 stretch of GOP dominance: Presidents Richard Nixon, Gerald Ford, Ronald Reagan and George H. W. Bush. The previous years of Democratic control and liberalism were replaced with conservatism using this strategy.

The social/political climate in America turned toxic for many whites during the Civil Rights Era. They felt too many favors were being given to black people, at their expense. So when Nixon euphemistically referred to those Whites, as "Middle American" and that they were the Americans being bereft of their rights, therefore the Republicans would restore things as they use to be! His message resonated overwhelmingly, particularly with southern Democrats. En masse they changed political parties – from Democrat to Republican. It was a remarkable turn-around since the days dating back to Abraham Lincoln. The Republican Party was always an anathema.

Another factor fueling the political uprising was change of direction of some Blacks in the Civil Rights Movement. "Black Power" voices increasingly challenged Dr. Martin Luther King, Jr.'s non-violent approach. The stridency of the counter group's preachments and the strong arm tactics provided further ammunition for driving the Democrats out of power. Nixon demanded law and order; Ronald Reagan pitched to Whites by kicking-off his presidential candidacy in 1980 at the infamous town of Philadelphia, Mississippi – the site where three civil rights workers were brutally murdered by white supremacists. Republican conservatism was in; Democratic liberalism was out.

This monumental national political shift put Blacks on guard – and for good reason. The age-old strategy of divide and conquer was at hand. Nixon and Reagan, during their term made and took deliberate actions to reform the judicial system. They deemed it to be too liberal and unfair – perpetrating "reverse discrimination." They, along with Presidents Gerald Ford and George H. W. Bush, appointed a total of eight justices of conservative tendencies to the U. S. Supreme Court, hoping to skew the rulings to the right. Another way the Republicans reshaped policies and conducted federal business was to gradually erode and/or unravel some of the Entitlement programs that had benefited Blacks under Democratic administrations.

So profoundly upset were Whites by the Democrats' civil rights policies, they stuck by the Republicans, steadfastly despite Nixon's resignation due to the Water-gate scandal. Thus the Republicans continued to maintain control of the White House save for Democrat Jimmy Carter's anemic one-term that was sandwiched between the Ford and Reagan years. Basically this Conservative v Liberalism period switch did not stop social-political gains of black people, but in some instances it did stall and /or slow their rate of advancement and achievement in the struggle against Jim Crow and racism.

LIBERALISM v CONSERVATISM END NOTES

1. Adams, 304.

2. Elizabeth Jewel, *U.S. Presidents Factbook.* (New York: Random House, 2005) 257.

3. DeGregorio, 285.

4. Jewel, 359-360.

5. _____, 360.

6. DeGregorio, 587. Also see Jewel, "Political Career," 259-262.

7. _____, 597-599. Also see Jewel, "Watergate and Nixon Resignation," 365-367.

8. Jewel, 376.

9. _____, 374-375.

10. _____, 375-376.

11. DeGregorio, 614.

12. Jimmy Carter, *An Hour Before Daylight: Memories of a Rural Boyhood* (New York: Simon & Schuster, 2001). Carter writes extensively about his relationships with Blacks as he was growing up in rural Georgia. He also discusses the attitude his mother had toward Blacks, as opposed to that of his segregationist father.

13. DeGregorio, 619, 621. Also see Jewel, 386-388.

14. _____, 622.

15. _____, 634. Also see Jewel, 397.

16. Reagan made these remarks in the commencement address he delivered to the Eureka graduates in 1982.

17. F.B.I. documents obtained under the Freedom of Information Act, by the "San Jose Mercury News," in 1985, revealed that Reagan, as an FBI informant, passed on names of actors he believed to be Communists.

18. DeGregorio, 667-669.

19. _____, 671-672. Also see Jewel, 415.

20. Jewel, "Political Career," 416-419.

21. The Legacy of the Civil Rights Era brought unprecedented black political and social changes. Many Whites felt too much was done for them. Republicans capitalized on the dissention. They began systematically weakening and dismantling some of the entitlement programs and laws, eroding many of the gains Blacks achieved under the Democrats.

22. Adams, 296-297. Also, Martin Luther King's assassination incited many Blacks to abandon non-violent belief and action. Notably was the Student Non-Violent Committee (SNCC). H. "Rap" Brown, as the leader, called for "Black Power" and "Burn Baby Burn."

23. DeGregorio, Names and information about the U.S. Supreme Court appointees can be found on the following pages: Nixon, 599; Ford, 614; Reagan, 658; Bush, 697.

24. Paul Johnson, *A History of American People* (New York: Harper Collins, 1999) 887. During this period of Republican dominance, when the country politics shifted to the right, the U.S. Supreme Court also shifted. Judges of the liberal court aged and retired, opening vacancies. Eight appointments were made. Reagan and Nixon together totaled five. Jimmy Carter, a Democrat, appointed none.

25. During Post Reconstruction, laws were passed that newly-gained rights of Blacks were not protected. As a result, racism was practiced and endorsed overtly and covertly, dejure and defacto. Thus a pivotal difference between Post Reconstruction and Post Civil Rights is that in the latter period Blacks had some semblance of Constitutional recourse.

26. McPherson, 268. Also see Adams, 304-305.

27. Adams, 305-309.

28. _____, 313.

PANEL 14

Neoconservatism v Moderate Liberalism

1993~2009

President Profiles

William J. Clinton
Term: 1993-2001

George W. Bush
2001-2009

President	Date	Birthplace	College	Profession	Party
42. William J. Clinton	1946 -	Arkansas	Georgetown	Lawyer	Democrat
43. George W. Bush	1946 -	Massachusetts	Yale	Business	Republican

They represented the first baby boomer presidents. **William Jefferson Clinton** and **George Walker Bush** followed the last of the Greatest Generation presidents Nixon, Ford, Carter, Reagan and Bush, the elder. "Baby boomer" is a term used to describe the post-war generation. There was a huge birth-rate increase after WWII between the years of 1946 to 1964 that created this distinct generation. The climate of the growing up and young adult years for Clinton and Bush was magnetic. Epoch events, of all sorts, evolutionized and revolutionized the baby boomer generation, both nationally and internationally:

- Economic prosperity stemmed from WWII
- A new, vibrant middle class emerged[1]
- The technological age began its advent – television/computers/cyber space
- A tug-of-war for world supremacy between the U.S. and the U.S.S.R. escalated and permeated throughout
- Fallout from the Civil Rights Movement spawn societal dynamics, such as the hippies,[2] integration, gay rights, women's liberation

- National political pendulum swung markedly from left to right – liberalism to conservatism
- Globalization

Changes occurred with electrifying and radical speed. Clinton and Bush's baby boomer world bore little resemblance to that of their Greatest Generation parents. Social scientists have called the boomer era a counter-culture phenomenon. Their anti-establishment attitude and life style helped precipitate the national veering from a very pronounced liberalism, to that of a dizzying conservatism.[3] It seems rather paradoxical that baby boomers Clinton and Bush became the change-agents to push the political pendulum even further right, spearheading their parties' quest to recapture the status quo began by President Nixon.

William Clinton and George Bush held many things in common besides being baby boomers. Both served as state governors; neither participated in the Vietnam War; each served two presidential terms; and each made religion a strong part of their political appeal.

However, there were some very definitive differences in their backgrounds.

William Clinton – Bill as he called himself – as only the second president from the Deep South since Reconstruction, endured a rather trying childhood growing up in Arkansas. Born William Jefferson Blythe – similar to Gerald Ford – had his name changed. His biological father, William Jefferson Blythe III, died before Bill was born. As a traveling salesman, he was on the road often. In May 1946, he was killed in an automobile accident; the future president was born in August. So Bill spent his early years fatherless and virtually motherless for a while. His mother left him. She needed to get more training to make a decent living for Bill and herself. She left him with her parents, while she took more nurse's training in New Orleans. Thus, during his toddler years, Bill had neither parent. Upon her return to Arkansas, having completed her training, his mother juggled working and caring for him. She struggled as a single parent. Then in 1950, when Bill was four, she remarried. Roger Clinton became his stepfather. The household situation suffered; Roger was an alcoholic, who, while in drunken rages beat and abused the mother. Bill, at the age of 14, confronted his stepfather, threatening him. The domestic upheaval abated. As part of the reconciliation with Roger Clinton, Bill legally changed his name from Blythe to Clinton.[4]

Bill Clinton was a bright and accomplished student. He played the saxophone in the all-state band. In his junior year in high school, he was one of two boys from the Arkansas American Legion Boys Program to go to Boys Nation in Washington, D.C. He and the group met with President John F. Kennedy. Clinton became further enamored with government and public service after meeting President Kennedy. Following graduating fourth in his high school class in 1964, he returned to Washington – only this time as a student at Georgetown University, and enrolled in the School of Foreign Service. Once again he found success and accomplishment. He was class president his freshman and sophomore years. He worked on political campaigns, and had a part-time job as assistant clerk for Arkansas U.S. Senator William Fulbright, chair of the Senate Foreign Relations Committee. Clinton became further immersed in politics – the country was embroiled in Civil Rights and the Vietnam War. In 1968, he graduated with a degree in international affairs. That summer he was awarded a prestigious Fulbright Scholarship for study in England, at the University College, Oxford. There he pursued politics, philosophy and economics. Also, while abroad, he traveled extensively. Clinton studied for two years at Oxford.

Rather than continue study at Oxford for a third year, Bill Clinton accepted a scholarship to Yale University Law School. Once again he co-mingled his studies with political campaign activities. By the time he graduated in 1973, he knew a political career was for him. At this time the Vietnam War still raged. Clinton did not serve; instead, he returned to Arkansas. For awhile, Clinton was a law professor at the University of Arkansas. Then, later he plunged, full-bore, into

Arkansas politics. Along the way he experienced both failure and success.[5] But, the latter far out surpassed the former. Twice as governor of Arkansas, he drew national attention and gained a reputation as an astute, forward-looking politician. In 1988, Democrats picked him to run against incumbent George H.W. Bush, the father of his successor, George W. Bush. Clinton won, but forced by the times, he moderated his liberalism.

George W. Bush – also dubbed Dubya for his middle initial – had a very different childhood and background. Although he was born in Connecticut into a family of aristocracy and wealth, his father's oil business pursuits led to a childhood in the West and Southwest. His early days were spent between small towns in California and Texas. But, as the elder Bush's oil enterprise boomed, the family – Dubya and his five siblings – settled permanently in Texas. Throughout his elementary school days, he received a public school education. Then from the eighth grade on, he attended prestigious private schools in the East. Younger Bush, like his father, was a skilled athlete, and when he attended Yale University – beginning in 1964 – he played varsity baseball. In 1968, he graduated with a degree in history.[6] Academically he did not apply his energy as much as he did toward extra-curricular social activities.

Upon graduating from Yale, Bush was eligible for the draft. The Vietnam War was raging. He did not want to go into the Army and be a soldier; he wanted to be a pilot, like his father, who flew fighter planes in WWII. Rather than to serve in the regular military, young George joined the Air National Guard. This committed him to 39 days of service for once a year, for six years. He learned to fly; however, there is some question as to his carrying out his National Guard commitment. Yet, he received an honorable discharge.[7]

This period in Bush's life he dubbed the "nomadic years." He partied – and generally, led a socially out-of-control life. Although he tangentially worked on political campaigns, he was largely apolitical, and somewhat detached from the socio-political turbulence sweeping America. Then he turned his attention toward graduate study. First, he applied to the University of Texas Law School. His admission was denied. So in 1973, he set his sights on business and gained admission to Harvard Business School. Bush completed the course of study successfully and received his MBA degree in 1975. He returned to Texas. Like elder Bush, he entered the oil business. He made political contacts, and in 1978 he ran on a conservative, pro-business, anti-regulation platform, to take a seat in the U.S. House of Representatives. But he lost, defeated by the Democratic candidate. He continued for a time in the oil business, which was something of a roller-coaster. After leaving it in 1989, he organized a group of investors who bought the Texas Rangers, a Major League baseball team. His prominent identification with the Rangers raised his profile in Texas. With his father's political machine backing him, Dubya ran for governor in 1993. He won. His sweeping reforms in education, relaxed gun laws, and stronger guidelines in prosecuting juvenile offenders, engendered him to the Texas voter. Overwhelmingly, he was re-elected. From this political leap, he entered the U.S. Presidential race in 2000. Although his victory cast clouds of suspicion, George W. Bush became the 43rd president.[8]

NEOCONSERVATISM

V

MODERATE LIBERALISM
ISSUES & ACTIONS

- **Republican Party (GOP) Control**
- **Religious Right**
- **Clinton Impeachment**
- **Bush Elections**
- **9/11 Attack**
- **Iraq War**
- **Hurricane Katrina**
- **Clinton/Bush Appointments**
- **Clinton/Bush Legacies**

This sixteen year period of Neoconservatism v Moderate Liberalism, saw American politics continue to move more and more to the right under the auspices of Presidents William (Bill) Clinton) and George W. Bush. Although the White House during this era was split between the Democrat Clinton and the Republican Bush, the GOP controlled Congress. Therefore its right-politics dictated public policy and social-cultural issues.

In the '80's, Ronald Reagan injected religion into the social-cultural politics. He continuously expounded on and rhapsodized about the virtues of the "moral majority." Initially his aim targeted Nixon's "Middle America" white people. In time it morphed into subsequent administrations as a faith-based political plank of the Republican Party: the Religious Right. No longer was the message exclusively aimed to attract Whites to the GOP, but the net spread into the religious black community too.

The religious right dictum of Republicans played pivotal roles in Clinton's forced moderation and the stymieing impeachment. Initially targeted by the GOP controlled Congress were his Democrat liberal-leanings. It was determined to minimize and/or to prevent his instituting New Deal-type social programs. By the time of Clinton's second term, the religious right-led faction turned up the heat. Clinton's dalliances were the lightning rod.

Due to this religious-driven political witch hunt leading to the Clinton impeachment, plus term limits, Republicans managed to regain the White House. They got George W. Bush elected – not once, but twice. His first election generated suspicion; the second time he owed some of his success to more Blacks attracted to the GOP religious right politics.

Two unforeseen catastrophic events shaped Bush's two terms: the 9/11 Attack during the initial term and Hurricane Katrina's last term impact. Each had diametrically different results in decidedly political and social ways. The issues created caused epic controversies: the Iraq War and the FEMA incident.

Presidential appointments highlighted this era, also, especially those to the U.S. Supreme court. They brought a stir. Openings occurred during both Clinton and Bush administrations. Their selections excited both the neocons and the moderate-liberals. In addition to their judicial appointments, both presidents included many Blacks in key administrative positions.[9]

Black life under Bill Clinton and George W. Bush, reflected the social-economic situation of the average American. Class and race as usual – when conservatism dominates politics and policies – brought social and economic divide. A myriad of these factors of class conspired to cast less than sterling assessments of the Clinton and Bush legacies for this reason.

REPUBLICAN PARTY (GOP) CONTROL

Beginning with the Nixon administration, the nation's social and political policies and actions, under Republican conservatism, veered right. The previous years of Democratic dominance, from Franklin Roosevelt's New Deal through to Lyndon Johnson's Great Society, the federal government, interfered too much, the GOP charged.[10] They called for less government. Big government meant intrusion and encroachment on states rights, plus American Big Business was throttled, Republicans bugled. The American electorate embraced anti-liberalism and put the Republicans in control and forced Clinton, a Democrat to moderate policies and actions, as Jimmy Carter was pressed to do before him.

Under George W. Bush, Republican control emboldened him to push economic, political and social issues and actions further right to neo-conservatism. Regulations were all but lifted on how the corporate world did business. So amok was Big Business that the American economy verged on collapse. Its reckless practices precipitated peril world wide. Also, entitlement programs took hits; affirmative action, social security, health-medical care, and welfare headed the targets. Through statute and court rulings erosion, modification and nullification, Blacks found their quality of life in shambles thanks to the economic, political and social tactics of the Republican dictates carried out by neocon, George W. Bush.

RELIGIOUS RIGHT

Vestiges of Christian Sectarian religion had been manifest in American politics from the nation's inception; at times stronger than others. But in modern times, its influence under the George W. Bush regime was unprecedented. The coalition of fundamentalists and evangelicals, known as the Religious Right, led the neoconservative Republicans to base much of their domestic and foreign policies as well as politics on religion. Family values framed their preachments, a social-cultural message so that an appreciable number of Blacks embraced them.

Religion and the church have always been central in black life.[11] So when the Republicans used this political hook to entice black people from the Democrats, it was understandable why they succeeded with an appreciable number of black people. Controversial issues opposed by GOP, such as abortion, same-sex marriage, homosexuality and the theory of evolution resonated with Blacks. Many black preachers influenced their followers that these beliefs and practices were against biblical teachings; therefore sinful. This wedge helped elect George W. Bush both times.

CLINTON IMPEACHMENT

Bill Clinton defeated George W. Bush's father to preside over the 42nd U. S. presidential administration. Black voters contributed greatly to his successful elections. Ironically his southern religious roots were akin to theirs. It made him immensely popular with black people.[12] He began his first term in the fashion of the FDR New Deal and Johnson's Great Society mode. The controlling GOP congress disliked his liberal-leanings. They began forcing his issues and actions further toward the middle of the political spectrum. And when Clinton was elected to a second term, the Republicans stepped up their campaign to forestall him even more so.

Historian David Osborne said Clinton had what it took to be a great president. "A natural-born politician ... he was warm, physical, commanding, exuberant, soulful, tireless and empathetic." In addition, he had a brilliant mind capable of mastering the subject at hand. But unfortunately he had a propensity for foolish dalliances.[13] Some historians feel that they short-circuited his potential in reaching greatness among our American presidents. Yet these acts tended not to diminish Clinton's standing in the eyes of many in the black community.

Plotting Republicans strategists, aware of Clinton's weaknesses, trapped him. They left no stone unturned, they squandered untold tax-payer dollars and they drew up a list of offenses. The GOP-controlled House handed over the impeachment list to the Senate. It placed Clinton on trial. He was only the second American president to be impeached – Andrew Johnson was by the Radical Republicans in 1868. And like Johnson, Clinton was not found guilty. However so much damage was done to him, he limped dysfunctional through the balance of his last term as a political cripple. The GOP had done their job.

BUSH ELECTIONS

Elections are always an important function of the democratic process. Unless they are carried out orderly and fairly, some citizens are disenfranchised being denied the power of the ballot box. One man (woman) and one vote ensures one's right of having a say in the nation's business. The 2000 presidential election pitting George W. Bush, the Republican, against Albert Gore, Jr., the Democrat, Clinton's Vice President, came under a cloud – because some peoples' vote for Gore were not allowed due to a questionable ruling by the U.S. Supreme Court.[14] As a result, George W. Bush's claim to the presidency shall forever bear a stigma. In the voting, he garnered 9% of the black vote.

Four years later in the 2004 presidential election, Bush won, this time without any glaring irregularities. He also increased his black voter support by 3%. Much of the reason might be chalked up to those Blacks embracing the politics of the religious right.

9/11 ATTACK

September 11, 2001 is an American history date comparable in infamy to the Japanese attack on Pearl Harbor, Hawaii, in 1941 on December 7.[15] The 9/11 Attack was perpetrated by an Islamic terrorist group called al Qaeda. A number of its members hijacked four large commercial jet passenger planes. Two of the planes crashed into the North and South Towers of New York City's World Trade

Center, the third rammed the Pentagon near Washington, D.C. and the fourth jet plummeted into a field in rural Pennsylvania. It is believed that had the heroic passengers on the fourth plane not struggled with the terrorists, forcing them off course, they might have succeeded in obliterating the White House!

These brazen acts that claimed countless lives set the course for the Bush administration. Its policies – home and abroad – revolved around the mantra of "fighting the war on terror." The Republicans, during both the 2000 and 2004 presidential elections, called for patriotism.[16] So the 9/11 Attack fueled the fervor when it happened. Americans gave Bush a governing mandate, carte blanche; allowing him to abuse his new-found power.

IRAQ WAR

The first election of George W. Bush left a bitter taste for many Americans. As a result, the early months of his leadership met with somewhat suspicion, a tentativeness. But that changed after September 11, 2001 following the al Qaeda terrorist attack. Bush unleashed his hubris, became overarching with the resultant governing mandate. He took America into an unproved-war and alienated many countries by his brazen unilateralism.

On March 19, 2003, the United States opened war on Saddam Hussein and Iraq. Bush claimed they had weapons of mass destruction (WMD).[17] None were ever found, nor was there any connection to al Qaeda, another Bush claim. Hussein was defeated; but that did not end the war. The Iraq War has turned into a re-run of Vietnam. Even Bush's changed excuse of bringing liberation to a people who did not ask for it, did not bode well neither home nor abroad.

George Bush's unilateral policy caused national and international alienation. His recklessness cost the GOP congressional control in the 2006 off-year election. His "stay-the-course" stubbornness caused his high approval rating to plummet, all but tanking. Unnecessary debt, needless loss of life and other war-related ills affected Americans of all stripes.[18] Black people felt the impact considerably. Many young black men and women belonged to the National Guard and military reserve organizations. But probably the segment most targeted and involved were the career military. Many of whom graduated from the nation's military academies.

HURRICANE KATRINA

George Bush's approval was slipping by mid 2005. The war in Iraq was not the shock-and-awe quickie he promised. Besides, it was later proven that he lied to the American people about weapons of mass destruction as a reason for going to war. The climbing death toll and mounting national debt caused Bush support to further unravel. Americans were getting fed up with him and his ineptitude. He was becoming an embarrassment to many. Then came Hurricane Katrina.

Hurricane Katrina compounded George Bush's mire. A Category V hurricane – one of the most destructive ratings – Katrina hit landfall on August 29, 2005. It cut a 150-mile swath along the coastal areas of Texas, Mississippi and Louisiana. New Orleans bore the brunt. The ferocity of its winds and rains left chaos and untold havoc in its wake. The levees collapsed; the city flooded. Death and destruction stalked the city. People suffered; casualties mounted. Yet four days elapsed before New Orleans drew any attention from Bush and the federal government!

Representing the Bush administration, alas, FEMA (Federal Emergency Management Agency) finally showed. But it exhibited little direction or focus. Its most glaring disorganization and disarray flashed across the nation, and the world via television. It centered around New Orlean's Ninth Ward, an area peopled principally by Blacks, largely poor.[19] Days passed before their misery, mayhem and ravished conditions received any competent and concerted effort. Images of them and their situations were likened to those to be found in the

Third World. An embarrassment; black-eye-for America. Questions swirled about reasons and causes for the delay; and seemingly unconcern. Was it racism? Was it classism? Whatever the reasons and the causes, George W. Bush has been blamed – lowering his stature among majority black people.

CLINTON & BUSH APPOINTMENTS

Appointments to the U.S. Supreme Court by presidents leave a lasting impression. Their political imprint can last for years through the person(s) they choose and the actions the appointee takes since the judgeship is a lifetime job. Contrary to some "pursuits," the appointments are political. So when openings occur, a president gets an opportunity to influence the social, political and economic direction of the country in years to come.

During their tenures, Presidents Clinton and Bush made two appointments each. One of the Clinton picks differed from the norm: he selected only the second woman in history to the Court. She along with Clinton's male appointee were liberals; he hoped to keep his political point of view on the bench. Bush did likewise. He selected two judges reflecting his conservative viewpoint.[20] Neither president considered a black person. Suppose if either had, think of some of the possible ways history could have been altered. Perhaps some of the affirmative action cases such as the recent University of Michigan case (Grutter v Bollinger) and the Parents Involved in Community Schools v Seattle School District case, where race as a bases for determining diversity of integration, were over-turned and condemned. Both of the Bush appointees sided with the majority opinions. These are examples of how usually the appointees' votes represent the same politics as the appointing president.

Besides making judicial appointments, presidents pick people for key positions in their administration, especially those of their cabinet. Usually the selections reflect the political views of the president and his political party. Clinton and Bush appointees generally fit this mold. Both men selected numerous minorities of this stripe. Among them were several black officials, representing both the Democratic and the Republican Parties.[21]

CLINTON & BUSH LEGACIES

Clinton's presidency started imbuing hope for most black people. Their previous years under the Republicans tended to disappoint. Most had enjoyed the spoils of the Johnson years that bettered their social, political and economic status. So with the Democrats' return to the White House, majority of black people looked to regain some of the ground that slipped under the GOP. Unfortunately it did not happen. Republican control of the Congress, conservative-leaning of the courts and a nation being disenchanted with liberal politics was the backdrop during Bill Clinton's tenure. Forced to moderation, he had little footing to do much to further the cause of black people. In fact, some Blacks felt Clinton tarnished his legacy by playing too moderate politics. He compromised on the Welfare Reform Act and he was no more forceful in protecting affirmative action as well as his mishandling of the abortive Lani Guinier nomination – a black woman he picked for Attorney General.[22] Yet, despite President Clinton's inability to fulfill many of their expectations, most Blacks looked upon him favorably, recognizing the constraints placed upon him by the Republicans.

George W. Bush declared history must judge his legacy – it is much too premature to reach any formative conclusions. Perhaps, he had a legitimate point, but his record as it presently stands appears not too favorable for most Americans, Black included. Whether they were on the national or international front, Bush's actions were divisive and destructive.

Bush decisions gave free reign to the greedy grafty Wall Street, literally destroying Main Street[23] putting America in a recession. The economy virtually collapsed. Fraudulent investment and banking practices that netted bankruptcies, home foreclosures, unemployment and business failures created a nearly two class society, the have and the have-nots. And it left the government and the American people drowning under an avalanche of debt that spawn not only heaps of economic problems, but social and political ones too. With these calamities representing just the tip of the iceberg, President Bush's legacy may not find too high a rating among the pantheon of American presidents, nor among most middle class Americans, black Americans included.[24]

NEOCONSERVATISM

V

MODERATE LIBERALISM
Analytical Summary:
EFFECTS ON BLACKS

- Entitlements Further Eroded
- Some Leave Democrats for Republican Party
- Progress Stymied
- Division Over Religion and War
- Bush Gained Added Power
- Many Drawn in to Being Career Military
- Many Casualties and Victims Attributed to
  FEMA (Federal Emergency Management Agency)
  Neglect/Ineptness
- Reflective of Party Politics
- Mixed Reviews

Political ideology has always determined the economic and social-cultural direction of this country. From the beginning of nationhood the ideology was conservative. The Founding Fathers wanted not to relinquish their wealth and power; they gained and maintained them courtesy of free black labor and unfettered production. Hence they strove to conserve the institute of slavery. Most of the ensuing eras, however, had ideological tugs-of-war: yanking from right to left – and back again, many times over. These roller coaster actions of many presidents, during some historical American years, tend to epitomize the political vicissitudes. Invariably, in one way or another, Blacks have been the thrown-rock that kept the political pool roiling. And oft-times religious issues caused further agitation skewing the political direction. The preachments figured prominently in the movement to the right when the Republicans took control, following Richard Nixon's ascent to the White House in 1969, and Ronald Reagan's added pro-white stance in 1981.

Prior to that, Republicans and their conservative politics, were all but shut out of the political discourse. For over thirty-five years, liberal Democrats reigned. After awhile, Franklin Roosevelt's New Deal and Lyndon Johnson's civil rights-laden Great Society abraded many Whites – those whom Nixon called "middle America" and Reagan named the "moral majority." They vehemently and fervently held beliefs that all Blacks received preferential treatment at their expense. A massive political backlash resulted swinging 180 degrees to the right. Swept into the fold were countless party-switching southern Whites – changing from Democrats to Republicans. This transformation led to a GOP-controlled Congress. And the two Democrat administrations squeezed amid the five GOP administrations were forced to moderate their liberalism, moving them center. Then as a consequence, an appreciable number of entitlement programs, rulings and/or laws that had benefited black people, were eroded, modified, and in some cases, completely nullified. Of course, Clinton's impeachment during his second term, stymied his progress even more. Conservatism held sway and grew stronger with the advent of George W. Bush.

Bush brought a more intense rightist ideology to Washington: a neo-conservatism; politics laced with religious issues. So powerful was this plank to the Republican agenda, called the Religious Right, black preachers embraced it – and influenced many of their flock to vote GOP. In fact, the black vote made a considerable impact in both of George Bush elections, enabling him and the neo-conservatives to govern the country for eight destructive and divisive years. Years so ruinous that few average Americans benefited. His administration courted the wealthy and catered to Big Business. The virtual mandate of governance he received after the 9/11 Attack freed him to conduct that nation's business, literally without impunity. Lack of accountability proved disastrous for the country. His political behavior of ineptitude and hubris was exhibited throughout, especially the unprovoked Iraq War handling, the Katrina debacle and the wrecking of the economy. It was not a good show ending with a catastrophic recession.

This brings up the subject of legacies – President Bill Clinton's and President George W. Bush's. Both men were "Baby Boomers." They grew up amid magnetic changes in America, particularly social relations between black and white Americans. De jure segregation succumbed to integration and affirmative action opened educational, economic and political doors, yielding opportunities for black people. These national changes were reflected in each presidential administration. Most prominently they showed in the appointments each made, and the manner in which each party encouraged black involvement. These are plusses for both men. But there are other variables in the legacy equations.

Probably the more important determinants for rating a president are the issues and how he acted in his governance. Clinton faced a hostile Congress. On issues such as welfare and affirmative action, he equivocated, waffled and compromised. He endorsed the North American Free Trade Agreement (NAFTA). That cost Americans jobs. Clinton's actions, in general, disappointed and disillusioned many Blacks, who supported him nearly unconditionally. And these feelings grew more deflated, when in the second term his indiscretions led to impeachment. These actions belied what Clinton promised, when on the campaign trail – a kind of liberal people – friendly administration; not market-driven moderation. Overall Clinton's watch yielded few positives or advancements for the majority of black people.

On the other hand, George W. Bush made no pretense as to what political course he would take. It was clear he planned to continue, in embellished form, the Reaganesque conservative policies favoring the wealthy and the Big Business powerful. The "little people" – the average Americans – were used by him as the foil to further the gains of the upper 1 to 2%, who already controlled over half of the nation's wealth! He supported, endorsed and under wrote all sorts of corporate greed and graft. At the end of his eight years, Bush left the nation a debt-ridden economy, in near-collapse: foreclosures, bankruptcies, unemployment, homelessness, crumbling banking system and a failing auto industry. America plunged into a deep recession. Blacks shared the brunt of this adversity along with the rest of the Americans.

Legacy. Webster's Dictionary defines it figuratively, something that has been handed down from an ancestor or a predecessor. Also, a legacy is not static; it is forever evolving. In addition, the source of the appraisal, and the time when the appraisal is made, figure significantly in any legacy.

So what did Clinton hand down to black people? His actions left much to be desired, after such a promising beginning that some even called him "the first black president." Obstacles were, however formidable: a Republican controlled Congress, an anti-liberal national political mood, and his own personal transgressions. Given the circumstances of this neo-conservative/moderate liberal era Bill Clinton, while he did not do too much to advance the cause of black people, his actions overall were not too damaging either. So among many Blacks, they view the Clinton performance with ambivalence.

George Bush defended his actions as president. He cautioned against rash conclusions – let history be the judge. He pointed out, as an example, how over the years, the way time favorably altered Harry S. Truman's perceived presidency. Perhaps. But a review of the Bush administrations – at this time – the indicators of his legacy are not commendable. In his wake, in addition to leaving America in a recession, he also left the middle class diminished, the society culturally divided, the national debt staggering, the resource-draining war unresolved and a lingering unfavorable world reputation.

At this juncture, the right-driven policies of Presidents Clinton and Bush, for various reasons, appear mixed, and by some – Blacks included – to be none too favorable presidential performances. Yet their histories are very short. Many shifts and changes, in subsequent American life, could influence later historians to bear out George Bush's admonition about legacies.

NEOCONSERVATISM v MODERATE LIBERALISM
END NOTES

1. Federal entitlements and subsidies for returning service personnel and Corporate industries translated into good paying jobs, improved education and training opportunities following WWII. This created a sizeable middle class among Blacks and other Americans.

2. Hippies were a counter-culture group comprised mainly of middle-class white kids. They espoused "making love, not war." A lifestyle of free speech, sex, drugs, and self-indulgenced dubbed them as the ME generation.

3. See Panel 13 end notes. "Middle America," 26.

4. Bill Clinton, *My Life*. (New York: Alfred Knopf.) 2004.

5. DeGregorio, 712-718.

6. Jewel, 449-450.

7. _____,450.

8. _____, 451-453.

9. Both Clinton and Bush appointed Blacks to positions in their administrations. Clinton: Ron Brown, Secretary of Commerce; Mike Asby, Secretary of Agriculture; Hazel O'Leary, Secretary of Energy; Jesse Brown, Veterans' Affairs; Joyce Elder, Surgeon General; Vernon Jordan, Advisor. Bush: Colin L. Powell, Secretary of State (first term) Condoleeza Rice, Secretary of State (2nd term); Ron Paige, Secretary of Education (first term).

10. McPherson, 268, 269.

11. In April/May 2005 issue of Savoy - an African American magazine - the article, "The Souls of Black Folk: black ministers battle over the devil they know and the one some want to get to know," provides profound insights into how George Bush used the black clergy to deliver the black vote for him, during the 2004 presidential election, 72-75.

12. _____, 73.

13. McPherson, 303-306.

14. _____, 308.

15. The 9/11 Attack was the first the U.S. had ever been attacked by a foreign political group on American soil, of that magnitude.

16. In the 2004 election, it went in favor of George Bush and the Republicans because the issues of fear and homeland security intimidated majority of voters to keep the incumbents in office.

17. The Weapons of Mass destruction (WMD) – the UN inspectors proved that they did not exist.

18. Many Blacks were career military. They found opportunities there that were not afforded them in the civilian sector.

19. *Time*, "Special Report: Why New Orleans still isn't safe," 6, 28-44.

20. Besides appointing conservative justices to the U. S. Supreme Court, the Bush administration directed the Attorney General Robert Gonzales to fire or replace lower court judges deemed to be too liberal.

21. See note #9.

22. Adams, 316 – 319.

23. *Time*, "Inside Breakdown at SEC," 34 – 37. March 9, 2009.

24. Large numbers of black people gained middle-class status during the Johnson era and under Democrat control of the federal government. But once the Republicans took over beginning with Richard Nixon, and subsequent GOP administrations, Big Business and the wealthy one-percent were courted. Laissez faire policies were increasingly implemented: deregulation, outsourcing, tax-cuts for the rich, eliminating or reducing entitlement programs. During George W. Bush's term these practices accelerated, so much so that the middle-class – Blacks and others – have precipitously been relegated to the ranks of "have-nots."

ADDENDUM:
A NEW ERA OF HOPE

The 44th United States President,
Barack Hussein Obama, Jr.

"Perhaps it takes a new face to see the promise in a future that now looks dark...."
– Massimo Calabresi and Michael Duffy, "Person of the Year,"
Time Magazine, December 29, 2008 – January 5, 2009.

On January 20, 2009, when Barack Obama placed his hands on the Bible, and repeated the presidential oath, America more than made history. The new face was black; the new president was African-American! In every sense: the son of a black Kenyan African father and a white Kansan American mother. Three hundred and ninety years after Antony, Isabela and the eighteen other Africans were brought ashore at Jamestown, Virginia, Obama's election represented rebirth, redemption and hope for America – A new beginning, a new era where race – hopefully becomes history.

Calabresi and Duffy observed that "His (Obama) arrival on the scene feels like a step into the next century... his genome is global, his world is net worked, and his spirit is democratic." No other president in American history ever inherited and never confronted the twin debacle of both domestic and global entanglements. Presidents George Washington, Abraham Lincoln and Franklin Roosevelt could never have fathomed such a multi-morphed-morass. President Obama faces and will continue to face this throughout his presidency. And to focus only on his actions on those issues affecting Blacks will be hard to differentiate and a bit short sighted. In this New Era – this new beginning – it is hopeful that Barak H. Obama, as the first black American president, will inspire and foster in leaders the wisdom to seek answers to the assorted human dilemmas by exploring areas beyond the strictures of RACE.

September 30, 2009

Epilogue

As noted in the preface, our book, *Blacks Through the 'Ayes' of Our American Presidents,* resulted from Taylor's two questions: Why are black people in America still treated as second-class citizens and why can't we get beyond this? Webster defines epilogue as the concluding part of literary work used for author summarization and interpretation. 'Ayes' epilogue is that kind of reprise. Beginning at Jamestown in 1619 with the introduction of Africans (black people) into America, and the tracing of the timeline from era to era ending on 2009, considerable is revealed. Defined are the important issues and the actions the Founding Fathers and the Presidents took as they related the evolution of how Blacks have fit and do now fit in American history. Why then would Taylor's questions epitomize the knowledge-void felt by so many?

Answers, or the lack of such, have largely been due to unfortunate writing, reading, and teaching of history, in general. Kenneth C. Davis in an excerpted article from his book, *Don't Know Much About History,* addresses a commonly-cited reason for not knowing, it is boring, because of rote-based teaching and "learning of dates, names and battles." He offers a solution. "If people only heard real stories of real people in real places, nobody could possibly claim to be 'bored' by history." Truth might be, also added to the equation. Too frequently, writing, reading and teaching about history, and in our case in point – American history – have not dealt with "the real." Cherry-picked, glorified tales permeate throughout. Our political beginnings and subsequent political journey that are consummated in the American presidency, thus mislead, omit and/or distort.

Blacks Through the 'Ayes' of Our American Presidents brings and presents a reality. It brings and presents a reality to a phase of American history that is fraught with legend, myth, hypocrisy and lies. These perpetrations fueled and funded the Founding Fathers philosophy about African's (Black's) inferiority. It started from 1619, at Jamestown, Virginia, when Isabela and Antony, along with the other eighteen black indentured servants, were purchased and brought ashore, seeds of racism took root. In time, slavery sprouted! Rationalizations of all sorts proliferated creating a national mythology about race; a mythology that evolved into a racial philosophy. The Declaration of Independence, the United States Constitution & the Bill of Rights – the cornerstones of our nation – reflect and represent this thinking. Some of it is through omission, other evidences through commission. It is often said that belief dictates behavior. Therefore, it follows that American history and the incumbent American culture stem from a race-based philosophy. So then, when our American presidents take the oath of office, and swear to uphold the Constitution – "to the best of my ability" – they ostensibly pledge allegiance, and fully endorse a race-based philosophy of society. The above background of America, somewhat explains the "what" of Jane's second question – circumstances leading to the attitude for the Blacks' continued second-class treatment.

The "why" of her first question can largely be answered by reviewing how American history is transmitted and perpetuated. Kenneth C. Davis observes that by our not viewing people as real people, particularly our presidents, speaks to the pitfalls. Beginning with George Washington, his biography too often reads of saintliness, devoid of human frailties. These type-tales ditto their way into teaching about the presidents and the presidencies. Early presidents such as Thomas Jefferson, Andrew Jackson and Abraham Lincoln standout, considerably, as bigger-than-life figures; added to the lexicon are recent anointees FDR, IKE and JFK. Little credence is given to the "real" man. A feature of 'Ayes' begins each Panel with the President Profile. Each sketches an overview of the life and times. It is hoped, by the reader having this knowledge and picture, there will be better understanding and insight, as to why the president made certain decisions; and why he acted or reacted the way he did to issues and events.

When one is up-close and an eyewitness, reflections are at a premium; on the other hand, hind-sight offers one a marvelous luxury to ponder and to explore the "what-ifs" and the "why-nots." That points up the need and the importance of knowing one's history. Some claim history "done and gone" … it's boring. Pause a minute …William Faulkner's sage: "The past isn't dead and buried. In fact, it isn't even past …."

Blacks Through the 'Ayes' of Our American Presidents is written with this in mind. America's past is its present. America is an anomaly, much of this attributable to race. By reviewing and revealing history gleaned from the actions and the policies of the American presidents relative to American black people, we – Taylor, Tollette, and Scott – hope that 'Ayes' will inspire reflective thought, and spur critical dialog toward resolving our dilemma over race and racism as it relates to the American ethos. Plus, we also encourage the utilization of the various features – Appendix, Bibliography, Chronology, Glossary, and/or Index – as a resource tool to further enhance one's learning and knowledge.

CHRONOLOGY

1619   Twenty Africans brought to Jamestown, Virginia; became indentured servants.

1641   Massachusetts colony first to legalize slavery.

1676   Black and white indentured servants rebelled in Virginia.

1688   Quakers in Pennsylvania make first formal protest against slavery.

1700   Blacks makeup 11% of the population of the colonies.

1750   Blacks makeup 20% of the colonies' population.

1770   Black population increases to 21%. Crispus Attucks, a fugitive slave, is first killed in the Boston Massacre.

1775   Lord Dunmore offers freedom to all slaves who fight for England.

1776   Signers of the Declaration of Independence remove section denouncing slavery.

1778   Continental Congress authorizes George Washington to recruit free Blacks. Five thousand served in the Continental Army.

1787   U.S. Constitution adopted. The words "slave" and "slavery" do not appear in it.

1789   George Washington, a slave owner, becomes the first U.S. President.

1790   Black Population makes up 19%.

1793   Eli Whitney invents the Cotton Gin. The first Fugitive Slave Law is passed.

1800   Gabriel Prosser leads a slave revolt in Richmond, Virginia. It fails; he is hanged.

1808   Congress bans U.S. involvement in international slave trade.

1820   Missouri compromise maintains balance of slave and free states.

1821   Liberia founded in Africa as a settlement for former slaves.

1822   Denmark Vesey's planned slave rebellion in Charleston, South Carolina fails; 35 slaves executed.

1833   Slavery abolished in the British Empire. American Anti-Slavery Society founded.

1838   Frederick Douglass escapes from slavery.

1849   Harriet Tubman escapes from slavery.

1852   Harriet Beecher Stowe publishes *Uncle Tom's Cabin.*

1854   Armed conflict breaks out in Kansas after passage of Kansas-Nebraska Act.

1857   U.S. Supreme Court hands down the pro-slave Dred Scott Decision.

1860   Abraham Lincoln elected as the first Republican president. Blacks make up 14% of population.

1861   Civil War begins; Blacks banned from military service.

1862   Lincoln issues Emancipation Proclamation; Blacks authorized to fight.

1865   The 13th Amendment, passed and ratified, abolishing slavery.
Civil War ends; Lee surrenders at Appomattox, April 9th.
Lincoln shot April 14th, dies the next day.
Andrew Johnson becomes President; Mississippi Black Codes enacted.

1866   The 14th Amendment passed giving Blacks citizenship.

1868   The 14th Amendment ratified.
Johnson impeached, not guilty.
Ulysses S. Grant elected U.S. President.

1869   The 15th Amendment passed, granting voting rights (to all men).

1870   Hiram R. Revels, from Mississippi, becomes first Black elected to the U. S. Senate.
        Fifteenth Amendment ratified.

1875   Congress passes Civil Rights Act prohibiting discrimination in public accommodations.

1877   Rutherford B. Hayes gets contested presidency, after a deal to withdraw troops from the South, ending Reconstruction.
        Black town of Nicodemus, Kansas is founded.

1883   U.S. Supreme Court declares the Civil Rights Act of 1875 unconstitutional.

1884   Robert Smalls elected from South Carolina to the U. S. House of Representatives.

1895   Booker T. Washington delivers Atlanta Compromise speech at Cotton States Exposition.
        Frederick Douglass dies.

1896   U.S. Supreme Court legalizes segregation by establishing the doctrine of separate but equal in Plessy v Ferguson Decision.

1898   Widespread outbreaks of racial violence erupts, punctuated by riots, lynchings, and progress disenfranchisement of Blacks.

1901   George White becomes the last U.S. House of Representative member of the Blacks elected during Reconstruction; another black is not elected to the U. S. Congress until 1929.

1905   The first issue of *The Chicago Defender* is published.

1906   The Brownsville, Texas uprising broke out between black soldiers and white citizens. Theodore Roosevelt court-martialed the soldiers.

1909   National Association for the Advancement of Colored People (NAACP) founded.

1911   National Urban League founded.

1913   Woodrow Wilson declares black and white workers use separate facilities.

1915   Northern Migration starts.
        Ku Klux Klan reemerges.
        Booker T. Washington dies.

1917   The U.S. enters WWI.
        Blacks join through Selective Service.

1918   WWI ends.
        Over 371,000 Blacks serve, over half served in France.

1919   More than 20 race riots erupt in the U.S.
        Dubois tabbed it the "Red Summer."

1921   Race riots continue in more than 26 cities, Tulsa, Oklahoma one of the worst.

1923   Marcus Garvey's black nationalist Universal Negro Improvement Association
        membership purported to be over half million.

1925   A. Phillip Randolph organizes the black union, Brotherhood of Sleeping Car
        Porters and Maids.

1927   Marcus Garvey deported to Jamaica as an undesirable alien.

1929   Stock Market collapses; Blacks economic situation worsened.

1932   Franklin D. Roosevelt elected; the New Deal began, Blacks benefit.

1941   First class of black pilots graduate from segregated aviation school at Tuskegee
        Army Air Field in Alabama – March 7th.
        Japan attacks Pearl Harbor Hawaii – December 7th.
        America enters WWII.

1942   All-black 323 Fighter Group activated.
        During the War, 95 of the all-black fighter pilots were awarded the
        Distinguished Flying Cross.

1944   U.S. Supreme Court rules all-white primaries unconstitutional.

1945   WWII ends.
        Germany surrenders May 9th; Japan September 2nd.
        Approximately a million Blacks serve in segregated units.
        Franklin Roosevelt dies April 12th; Harry S Truman becomes President.

1948   Truman issues an executive order unifying and desegregating the military.

1950   Korean War begins; American military fights in integrated units, first time
        in U.S. history.

1953   Dwight Eisenhower becomes President; he appoints Earl Warren Chief Justice
        of U.S. Supreme Court.

1954   Warren Court strikes down Plessy v Ferguson Decision, outlawing segregation,
        by handing down the Brown v Board of Education Decision – May 17th.

1955   Rosa Parks refuses to vacate her seat; the Montgomery Bus Boycott begins
        Dec. 1st, Martin Luther King leads.

1956   Montgomery Bus Boycott ends-December; Federal District Court rules
        segregation illegal in public transportation.

1957   Eisenhower federalized troops to protect nine black students in their effort
        to integrate Central High School in Little Rock, Arkansas.
        Eisenhower signed the Civil Rights Act that establishes the Civil Rights
        Commission.

1960   Eisenhower signs another Civil Rights Act that provides greater protection
        of voting rights.

1961   John F. Kennedy took office; Black vote helped get him elected.

1963   More than 250,000 Whites and Blacks staged a March on Washington for civil
        rights. Dr. King makes his famous "Dream Speech," August 28th.
        Kennedy assassinated in Dallas, Texas, November 22nd.
        Lyndon B. Johnson becomes President.

1964   Johnson signs Civil Rights Act – July 10th. It includes public accommodations
        and fair employment sections.

1965   Johnson signs the Voting Rights Act. It provides new enforcement tools to implement Civil Rights Acts of 1957, 1960, and 1964.

1966   Two black civil rights organizations – Student Non-Violent Coordinating Committee (SNCC) and Congress of Racial Equality (CORE) – announce a "BLACK POWER" policy.

1967   Johnson appoints Thurgood Marshall as the first Black justice to the U.S. Supreme Court.

1968   Martin Luther King, Jr. is assassinated. Riots erupt in black ghettos. Richard Nixon is elected President.

1972   Plumbers break-in to the Democratic Party Headquarters at Watergate.

1974   Nixon resigns over Watergate scandal – Aug. 9th. Violence erupts in Boston over court-ordered school busing – Sept. 12th.

1976   Jimmy Carter becomes President. He receives majority of black votes.

1978   The U.S. Supreme Court rules in the Allan P. Bakke case that racial quotas are unconstitutional, a practice of affirmative action.

1980   Ronald Reagan announces his candidacy for President in Philadelphia, Mississippi where 3 civil rights workers were murdered in 1964. Reagan is elected. Many southern Whites leave the Democratic Party, and become Republicans. Conservatives control the government.

1988   George Herbert Walker Bush elected President.

1991   Bush appoints Clarence Thomas to the U.S. Supreme Court; he becomes the second black justice.

1992   William J. Clinton President; Receive heavy black voter support. Clinton appoints 4 Blacks to his cabinet.

1996   Clinton signs Welfare Reform Act. Changes individual payment to bloc grants – Aug. 22nd. Clinton reelected; Blacks continue to vote for him.

1999   Clinton is impeached, but not found guilty.

2000   George Walker Bush elected President. Disputed Florida electoral votes awarded to him over Al Gore who won the majority vote.
Bush appoints 2 Blacks to his cabinet: Colin Powell, Secretary of State; Condoleeza Rice, National Security Advisor.

2001   Al Qaeda terrorist attack on World Trade Center and the Pentagon – Sept. 11th.

2003   Congress gives Bush the authority to go to war against Iraq – March 19th.

2004   Bush reelected; gets 12% black vote, up from 9% in 2000 election.
Bush appoints Condoleezza Rice Secretary of State; Colin Powell resigns.

2005   Hurricane Katrina strikes – Aug. 29th – New Orleans heavily hit. Thousands of Blacks affected.
Bush slow to act; FEMA (Federal Emergency Management Agency) responds after four days passed.

2006   Bush signs renewal of the Voting Rights Act of 1965.

2007   Bush awards 350 Tuskegee Airmen, veterans of WWII, the Congressional Medal – March 28th.
The U.S. Supreme Court rules in two school integration cases – Seattle, Washington and Louisville, Kentucky – that using race in their integration programs violates the Constitution's guarantee of equal protection – the 14th Amendment – June 28th.

2008   Barack Obama is elected President of the United States.

Glossary

Affirmative Action: a plan or program to remedy the effects of past discrimination in employment, education, or other activities.

Al Qaeda: a terrorist organization with Islamic leanings.

Black Codes: regulations passed by southern state governments during Reconstruction to deprive newly-freed Blacks of their civil rights.

Black Power: a Philosophy practiced by some organizations that embraced Black Nationalism.

Brown v. Board of Education of Topeka (1954): a U.S. Supreme Court Decision which declared "separate but equal" education to be inherently unequal, which led to the outlawing of segregation.

Capitalism: an economic system where production and distribution of goods and services are privately owned and operated for profit in a competitive market.

Civil Rights: fundamental rights belonging to each member of society.

Civil War Amendments: the Thirteenth, Fourteenth, and Fifteenth Amendments of the U.S. Constitution passed following the Civil War which freed the slaves, granted them citizenship and guaranteed them rights of citizens.

Continental Congress: the assembly of representatives from the colonies that first met in 1774 to protest England's oppressive rule.

Constitutional Convention: the 1787 meeting held in Philadelphia where and when the U. S. Constitution was drafted.

Conservatism: a political philosophy that believes in maintaining the status quo, considered to be right in the political spectrum.

Democracy: a form of government where the people exercise control.

Depression: a period of slow business activity and high unemployment.

Diversity: variation among the members of a community or society.

Dred Scott v Sanford (1857): a Supreme Court case which held that Blacks were not U.S. Citizens and that slavery was legal in western territories.

Electoral College: the group of presidential electors that casts the official votes for president after a presidential election.

Entitlement Programs: programs federally funded to benefit various segments of the society.

FEMA: Federal Emergency Management Agency assists the nation's states and communities when disasters occur.

Genocide: mass killings of national, racial or religious groups.

Impeach: to bring charges of wrongdoing against government officials.

Imperialism: a policy of expanding national power by acquiring foreign territories or assuming political and economic control over them.

Indentured Servant: a person who agreed to work for a certain period of years in exchange for passage to America.

Isolationism: a policy that favors keeping a nation aloof from foreign involvement.

Jim Crow: laws and customs segregating Blacks from Whites: a term derived from a black character in a popular minstrel show.

Liberalism: a political philosophy that believes in change where and when necessary, considered to be left on the political spectrum.

Literacy Test: a suffrage qualification used to determine fitness for voting, used against Blacks in the South. Congress suspended its use in the Voting Rights Act (1965).

Middle America: a euphemism used by Nixon to direct government attention toward Whites, putting aside civil rights and Blacks.

Minutemen: the civilian armies of the American Revolution, so called because of their readiness for battle.

Moderantism: a political philosophy that believes a middle of the road posture to be the best approach.

Moral Majority: a euphemism used by Reagan and conservative Republicans to appeal to the "religious right."

NAACP: National Association for the Advancement of Colored People is an interracial organization founded in 1909; it advocates for Black peoples' rights, primarily through legal and political action.

Nationalism: is loyalty to one's nation and support of its interests.

Neo[-]conservatism: the reapplying of a newer and more orthodox form of conservatism.

New Deal: the political policies and programs of Franklin Roosevelt's tenure.

Nonviolent direct action: peaceful tactics used as a means of gaining one's civil or political rights.

Political Rights: all of the implicit rights guaranteed constitutionally and the implied rights found in the philosophy of natural laws.

Poll Tax: voters in many southern states were required to pay taxes to vote; the taxes were declared unlawful in 1966.

Popular Sovereignty: the ultimate political authority rests with the people.

Populism: a political bloc originating from a grassroots source.

Progressivism: a political movement that aims to improve general societal conditions.

Quotas: a method or system devised to foster political equity.

Racism: a belief that one race is superior to others; racial supremacy.

Plessy v Ferguson (1896): a Supreme Court ruling that segregation was legal by virtue of the "separate but equal" proviso.

Radical: the advocating of extremes or revolutionary changes, especially in politics or government.

Ratification: the formal approval of the U.S. Constitution by the states.

Secession: in U.S. history, the act of a state leaving the Union.

Sectionalism: a strong alliance to local interests over those of the whole nation.

Segregation: the act of separation or isolation of a race, a class, or ethnic group from the rest of the society.

The National Urban League: an organization founded in 1911 to fight discrimination in employment and industrial skills against Blacks.

Three-fifths Clause: a clause in the U.S. Constitution, no longer in effect, that each slave was not a whole person, and extrapolated to mean the status of all Blacks.

Unalienable (inalienable) Rights: the fundamental rights of the people that may not be taken away.

Veto: the constitutional power of the president to refuse to sign a bill passed by Congress.

Watergate: the site in Washington, D.C. where the scandal occurred that led to Richard Nixon's resignation from the presidency.

World Trade Center of New York: the site of one of the terrorist attacks on September 11, 2001.

BIBLIOGRAPHY

Adams, Francis D., and Barry Sanders. *Alienable Rights: the Exclusion of African Americans in a White Man's Land, 1619 – 2000.* New York: Harper Collins Publishers, 2003.

Allport, Gordon A. *The Nature of Prejudice.* New York: Doubleday, 1958.

Amar, Akhill Reed. *America's Constitution: A Biography.* New York: Random House, 2005.

Athearn, Robert G. *In Search of Canaan.* Lawrence: Regents Press of Kansas, 1978.

Bennett, Lerone, Jr. *Before the Mayflower: A History of the Negro in America 1619-1964.* Baltimore: Pelican Books, 1969.

Bennett, Lerone, Jr. *Forced Into Glory: Abraham Lincoln's Dream.* Chicago: Johnson Publishing Company, 1999.

Brown, Dee. *Bury My Heart At Wounded Knee.* New York: Holt, Rinehart & Winston, 1973.

Caro, Robert A. *The Years of Lyndon Johnson.* New York: Alfred Knopf, 1990.

Carter, Jimmy. *An Hour Before Daylight.* New York: Simon & Schuster, 2001.

Clinton, Bill. *My Life.* New York: Alfred Knopf, 2004.

DeGregorio, William A. *The Complete Book of U.S. Presidents.* New York: Random House, 1997.

Franklin, John Hope. *From Slavery to Freedom: A History of American Negroes.* New York: Vintage Books, 1969.

Good, Donnie D. *The Buffalo Soldier.* Tulsa: Thomas Gilcrease Institute of American History, 1970.

Goodwin, Doris Kearns. *Team of Rivals: The Political Genius of Abraham Lincoln.* New York: Simon & Schuster, 2005.

Hagedorn, Ann. *Savage Peace: Hope and Fear in America 1919.* New York: Simon & Schuster, 2007.

Hodges, Norman E.W. *Breaking the Chains of Bondage: Black History From Its Origins in Africa to the Present.* New York: Simon & Schuster, 1972.

Horton, James Oliver, and Lois E. Horton. *Slavery and the Making of America,* companion book. New York: Oxford Press, 2005.

Jewel, Elizabeth. *U.S. Presidents Factbook.* New York: Random House, 2005.

Johnson, Paul. *A History of the American People.* New York: Harper Collins, 1999.

Jones, Arthur C. Wade in the Water. New York: Orbis Books, 1993.

Larson, Kate Clifford. *Bound for the Promise Land: Harriet Tubman, Portrait of an American Hero.* New York: Ballantine Books, 2004.

Lincoln, C. Eric. *The Negro Pilgrimage in America.* New York: Bantam Books, 1967.

McPherson, James M. General Editor. *To the Best of My Ability: The American Presidents.* New York: D.K. Publishing Company, 2000.

Mellon, T. Matthew. *Early American Views of Negro Slavery.* New York: Mentor Books, 1969.

Meier, August, and Elliott M. Rudwick. *From Plantation to Ghetto: An Interpretive History of American Negroes.* New York: Hill and Wang, 1969.

Miller, Merle. *Plain Speaking.* New York: Berkley Publishing, 1974.

Monk, Linda R. *The Words We Live By: Your Annotated Guide to the Constitution.* New York: Stonesong Press, 2005.

Nalty, Bernard C. *Strength for the Fight: History of Black Americans in the Military.* New York: MacMillan Free Press, 1986.

Ogletree, Charles J., Jr. *All Deliberate Speed: Reflections on the First Half Century of Brown v Board of Education.* New York: W. W. Norton, 2004.

Painter, Nell Irvin. *Exodusters: Migration to Kansas After Reconstruction.* Lawrence: University Press of Kansas, 1986.

Painter, Nell Irvin. *Standing at Armageddon: The United States, 1877-1919.* New York: W.W. Norton, 1987.

Phillips, Kevin. *American Theocracy: The Peril and Politics of Radical Religion, Oil, and Borrowed Money in the 21st Century.* New York: Viking, 2006.

Reeves, Pamela. *Ellis Island.* New York: Dorset Press, 1991.

Roberts, Paul M. and Paula A Franklin. *A Comprehensive United States History.* New York: AMSCO School Publications, 1986.

Schecter, Barnet. *The Devils Own Work: The Civil War Draft Riots and the Fight to Reconstruct America.* New York: Walker & Company, 2006.

Stamps, Kenneth M. *The Era of Reconstruction 1865-1877.* New York: Vintage Books, 1965.

Taranto, James. Editor. *Presidential Leadership: Rating the Best and the Worst in the White House.* New York: Wall Street Journal Book Free Press, 2004.

Time Magazine Editors. *The Making of America: Life, Liberty and the Pursuit of a Nation.* New York: Time Books, 2005.

Walker, Wyatt Tee. *Somebody's Calling My Name.* Valley Forge, Pa: Judson Press, 1979.

West, Cornel. *Race Matters.* New York: Vintage Books, 2001.

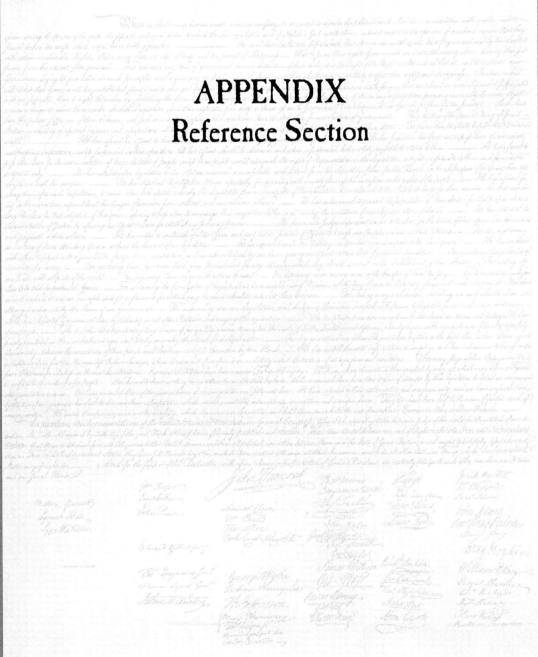

APPENDIX
Reference Section

Declaration of Independence

IN CONGRESS, JULY 4, 1776.

A DECLARATION

BY THE REPRESENTATIVES OF THE

UNITED STATES OF AMERICA,

IN GENERAL CONGRESS ASEMBLED.

When, in the course of human events, it becomes necessary for one people to dissolve the political bands which have connected them with another, and to assume among the powers of the earth, the separate and equal station to which the laws of nature and of nature's God entitle them, a decent respect to the opinions of mankind requires that they should declare the causes which impel them to the separation.

We hold these truths to be self-evident, that all men are created equal, that they are endowed by their Creator with certain unalienable rights, that among these are life, liberty and the pursuit of happiness. That to secure these rights, governments are instituted among men, deriving their just powers from the consent of the governed. That whenever any form of government becomes destructive to these ends, it is the right of the people to alter or to abolish it, and to institute new government, laying its foundation on such principles and organizing its powers in such form, as to them shall seem most likely to effect their safety and happiness. Prudence, indeed, will dictate that governments long established should not be changed for light and transient causes; and accordingly all experience hath shown that mankind are more disposed to suffer, while evils are sufferable, than to right themselves by abolishing the forms to which they are accustomed. But when a long train of abuses and usurpations, pursuing invariably the same object evinces a design to reduce them under absolute despotism, it is their right, it is

their duty, to throw off such government, and to provide new guards for their future security. Such has been the patient sufferance of these colonies; and such is now the necessity which constrains them to alter their former systems of government. The history of the present King of Great Britain is a history of repeated injuries and usurpations, all having in direct object the establishment of an absolute tyranny over these states. To prove this, let facts be submitted to a candid world.

He has refused his assent to laws, the most wholesome and necessary for the public good.

He has forbidden his governors to pass laws of immediate and pressing importance, unless suspended in their operation till his assent should be obtained; and when so suspended, he has utterly neglected to attend to them.

He has refused to pass other laws for the accommodation of large districts of people, unless those people would relinquish the right of representation in the legislature, a right inestimable to them and formidable to tyrants only.

He has called together legislative bodies at places unusual, uncomfortable, and distant from the depository of their public records, for the sole purpose of fatiguing them into compliance with his measures.

He has dissolved representative houses repeatedly, for opposing with manly firmness his invasions on the rights of the people.

He has refused for a long time, after such dissolutions, to cause others to be elected; whereby the legislative powers, incapable of annihilation, have returned to the people at large for their exercise; the state remaining in the meantime exposed to all the dangers of invasion from without, and convulsions within.

• This is the original text. Passages in brackets indicate that they were affected by Amendments.

He has endeavored to prevent the population of these states; for that purpose obstructing the laws for naturalization of foreigners; refusing to pass others to encourage their migration hither, and raising the conditions of new appropriations of lands.

He has obstructed the administration of justice, by refusing his assent to laws for establishing judiciary powers.

He has made judges dependent on his will alone, for the tenure of their offices, and the amount and payment of their salaries.

He has erected a multitude of new offices, and sent hither swarms of officers to harass our people, and eat out their substance.

He has kept among us, in times of peace, standing armies without the consent of our legislature.

He has affected to render the military independent of and superior to civil power.

He has combined with others to subject us to a jurisdiction foreign to our constitution, and unacknowledged by our laws; giving his assent to their acts of pretended legislation:

For quartering large bodies of armed troops among us:

For protecting them, by mock trial, from punishment for any murders which they should commit on the inhabitants of these states:

For cutting off our trade with all parts of the world:

For imposing taxes on us without our consent:

For depriving us in many cases, of the benefits of trial by jury:

For transporting us beyond seas to be tried for pretended offenses:

For abolishing the free system of English laws in a neighboring province, establishing therein an arbitrary government, and enlarging its boundaries so as to render it at once an example and fit instrument for introducing the same absolute rule in these colonies:

For taking away our charters, abolishing our most valuable laws, and altering fundamentally the forms of our governments:

For suspending our own legislatures, and declaring themselves invested with power to legislate for us in all cases whatsoever.

He has abdicated government here, by declaring us out of his protection and waging war against us.

He has plundered our seas, ravaged our coasts, burned our towns, and destroyed the lives of our people.

He is at this time transporting large armies of foreign mercenaries to complete the works of death, desolation and tyranny, already begun with circumstances of cruelty and perfidy scarcely paralleled in the most barbarous ages, and totally unworthy the head of a civilized nation.

He has constrained our fellow citizens taken captive on the high seas to bear arms against their country, to become the executioners of their friends and brethren, or to fall themselves by their hands.

He has excited domestic insurrections amongst us, and has endeavored to bring on the inhabitants of our frontiers, the merciless Indian savages, whose known rule of warfare, is undistinguished destruction of all ages, sexes and conditions.

In every stage of these oppressions we have petitioned for redress in the most humble terms: our repeated petitions have been answered only by repeated injury. A prince, whose character is thus marked by every act which may define a tyrant, is unfit to be the ruler of a free people.

Nor have we been wanting in attention to our British brethren. We have warned them from time to time of attempts by their legislature to extend an unwarrantable jurisdiction over us. We have reminded them of the circumstances of our emigration and settlement here. We have appealed to their native justice and magnanimity, and we have conjured them by the ties of our common kindred to disavow these usurpations, which, would inevitably interrupt our connections and correspondence. They too have been deaf to the voice of justice and of consanguinity. We must, therefore, acquiesce in the necessity, which denounces our separation, and hold them, as we hold the rest of mankind, enemies in war, in peace friends.

We, therefore, the representatives of the United States of America, in General Congress, assembled, appealing to the Supreme Judge of the world for the rectitude of our intentions, do, in the name, and by the authority of the good people of these colonies, solemnly publish and declare, that these united colonies are, and of right ought to be free and independent states; that they are absolved from all allegiance to the British Crown, and that all political connection between them and the state of Great Britain, is and ought to be totally dissolved; and that as free and independent states, they have full power to levy war, conclude peace, contract alliances, establish commerce, and to do all other acts and things which independent states may of right do. And for the support of this declaration, with a firm reliance on the protection of Divine Providence, we mutually pledge to each other our lives, our fortunes and our sacred honor.

Signed by ORDER and in BEHALF of the
CONGRESS,
JOHN HANCOCK, PRESIDENT

Signers of the Declaration of Independence

New-Hampshire
Josiah Bartlett,
Wm. Whipple,
Matthew Thornton.

Delaware
Casar Rodney,
Geo. Read,
(ThoM:Kean.)

Massachusetts-Bay.
Saml. Adams,
John Adams,
Robt. Treat Paine,
Elbridge Gerry.

**Rhode-Island
and Providence, &c.**
Step. Hopkins,
William Ellery.

Connecticut.
Roger Sherman,
Saml. Huntington,
Wm. Williams,
Oliver Wolcott.

New-York
Wm. Floyd,
Phil. Livingston,
Frans. Lewis,
Lewis Morris.

New-Jersey
Richd. Stockton,
Jno. Witherspoon,
Fras. Hopkinson,
John Hart,
Abra. Clark.

Pennsylvania
Robt. Morris,
Benjamin Rush,

Benjamin Rush,
Benja. Franklin,
John Morton,
Geo. Clymer,
Jas. Smith
Geo. Taylor,
James Wilson,
Geo. Ross.

Maryland
Samuel Chase,
Wm. Paca,
Thos. Stone,
Charles Carroll, of Carrollton.

Virginia
George Wythe,
Richard Henry Lee,
Ths. Jefferson,
Benja. Harrison,
Thos. Nelson, jr.
Francis Lightfoot Lee,
Carter Braxton.

North-Carolina.
Wm. Hooper Joseph Hewes,
John Penn.

South-Carolina.
Edward Rutledge,
Thos. Heyward, junr.
Thomas Lynch, junr.
Arthur Middleton.

Georgia.
Button Gwinnett,
Lyman Hall,
Geo. Walton.

According to the authenticated list printed by order of Congress of January 18,1777. Braces, spelling, and abbreviations of names conform to original printed list.

The Constitution of the United States of America

PREAMBLE

We the people of the United States, in order to form a more perfect Union, establish justice, insure domestic tranquility, provide for the common defense, promote the general welfare, and secure the blessings of liberty to ourselves and our posterity, do ordain and establish this Constitution for the United States of America.

ARTICLE I
Section One
Legislative Power

All legislative powers herein granted shall be vested in a Congress of the United States, which shall consist of a Senate and House of Representatives.

Section Two
House of Representatives, How Constituted Power of Impeachment

1. The House of Representatives shall be composed of members chosen every second year by the people of the several states, and the electors in each state shall have the qualifications requisite for electors of the most numerous branch of the state legislature.

2. No person shall be a Representative who shall not have attained to the age of twenty-five years, and been seven years a citizen of the United States, and who shall not, when elected, be an inhabitant of that state in which he shall be chosen.

3. [Representatives and direct taxes shall be ap-porioned among the several states which may be included within this Union, according to their respective numbers, which shall be determined by adding to the whole number of free persons, including those bound to service for a term of years, and excluding Indians not taxed, three fifths of all other persons.]* The actual enumeration shall be made within three years after the first meeting of the Congress of the United States, and within every subsequent term of ten years, in such manner as they shall by law direct. The number of Representatives shall not exceed one for every thirty thousand, but each state shall have at least one Representative; and until such enumeration shall be made, the state of New Hampshire shall be entitled to choose three, Massachusetts eight, Rhode Island and Providence Plantations one, Connecticut five, New York six, New Jersey four, Pennsylvania eight, Delaware one, Maryland six, Virginia ten, North Carolina five, South Carolina five, and Georgia three.

4. When vacancies happen in the representation from any state, the executive authority thereof shall issue writs of election to fill such vacancies.

5. The House of Representatives shall choose their speaker and other officers; and shall have the sole power of impeachment.

Section Three
The Senate, How Constituted

1. [The Senate of the United States shall be composed of two Senators from each state, chosen by the legislature thereof, for six years; and each Senator shall have one vote.]

2. Immediately after they shall be assembled in consequence of the first election, they shall be divided as equally as may be into three classes. The seats of the Senators of the first class shall be vacated at the expiration of the second year, of the second class at the expiration of the fourth year, and of the third class at the expiration of the sixth year, so that one third maybe chosen every second year; and if vacancies happen by resignation, or otherwise, during the recess of the legislature of any state, the executive thereof may make temporary appointments [until the next meeting of the legislature, which shall then fill such vacancies.]

3. No person shall be a Senator who shall not have attained to the age of thirty years, and been nine years a citizen of the United States, and who shall not, when elected, be an inhabitant of that state for which he. shall be chosen.

4. The Vice-President of the United States shall be president of the Senate, but shall have no vote unless they be equally divided.

5. The Senate shall choose their other officers, and also a president pro tempore, in the absence of the Vice-President, or when he shall exercise the office of President of the United States.

6. The Senate shall have the sole power to try all impeachments. When sitting for that purpose, they shall be on oath or affirmation. When the President of the United States is tried, the Chief Justice shall preside; and no person shall be convicted without the concurrence of two-thirds of the members present.

7. Judgment in cases of impeachment shall not extend further than to removal from office, and disqualification to hold and enjoy any office of honor, trust, or profit under the United States; but the party convicted shall nevertheless be liable and subject to indictment, trial, judgment, and punishment, according to law.

Section Four

Election of Senators and Representatives

1. The times, places, and manner of holding elections for Senators and Representatives shall be prescribed in each state by the legislature thereof, but the Congress may at any time by law make or alter such regulations except as to the place of choosing Senators.

2. [The Congress shall assemble at least once in every year, and such meeting shall be on the first Monday in December, unless they shall by law appoint a different day.]

Section Five

Powers, Quorum, Journals, Meetings, Adjournments

1. Each House shall be the judge of the elections, returns, and qualifications of its own members, and a majority of each shall constitute a quorum to do business; but a smaller number may adjourn from day to day, and may be authorized to compel the attendance of absent members, in such manner, and under such penalties as each House may provide.

2. Each House may determine the rules of its proceedings, punish its members for disorderly behavior, and, with the concurrence of two-thirds, expel a member.

3. Each House shall keep ajournai of its proceedings, and from time to time publish the same, excepting such parts as may in their judgment require secrecy; and the yeas and nays of the members of either House on any question shall, at the desire of one-fifth of those present, be entered on the journal.

4. Neither House, during the session of Congress, shall, without the consent of the other, adjourn for more than three days, nor to any other place than that in which the two Houses shall be sitting.

Section Six

Compensation, Privileges, Disabilities

1. The Senators and Representatives shall receive a compensation for their services, to be ascertained by law, and paid out of the Treasury of the United States. They shall in all cases, except treason, felony and breach of the peace, be privileged from arrest during their attendance at the session of their respective Houses, and in going to and returning from the same; and for any speech or debate in either House, they shall not be questioned in any other place.

2. No Senator or Representative shall, during the time for which he was elected, be appointed to any civil office under the authority of the United States, which shall have been created, or the emoluments whereof shall have been increased during such time; and no person holding any office under the United States shall be a member of either House during his continuance in office.

Section Seven

Procedure in Passing Bills, Orders, and Resolutions

1. All bills for raising revenue shall originate in the House of Representatives; but the Senate may propose or concur with amendments as on other bills.

2. Every bill which shall have passed the House of Representatives and the Senate, shall, before it become a law, be presented to the President of the United States; if he approve he shall sign it, but if not he shall return it, with his objections, to that House in which it shall have originated, who shall enter the objections at large on their journal, and proceed to reconsider it. If after such reconsideration two-thirds of that House shall agree to pass the bill, it shall be sent, together with the objections, to the other House, by which it shall likewise be reconsidered, and if approved by two-thirds of that House, it shall become a law. But in all such cases the votes of both Houses shall be determined by yeas and nays, and the names of the persons voting for and against the bill shall be entered on the journal of each House respectively. If any bill shall not be returned by the President within ten days (Sundays excepted) after it shall have been presented to him, the same shall be a law, in like manner as if he had signed it, unless the Congress by their adjournment prevent its return, in which case it shall not be a law.

3. Every order, resolution, or vote to which theconcurrence of the Senate and House of Representatives may be necessary (except on a question of adjournment) shall be presented to the President of the United States; and before the same shall take effect, shall be approved by him, or being disapproved by him, shall be repassed by two-thirds of the Senate and House of Representatives, according to the rules and limitations prescribed in the case of a bill.

Section Eight

Powers of Congress The Congress shall have power:

1. To lay and collect taxes, duties, imposts and excises, to pay the debts and provide for the common defense and general welfare of the United States; but all duties, imposts and excises shall be uniform throughout the United States;

2. To borrow money on the credit of the United States;

3. To regulate commerce with foreign nations, and among the several States, and with the Indian tribes;

4. To establish an uniform rule of naturalization, and uniform laws on the subject of bankruptcies throughout the United States;

5. To coin money, regulate the value thereof, and of foreign coin, and fix the standard of weights and measures;

6. To provide for the punishment of counterfeiting the securities and current coin of the United States;

7. To establish post offices and post roads;

8. To promote the progress of science and useful arts, by securing for limited time to authors and inventors the exclusive right to their respective writings and discoveries;

9. To constitute tribunals inferior to the Supreme Court;

10. To define and punish piracies and felonies committed on the high seas, and offenses against the law of nations;

11. To declare war, grant letters of marque and reprisal, and make rules concerning captures on land and water;

12. To raise and support armies, but no appropriation of money to that use shall be for a longer term than two years;

13. To provide and maintain a navy;

14. To make rules for the government and regulation of the land and naval forces;

15. To provide for calling forth the militia to execute the laws of the Union, suppress insurrections and repel invasions;

16. To provide for organizing, arming and disciplining the militia, and for governing such part of them as may be employed in the service of the United States, reserving to the states respectively, the appointment of the officers, and the authority of training the militia according to the discipline prescribed by Congress;

17. To exercise exclusive legislation in all cases whatsoever, over such district (not exceeding ten miles square) as may, by session of particular states, and the acceptance of Congress, become the seat of the government of the United States, and to exercise like authority over all places purchased by the consent of the legislature of the state in which the same shall be, for the erection of forts, magazines, arsenals, dockyards, and other needful buildings; - and

18. To make all laws which shall be necessary and proper for carrying into execution the foregoing powers, and all other powers vested by this Constitution in the Government of the United States, or in any department or officer thereof.

Section Nine
Limitations upon Powers of Congress

1. The migration or importation of such persons as any of the states now existing shall think proper to admit, shall not be prohibited by the Congress prior to the year one thousand eight hundred and eight, but a tax or duty may be imposed on such importation, not exceeding ten dollars for each person.

2. The privilege of the writ of habeas corpus shall not be suspended, unless when in cases of rebellion or invasion the public safety may require it.

3. No bill of attainder or ex post facto law shall be passed.

4. No capitation, or other direct, tax shall be laid, unless in proportion to the census or enumeration herein before directed to be taken.

5. No tax or duty shall be laid on articles exported from any state.

6. No preference shall be given by any regulation of commerce or revenue to the ports of one state over those of another; nor shall vessels bound to, or from one state, be obliged to enter clear, or pay duties in another.

7. No money shall be drawn from the treasury but in consequence of appropriations made by law, and a regular statement and account of the receipts and expenditures of all public money shall be published from time to time.

8. No title of nobility shall be granted by the United States: And no person holding any office of profit or trust under them, shall, without the consent of the Congress, accept of any present, emolument, office, or title, of any kind whatever from any king, prince, or foreign state.

Section Ten
Restrictions upon Powers of States

1. No state shall enter into any treaty, alliance, or confederation; grant letters of marque and reprisal; coin money; emit bills of credit; make any thing but gold and silver coin a tender in payment of debts; pass any bill of attainder, ex post facto law, or law impairing the obligation of contracts, or grant any title of nobility.

2. No state shall, without the consent of the Congress, lay any imposts or duties on imports or exports, except what may be absolutely necessary for executing its inspection laws; and the net produce of all duties and

imposts, laid by any state on imports or exports, shall be for the use of the treasury of the United States; and all such laws shall be subject to the revision and control of the Congress.

3. No state shall, without the consent of Congress, lay any duty of tonnage, keep troops, or ships of war in time of peace, enter into any agreement or compact with another state or with a foreign power, or engage in war, unless actually invaded, or in such imminent danger as will not admit of delay.

ARTICLE II
Section One
*Executive Powers, Electors, Qualifications
of the President*

1. The executive power shall be vested in a President of the United States of America. He shall hold his office during the term of four years, and, together with the Vice-President, chosen for the same term, be elected, as follows:

2. Each state shall appoint, in such manner as the legislature therefore may direct, a number of electors, equal to the whole number of Senators and Representatives to which the state may be entitled in the Congress; but no Senator or Representative, or person holding an office of trust or profit under the United States, shall be appointed an elector.

3. [The Electors shall meet in their respective states, and vote by ballot for two persons, of whom one at least shall not be an inhabitant of the same state with themselves. And they shall make a list of all the persons voted for, and of the number of votes for each; which list they shall sign and certify, and transmit sealed to the seat of the Government of the United States, directed to the President of the Senate. The President of the Senate shall, in the presence of the Senate and House of Representatives, open all the certificates, and the votes shall then be counted. The person having the greatest number of votes shall be the President, if such number be a majority of the whole number of electors appointed; and if there be more than one who have such majority, and have an equal number of votes, then the House of Representatives shall immediately choose by ballot one of them for President; and if no person have a majority, then from the five highest on the list the said House shall in like manner choose the President. But in choosing the President, the votes shall be taken by states, the representation from each state having one vote; a quorum for this purpose shall consist of a member or members from two-thirds of the states, and a majority of all the states shall be necessary to a choice. In every case, after the choice of the President, the person having the greatest number of votes of the electors shall be the Vice-President. But if there should remain two or more who have equal votes, the Senate shall choose from them by ballot the Vice-President.]

4. The Congress may determine the time of choosing the electors, and the day on which they shall give their votes; which day shall be the same throughout the United States.

5. No person except a natural born citizen, or a citizen of the United States, at the time of the adoption of this Constitution, shall be eligible to the office of President; neither shall any person be eligible to that office who shall not have attained to the age of thirty-five years, and been fourteen years a resident within the United States.

6. [In case of the removal of the President from office, or of his death, resignation, or inability to discharge the powers and duties of the said office, the same shall devolve on the Vice-President, and the Congress may by law provide for the case of removal, death, resignation or inability, both of the President and Vice-President, declaring what officer shall then act as President, and such officer shall act accordingly, until the disability be removed, or a President shall be elected.]

7. The President shall, at stated times, receive for his services, a compensation, which shall neither be increased nor diminished during the period for which he shall have been elected, and he shall not receive within that period any other emolument from the United States, or any of them.

8. Before he enter the execution of this office, he shall take the following oath or affirmation:

"I do solemnly swear (or affirm) that I will faithfully execute the office of President of the United States, and will to the best of my ability, preserve, protect and defend the Constitution of the United States."

Section Two
Powers and Duties of the President

1. The President shall be Commander in Chief of the army and navy of the United States, and of the militia of the several states, when called into the actual service of the United States; he may require the opinion, in writing, of the principal officer in each of the executive departments, upon any subject relating to the duties of their respective offices, and he shall have power to grant reprieves and pardons for offenses against the United States, except in cases of impeachment.

2. He shall have power, by and with the advice and consent of the Senate, to make treaties, provided two-thirds of the Senators present concur; and he shall nominate, and by and with the advice and consent of the Senate, shall appoint ambassadors, other public ministers and consuls, judges of the Supreme Court, and all other officers of the United States, whose appointments are not herein otherwise provided for, and which shall be established by law; but the Congress may by law vest the appointment of such inferior officers, as they think proper, in the President alone, in the courts of law, or in the heads of departments.

3. The President shall have power to fill up all vacancies that may happen during the recess of the Senate, by granting commissions which shall expire at the end of their next session.

Section Three
Powers and Duties of the President

He shall from time to time give to the Congress information of the state of the Union, and recommend to their consideration such measures as he shall judge necessary and expedient; he may, on extraordinary occasions, convene both Houses, or either of them, and in case of disagreement between them, with respect to the time of adjournment, he may adjourn them to such time as he shall think proper; he shall receive ambassadors and other public ministers; he shall take care that the laws be faithfully executed, and shall commission all the officers of the United States.

Section Four
Forfeiture of Offices for Crimes

The President, Vice-President and all civil officers of the United States, shall be removed from office on impeachment for, and conviction of, treason, bribery, or other high crimes and misdemeanors.

ARTICLE III
Section One
Judicial Powers, Tenure of Office

The judicial power of the United States, shall be vested in one Supreme Court, and in such inferior courts as the Congress may from time to time ordain and establish. The judges, both of the Supreme and inferior courts, shall hold their offices during good behavior, and shall, at stated times, receive for their services a compensation, which shall not be diminished during their continuance in office.

Section Two
Cases to Which Judicial Power Extends

1. The judicial power shall extend to all cases, in law and equity, arising under this Constitution, the laws of the United States, and treaties made, or which shall be made, under their authority, to all cases affecting ambassadors, other public ministers and consuls; to all cases of admiralty and maritime jurisdiction; to controversies to which the United States shall be a party; to controversies between two or more states; between a state and citizens of another state; between citizens of different states; between citizens of the same state claiming lands under grants of different states, and [between a state, or the citizens thereof, and foreign states, citizens or subjects.]

2. In all cases affecting ambassadors, other public ministers and consuls, and those in which a state shall be party, the Supreme Court shall have original jurisdiction. In all the other cases before mentioned, the Supreme Court shall have appellate jurisdiction, both as to law and fact, with such exceptions, and under such regulations as the Congress shall make.

3. The trial of all crimes, except in cases of impeachment, shall be by the jury; and such trial shall be held in the state where the said crimes shall have been committed; but when not committed within any state, the trial shall be at such place or places as the Congress may by law have directed.

Section Three
Treason, Proof, and Punishment

1. Treason against the United States, shall consist only in levying war against them, or in adhering to their enemies, giving them aid and comfort. No person shall be convicted of treason unless on the testimony of two witnesses to the same overt act, or on confession in open court.

2. The Congress shall have power to declare the punishment of treason, but no attainder of treason shall work corruption of blood or forfeiture except during the life of the person attainted.

ARTICLE IV
Section One

Faith and Credit among States Full faith and credit shall be given in each state to the public acts, records, and judicial proceedings of every other state. And the Congress may by general laws prescribe the manner in which such acts, records and proceedings shall be proved, and the effect thereof.

Section Two
Surrender of Fugitives

1. The citizens of each state shall be entitled to all privileges and immunities of citizens in the several states.

2. A person charged in any state with treason, felony, or other crime, who shall flee from justice, and be found in another state, shall on demand of the executive authority of the state, from which he fled, be delivered up, to be removed to the state having jurisdiction of the crime.

3. [No person held to service or labor in one state, under the laws thereof, escaping into another, shall, in consequence of any law or regulation therein, be discharged from such service or labor, but shall be delivered up on claim of the party to whom such service or labor may be due.]

Section Three
Admission of New States

1. New states may be admitted by the Congress into this Union, but no new state shall be formed or erected within the jurisdiction of any other state; nor any state be formed by the junction of two or more states, or parts of states, without the consent of the legislatures of the states concerned as well as of the Congress.

2. The Congress shall have power to dispose of and make all needful rules and regulations respecting the territory or other property belonging to the United States, and nothing in this Constitution shall be so construed as to prejudice any claims of the United States, or of any particular state.

Section Four
Guarantee of Republican Government

The United States shall guarantee to every state in this Union a republican form of government, and shall protect each of them against invasion; and on application of the legislature, or of the executive (when the legislature cannot be convened) against domestic violence.

ARTICLE V
Amendment of the Constitution

The Congress, whenever two-thirds of both Houses shall deem it necessary, shall propose amendments to this Constitution, or, on the application of the legislatures of two-thirds of the several states, shall call a convention for proposing amendments, which, in either case, shall be valid to all intents and purposes, as part of this Constitution, when ratified by A the legislatures of three-fourths of the several states, or by conventions in three-fourths thereof, as the one or the other mode of ratification may be proposed by the Congress; provided that no amendment which may be made prior to the year one thousand eight hundred and eight shall in any manner affect the first and fourth clauses in the ninth section of the first article; and that no state, without its consent, shall be deprived of its equal suffrage in the Senate.

ARTICLE VI
Miscellaneous Provisions

1. AU debts contracted and engagements entered into, before the adoption of this Constitution, shall be as valid against the United States under this Constitution, as under the confederation.

2. This Constitution, and the laws of the United States which shall be made in pursuance thereof; and all treaties made, or which shall be made, under the authority of the United States, shall be the supreme law of the land; and the judges in every state shall be bound thereby, anything in the Constitution or laws of any state to the contrary notwithstanding.

3. The Senators and Representatives before mentioned, and the members of the several state legislatures, and all executive and judicial officers, both of the United States and of the several states, shall be bound by oath or affirmation, to support this Constitu¬tion; but no religious test shall ever be required as a qualification to any office or public trust under the United States.

ARTICLE VII
Ratification and Establishment

The ratification of the conventions of nine states, shall be sufficient for the establishment of this Constitution between the states so ratifying the same.

Done in Convention, by the unanimous consent of the States present, the seventeenth day of September, in the year of our Lord one thousand seven hundred and eighty-seven, and of the independence of the United States of America the twelfth. In witness whereof we have hereunto subscribed our names.

George Washington, President,
and Deputy from Virginia.

(This Constitution was adopted on September 17, 1787 by the Constitutional Convention, and was declared ratified on July 2, 1788.)

Signers of the Constitution

New Hampshire
John Langdon
Nicholas Gilman

Massachusetts
Nathaniel Gorham
Rufus King

Connecticut
William Samuel Johnson
Roger Sherman

New York
Alexander Hamilton

New Jersey
William Livingston
David Brearley
William Paterson
Jonathan Dayton

Pennsylvania
Benjamin Franklin
Thomas Mifflin
Robert Morris
George Clymer
Thomas Fitzsimons
Jared Ingersoll
James Wilson
Gouverneur Morris

Delaware
George Read Gunning
Bedford, Jr. John
Dickinson Richard
Bassett Jacob Broom

Maryland
James McHenry
Daniel of St. Tho. Jenifer Daniel Carrol

Virginia
John Blair
James Madison, Junior.

North Carolina
William Blount
Richard Dodds Spaight
Hugh Williamson

South Carolina
John Rutledge
Charles Cotesworth Pinckney
Charles Pinckney
Pierce Butler

Georgia
William Few Abraham Baldwin
Attest: William Jackson, Secretary

AMENDMENTS TO THE CONSTITUTION

Since 1787, twenty-six amendments have been proposed by the Congress and ratified by the several states, pursuant to the fifth Article of the original Constitution.

Amendment I

Congress shall make no law respecting an establishment of religion, or prohibiting the free exercise thereof; or abridging the freedom of speech, or of the press; or the right of the people peaceably to assemble, and to petition the Government for a redress of grievances. (Ratified December, 1791.)

Amendment II

A well regulated Militia, being necessary to the security of a free State, the right of the people to keep and bear Arms, shall not be infringed. (Ratified December, 1791.)

Amendment III

No Soldier shall, in time of peace be quartered in any house without the consent of the Owner, nor in time of war, but in a manner to be prescribed by law. (Ratified December, 1791.)

Amendment IV

The right of the people to be secure in their persons, houses, papers, and effects, against unreasonable searches and seizures, shall not be violated, and no Warrants shall issue, but upon probable cause, supported by Oath or affirmation, and particularly describing the place to be searched, and the persons or things to be seized. (Ratified December, 1791.)

Amendment V

No person shall be held to answer for a capital, or otherwise infamous crime, unless on a presentment or indictment of a Grand Jury, except in cases arising in the land or naval forces, or in the Militia, when in actual service in time of War or public danger; nor shall any person be subject for the same offence to be twice put in jeopardy of life or limb; nor shall be compelled in any criminal case to be a witness against himself, nor be deprived of life, liberty, or property, without due process of law; nor shall private property be taken for public use, without just compensation. (Ratified December, 1791.)

Amendment VI

In all criminal prosecutions, the accused shall enjoy the right to a speedy and public trial, by an impartial jury of the State and district wherein the crime shall have been committed, which district shall have been previously ascertained by law, and to be informed of the nature and cause of the accusation; to be confronted with the witnesses against him; to have compulsory process for obtaining witnesses in his favor, w and to have the assistance of counsel for his defence. (Ratified December, 1791.)

Amendment VII

In Suits at common law, where the value in controversy shall exceed twenty dollars, the right of trial by jury shall be preserved, and no fact tried by a jury, shall be otherwise re-examined in any Court of the United States, than according to the rules of the common law. (Ratified December, 1791.)

Amendment VIII

Excessive bail shall not be required, nor excessive fines imposed, nor cruel and unusual punishments inflicted. (Ratified December, 1791.)

Amendment IX

The enumeration in the Constitution, of certain rights, shall not be construed to deny or disparage others retained by the people. (Ratified December, 1791.)

Amendment X

The powers not delegated to the United States by the Constitution, nor prohibited by it to the States, are reserved to the States respectively, or to the people. (Ratified December, 1791.)

Amendment XI

The Judicial power of the United States shall not be construed to extend to any suit in law or equity, commenced or prosecuted against one of the United States by Citizens of another State, or by Citizens or Subjects of any Foreign State. (Ratified February, 1795.)

Amendment XII

The Electors shall meet in their respective states, and vote by ballot for President and Vice-President, one of whom, at least, shall not be an inhabitant of the same state with themselves; they shall name in their ballots the person voted for as President, and in distinct ballots the person voted for as Vice-President, and they shall make distinct lists of all persons voted for as President, and of all persons voted for as Vice-President, and of the number of votes for each, which lists they shall sign and certify, and transmit sealed to the seat of the government of the United States, directed to the President of the Senate;—The President of the Senate shall, in the presence of the Senate and House of Representatives, open all the certificates and the votes shall then be counted;—The person having the greatest number of votes for President, shall be the President, if such number be a majority of the whole number of Electors appointed; and if no person have such majority, then from the persons having the highest numbers not exceeding three on the list of those voted for as President, the House of Representatives shall choose immediately, by ballot, the President. But in choosing the President, the votes shall be taken by states, the representation from each state having one vote; a quorum for this purpose shall consist of a member or members from two-thirds of the states, and a majority of all the states shall be necessary to a choice. [And if the House of Representatives shall not choose a President whenever the right of choice shall devolve upon them, before the fourth day of March next following, then the Vice-President shaU act as President, as in the case of the death or other constitutional disability of the President.] The person having the greatest number of votes as Vice-President, shall be the Vice-President, if such number be a majority of the whole number of Electors appointed, and if no person have a majority, then from the two highest numbers on the list, the Senate shall choose the Vice-President; a quorum for the purpose shall consist of two-thirds of the whole number of Senators, and a majority of the whole number shall be necessary to a choice. But no person constitutionally ineligible to the office of President shall be eligible to that of Vice-President of the United States. (Ratified June, 1804.)

Amendment XIII

Section 1. Neither slavery nor involuntary servitude, except as a punishment for crime whereof the party shall have been duly convicted, shall exist within the United States, or any place subject to their jurisdiction.

Section 2. Congress shall have power to enforce this article by appropriate legislation. (Ratified December, 1865.)

Amendment XIV

Section 1. All persons born or naturalized in the United States, and subject to the jurisdiction thereof, are citizens of the United States and of the State wherein they reside. No State shall make or enforce any law which shall abridge the privileges or immunities of citizens of the United States; nor shall any State deprive any person of life, liberty, or property, without due process of law; nor deny to any person within its jurisdiction the equal protection of the laws.

Section 2. Representatives shall be apportioned among the several States according to their respective numbers, counting the whole number of persons in each State, excluding Indians not taxed. But when the right to vote at any election for the choice of electors for President and Vice President of the United States, Representatives in Congress, the Executive and Judicial officers of a State, or the members of the Legislature thereof, is denied to any of the male inhabitants of such State, being twenty-one years of age, and citizens of the United States, or in any way abridged, except for participation in rebellion, or other crime, the basis of representation therein shall be reduced in the proportion which the number of such male citizens shall bear to the whole number of male citizens twenty-one years of age in such State.

Section 3. No person shall be a Senator or a Representative in Congress, or elector of President and Vice-President, or hold any office, civil or military, under the United States, or under any State, who, having previously taken an oath, as a member of Congress, or as an officer of the United States, or as a member of any State legislature, or as an executive or judicial officer of any State, to support the Constitution of the United States, shall have engaged in insurrection or rebellion against the same, or given aid or comfort to the enemies thereof. But Congress may by a vote of two-thirds of each House, remove such dis-ability.

Section 4. The validity of the public debt of the United States, authorized by law, including debts incurred for payment of pensions and bounties for services in suppressing insurrection or rebellion, shall not be questioned. But neither the United States nor any State shall assume or pay any debt or obligation incurred in aid of insurrection or rebellion against the United States, or any claim for the loss or emancipation of any slave; but all such debts, obligations and claims shall be held illegal and void.

Section 5. The Congress shall have power to enforce, by appropriate legislation, the provisions of this article. (Ratified July, 1868.)

Amendment XV

Section 1. The right of citizens of the United States to vote shall not be denied or abridged by the United States or by any State on account of race, color, or previous condition of servitude.

Section 2. The Congress shall have power to enforce this article by appropriate legislation. (Ratified February, 1870.)

Amendment XVI

The Congress shall have power to lay and collect taxes on incomes, from whatever source derived, without apportionment among the several States, and without regard to any census or enumeration. (Ratified February, 1913.)

Amendment XVII

The Senate of the United States shall be composed of two Senators from each State, elected by the people thereof, for six years; and each Senator shall have one vote. The electors in each State shall have the qualifications requisite for electors of the most numerous branch of the State legislatures.

When vacancies happen in the representation of any State in the Senate, the executive authority of such State shall issue writs of election to fill such vacancies: *Provided*, That the legislature of any State may empower the executive thereof to make temporary appointments until the people fill the vacancies by election as the legislature may direct.

This amendment shall not be so construed as to affect the election or term of any Senator chosen before it becomes valid as part of the Constitution. (Ratified April, 1913.)

Amendment XVIII

[Section 1. After one year from the ratification of this article the manufacture, sale, or transportation of intoxicating liquors within, the importation thereof into, or the exportation thereof from the United States and all territory subject to the jurisdiction thereof for beverage purposes is hereby prohibited.

Section 2. The Congress and Several States shall have concurrent power to enforce this article by appropriate legislation.

Section 3. This article shall be inoperative unless it shall have been ratified as an amendment to the Constitution by the legislatures of the several States, as provided in the Constitution, within seven years from the date of the submission hereof to the States by the Congress.] (Ratified January, 1919.)

Amendment XIX

The right of citizens of the United States to vote shall not be denied or abridged by the United States or by any State on account of sex.

Congress shall have power to enforce this article by appropriate legislation. (Ratified August, 1920.)

Amendment XX

Section 1. The terms of the President and Vice President shall end at noon on the 20th day of January, and the terms of Senators and Representatives at noon on the 3d day of January, of the years in which such terms would have ended if this article had not been ratified; and the terms of their successors shall then begin.

Section 2. The Congress shall assemble at least once in every year, and such meeting shall begin at noon on the 3d day of January, unless they shall by law appoint a different day.

Section 3. If, at the time fixed for the beginning of the term of the President, the President elect shall have died, the Vice President elect shall become President. If a President shall not have been chosen before the time fixed for the beginning of his term, or if the President elect shall have failed to qualify, then the Vice President elect shall act as President until a President shall have qualified; and the Congress may by law provide for the case wherein neither a President elect nor a Vice President elect shall have qualified, declaring who shall then act as President, or the manner in which one who is to act shall be selected, and such person shall act accordingly until a President or Vice President shall have qualified.

Section 4. The Congress may by law provide for the case of the death of any of the persons from whom the House of Representatives may choose a President whenever the right of choice shall have devolved upon them, and for the case of the death of any of the persons from whom the Senate may choose a Vice President whenever the right of choice shall have devolved upon them.

Section 5. Sections 1 and 2 shall take effect on the 15th day of October following the ratification of this article. Section 6. This article shall be inoperative unless it shall have been ratified as an amendment to the Constitution by the legislatures of three-fourths of the several States within seven years from the date of its submission. (Ratified January, 1933.)

Amendment XXI

Section 1. The eighteenth article of amendment to the Constitution of the United States is hereby repealed. Section 2. The transportation or importation into any State, Territory, or possession of the United States for delivery or use therein of intoxicating liquors, in violation of the laws thereof, is hereby prohibited.

Section 3. This article shall be inoperative unless it shall have been ratified as an amendment to the Constitution by conventions in the several States, as provided in the Constitution, within seven years from the date of the submission hereof to the States by the 4fc Congress. (Ratified December, 1933.)

Amendment XXII

Section 1. No person shall be elected to the office of the President more than twice, and no person who has held the office of President, or acted as President, for more than two years of a term to which some other person was elected President shall be elected to the office of the President more than once. But this Article shall not apply to any person holding the office of President when this Article was proposed by the Congress, and shall not prevent any person who may be holding the office of President, or acting as President, during the term within which this Article becomes operative from holding the office of President or acting as President during the remainder of such term.

Section 2. This article shall be inoperative unless it shall have been ratified as an amendment to the Constitution by the legislatures of three-fourths of the several States within seven years from the date of its submission to the States by the Congress. (Ratified February, 1951.)

Amendment XXIII

Section 1. The District constituting the seat of Government of the United States shall appoint in such manner as the Congress may direct:

A number of electors of President and Vice President equal to the whole number of Senators and Representatives in Congress to which the District would be entitled if it were a State, but in no event more than the least populous State; they shall be in addition to those appointed by the States, but they shall be considered, for the purposes of the election of President and Vice President, to be electors appointed by a State; and they shall meet in the District and perform such duties as provided by the twelfth article of amendment.

Section 2. The Congress shall have power to enforce this article by appropriate legislation. (Ratified March, 1961.)

Amendment XXIV

Section 1. The right of citizens of the United States to vote in any primary or other election for President or Vice President, for electors for President or Vice President, or for Senator or Representative in Congress, shall not be denied or abridged by the United States or any State by reason of failure to pay any poll tax or other tax.

Section 2. The Congress shall have power to en-* force this article by appropriate legislation.
(Ratified January, 1964.)

Amendment XXV

Section 1. In case of removal of the President from office or of his death or resignation, the Vice President shall become President.

Section 2. Whenever there is a vacancy in the office of the Vice President, the President shall nominate a Vice President who shall take office upon confirmation by a majority vote of both Houses of Congress.

Section 3. Whenever the President transmits to the President pro tempore of the Senate and the Speaker of the House of Representatives his written declaration that he is unable to discharge the powers and duties of his office, and until he transmits to them a written declaration to the contrary, such powers and duties shall be discharged by the Vice President as Acting President.

Section 4. Whenever the Vice President and a major-

ity of either the principal officers of the executive departments or of such other body as Congress may by law provide, transmit to the President pro tempore of the Senate and the Speaker of the House of Representatives their written declaration that the President is unable to discharge the powers and duties of his office, the Vice President shall im¬mediately assume the powers and duties of the office as Acting President.

Thereafter, when the President transmits to the President pro tempore of the Senate and the Speaker of the House of Representatives his written declaration that no inability exists, he shall resume the powers and duties of his office unless the Vice President and a majority of either the principal officers of the executive department or of such other body as Congress may by law provide, transmit within four days to the President pro tempore of the Senate and the Speaker of the House of Representatives their written declaration that the President is unable to discharge the powers and duties of his office. Thereupon Congress shall decide the issue, assembling within forty-eight hours for that purpose if not in session. If the Congress, within twenty-one days after receipt of the latter written declaration, or, if Congress is not in session, within twenty-one days after Congress is required to assemble, determines by two-thirds vote of both Houses that the President is unable to discharge the powers and duties of his office, the Vice President shall continue to discharge the same as Acting President; otherwise, the President shall resume the powers and duties of his office. (Ratified February, 1967.)

Amendment XXVI

Section 1. The right of citizens of the United States, who are eighteen years of age or older, to vote shall not be denied or abridged by the United States or by any State on account of age.

Section 2. The Congress shall have power to enforce this article by appropriate legislation. (Ratified July, 1971.)

The Emancipation Proclamation

Whereas on the 22nd day of September, A.D. 1862, a proclamation was issued by the President of the United States, containing, among other things, the following, to wit:

"That on the 1st day of January, A.D. 1863, all persons held as slaves within any State or designated part of a State the people whereof shall then be in rebellion against the United States shall be then, thenceforward, and forever free; and the executive government of the United States, including the military and naval authority thereof, will recognize and maintain the freedom of such persons and will do no act or acts to repress such persons, or any of them, in any efforts they may make for their actual freedom."

"That the executive will on the 1st day of January aforesaid, by proclamation, designate the States and parts of States, if any, in which the people thereof, respectively, shall then be in rebellion against the United States; and the fact that any State or the people thereof shall on that day be in good faith represented in the Congress of the United States by members chosen thereto at elections wherein a majority of the qualified voters of such States shall have participated shall, in the absence of strong countervailing testimony, be deemed conclusive evidence that such State and the people thereof are not then in rebellion against the United States."

Now, therefore, I, Abraham Lincoln, President of the United States, by virtue of the power in me vested as Commander-in-Chief of the Army and Navy of the United States in time of actual armed rebellion against the authority and government of the United States, and as a fit and necessary war measure for supressing said rebellion, do, on this 1st day of January, A.D. 1863, and in accordance with my purpose so to do, publicly proclaimed for the full period of one hundred days from the first day above mentioned, order and designate as the States and parts of States wherein the people thereof, respectively, are this day in rebellion against the United States the following, to wit:

Arkansas, Texas, Louisiana (except the parishes of St. Bernard, Palquemines, Jefferson, St. John, St. Charles, St. James, Ascension, Assumption, Terrebone, Lafourche, St. Mary, St. Martin, and Orleans, including the city of New Orleans), Mississippi, Alabama, Florida, Georgia, South Carolina, North Carolina, and Virginia (except the forty-eight counties designated as West Virginia, and also the counties of Berkeley, Accomac, Morthhampton, Elizabeth City, York, Princess Anne, and Norfolk, including the cities of Norfolk and Portsmouth), and which excepted parts are for the present left precisely as if this proclamation were not issued.

And by virtue of the power and for the purpose aforesaid, I do order and declare that all persons held as slaves within said designated States and parts of States are, and henceforward shall be, free; and that the Executive Government of the United States, including the military and naval authorities thereof, will recognize and maintain the freedom of said persons.

And I hereby enjoin upon the people so declared to be free to abstain from all violence, unless in necessary self-defence; and I recommend to them that, in all case when allowed, they labor faithfully for reasonable wages.

And I further declare and make known that such persons of suitable condition will be received into the armed service of the United States to garrison forts, positions, stations, and other places, and to man vessels of all sorts in said service.

And upon this act, sincerely believed to be an act of justice, warranted by the Constitution upon military necessity, I invoke the considerate judgment of mankind and the gracious favor of Almighty God.

NEGRO SPIRITUALS

The Negro Spirituals speak to the oral tradition of Africa in how they define the American black people's quest and determination to be free. These original musical gems are unique to America. They stemmed from African seed, took root in the slave soil of the South, and ripened into a fruitful inspiration for all mankind seeking social and political justice.

At the onset, the old Roman method of "divide and conquer" worked well for American slave owners. Hailing from many West African tribes, the slaves spoke many different languages. The slavers deliberately mixed up the individual tribal members. Having no common tongue among them, negated – or reduced – the opportunity for group rebellion. Drums, a common African medium for communicating, were forbidden. However, the slaves ingeniously created and developed over time, their own music-based language. It started with humming, moaning, and groaning. Then when the Whites introduced Blacks to Christianity, the Bible provided the vehicle, the message, and the words to the melodies. From this background evolved the Negro Spiritual, an amalgam of African oral tradition and European religion.

In Wyatt Tee Walker's book, *Somebody's Calling My Name,* he cites the works of John Lovell, Black Song: The Forge and the Flame, of having "the fullest and best organized exposition that details precisely how the music of the Spirituals choreographed the dynamics of the slave community: 1. to give the community a true, valid, useful song 2. to keep the community invigorated 3. to inspire the uninspired individual 4. to enable the group to face its problems 5. to comment on the slave situation 6. to stir each member to personal solutions and to a sense of belonging in the midst of a confusing and terrifying world, and 7. to provide a code language for emergency uses."

This synopsis about Negro Spirituals gives examples of them; some are just the words, and others include both words and music. As one reads, sings and/or plays these spirituals, review Lovell's list of their purpose, their dynamics, and their importance to the slave community. This is particularly true as to their inspiration and influence on the Underground Railroad, and on Dr. Martin Luther King, Jr. and the latter day Civil Rights Movement.

Added note: This Appendix synopsis elaborates for the reader to better understand the fundamental and special significance that Negro Spirituals played in those dark days of slavery. We feel this elaboration to be pivotal, when placed in the context of Panel 1, Background, in the Notes, "The Slave System;" and Panel 4, Slavery Sectionalism; in the Notes "The Underground Railroad."

More Information / Links to Negro Spirituals

M. PORTER.   E. W. WATKINS.   H. D. ALEXANDER.   F. J. LOUDIN.   T. RUTLIN.
JENNIE JACKSON.   MABEL LEWIS.   ELLA SHEPPARD.   MAGGIE CARNES.   AMERICA W. ROBINSON.

Portrait of The Fisk Jubilee Singers, taken from J.B.I. Marsh, ed.,
The Story of the Jubilee Singers, London: Hodder and Stoughton, 1877.
http://xroads.virginia.edu/~HYPER/TWH/Fiskimage.html

For more information about Negro Spirituals search:
www.google.com then in the search box type: "Negro Spirituals"

Negro Spiritual Lyrics and more information:
http://www.negrospirituals.com/news-song/index.htm

Enjoy Negro Spirituals Sung:
www.youtube.com then, in the search box type the name of the Spiritual
you would like to hear (see the lists above)

The Negro National Anthem
"Lift Every Voice and Sing"
By: James Weldon Johnson

Lift Every Voice and sing till earth and heaven ring
Ring with the harmonies of liberty
Let our rejoicing rise high as the listening skies
Let it resound loud as the rolling sea

Sing a song, full of the faith that the dark past has taught us
Sing a song, full of the hope that the present has brought us
Facing the rising sun of our new day begun
Let us march on till victory is won

Stony the road we trod, bitter the chastening rod
felt in the days when hope unborn had died
yet with a steady beat, have not our weary feet
come to the place for which our fathers sighed?

We have come, over a way that which tears has been watered
We have come, treading our path through the blood of the slaughtered
Out of the gloomy past, till now we stand at last,
Where the white gleam of our bright star is cast

GOD of our weary years, GOD of our silent tears
Thou Who has brought us thus far on the way
Thou Who hast by Thy might, led us into the light
Keep us for-e-ver in the path we pray

Lest our feet, stray from the places our GOD where me met thee
Lest our hearts, drunk with the wine of the world we forget Thee
Shadowed beneath thy hand, may we forever stand
TRUE TO OUR GOD, TRUE TO OUR NATIVE LAND

http://seemeonline.com/fasr/anthem.html

NOTE: "A group of young men in Jacksonville, Florida, arranged to celebrate Lincoln's birthday in 1900. My brother, J. Rosamond Johnson, and I decided to write a song to be sung at the exercise. I wrote the words and he wrote the music. Our New York publisher, Edward B. Marks, made mimeographed copies for us and the song was taught to and sung by a chorus of five hundred colored school children.

"Shortly afterwards my brother and I moved from Jacksonville to New York, and the song passed out of our minds. But the school children of Jacksonville kept singing it, they went off to other schools and sang it, they became teachers and taught it to other children. Within twenty years, it was being sung over the South and in some other parts of the country. Today, the song, popularly known as the Negro National Hymn, is quite generally used.

"The lines of this song repay me in elation, almost of exquisite anguish, whenever I hear them sung by Negro children."

               – James Weldon Johnson, 1935

INDEX

Index Note:
See *Appendix* (281-299) for the copy of the complete text of the Declaration of Independence, the United States Constitution & The Bill of Rights and the Emancipation Proclamation.

ABOUT THE AUTHORS

Gwendolyn H. Scott, Historian

As a historical re-enactor, Ms. Scott portrays Clara Brown and others. She has a BFA and M.A. in elementary education from the University of Denver and was awarded Fulbright scholarships to India and Kenya. Ms. Scott has taught in both elementary and high school. Her most recent retirement in 2000 was from an adjunct professorship in Denver University's Teacher education program.

Wallace Yvonne Tollette, Independent Historian/Author

Ms. Tollette holds a B.A. in English, speech and drama and an M.A. in communication and theatre from the University of Colorado. She served as administrator (3 years) and executive director (6 years) of the Black American West Museum & Heritage Center in Denver. She is also an independent publisher having written five books featuring Black people in leadership positions across Colorado.

Jane Taylor, Learning Specialist and Project Coordinator

Ms. Taylor holds a B.A. in education and a M.A. in curriculum and supervision from the University of Connecticut. She has taught children, preschool to high school. A personal interest includes researching and interpreting Western black history. Her last job was at Denver Academy as a literacy specialist for elementary through high school students.

ACKNOWLEDGEMENTS

The authors of *Blacks Through the 'Ayes' of our American Presidents*, wish to extend their heartfelt thanks to a large number of people for all their help, encouragement and expertise in the compilation of this history. They participated on several levels; as proofreaders for accuracy; technical and scholarly assistance; lots of encouragement for our dedication to such behemoth project and being our pilot program testers.

We apologize for any omissions and/or errors. Whenever names are listed, there is always the possibility that someone will be omitted. If that is the case, please know that it was not intentional and do call our attention to it.

Our supporters (in no particular order)
Charleszine Nelson, Blair-Caldwell African American Research Library
Danny Walker, Blair-Caldwell African American Research Library
Carolyn Jones, Ph.D., Founder-Principal, Challenges,
Choices and Images Charter School
Jack and Jill of America
Grace Stiles, Stiles African American Heritage Center
Patricia 'Tish' Richard, Ph.D.
Rebecca Hunt, Ph.D.
Geoffrey Hunt, Ph.D.
Modupe Labode, Ph.D.
Gene Grier, Ford-Warren Library
James P. Beckwourth Mountain Club and all the historical re-enactors
Charlotte S. Waisman, Ph.D. and Jill S. Tietjen, co-authors,
Her Story: A Timeline of the Women Who Changed America
Carey Jones-Eskesen
Claudia Hinds
Roy Scott
Vicki Vitatoe
Jessica Vitatoe
Kenneth D. Taylor, Ph.D.
Nick Zelinger
Dan Dillon

A big "thank you" to all of you from the authors and program facilitators.

A SPECIAL ACKNOWLEDGEMENT

The authors wish to acknowledge and say an appreciative "thank you" to Carey Jones-Eskesen, Senior English Teacher at Denver Academy. We are indebted to Ms. Jones-Eskesen for her dedication, spending numerous hours aiding in the preparation and editing of this behemoth project.

> With appreciation,
> The Authors:
> Jane Taylor, Project Leader
> Gwendolyn Scott, Historian
> Wallace Yvonne Tollette, Independent Historian/Author
> Nick Zelinger, NZ Graphics

The Write Group is available for public programs
to discuss the material in this book.

If you or your organization would be interested
in a public program, please contact:

The Write Group
6632 East Asbury Ave.
Denver, CO 80224
303-756-0198
or
Email: Jtaylorbiz@msn.com

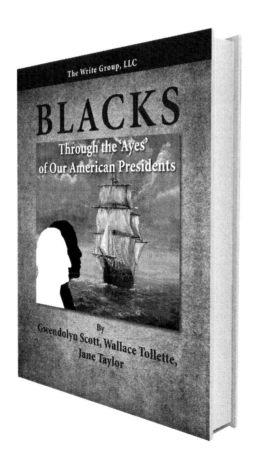